POP MUSIC
TECHNOLOGY AND CREATIVITY

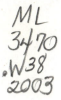

Pop Music
Technology and Creativity

Trevor Horn and the Digital Revolution

by

TIMOTHY WARNER
Lecturer in Music
at the University of Salford

ASHGATE

Published by
Ashgate Publishing Limited
Gower House
Croft Road
Aldershot
Hants GU11 3HR
England

Ashgate Publishing Company
Suite 420
101 Cherry Street
Burlington, VT 05401–4405
USA

Ashgate website: http://www.ashgate.com

British Library Cataloguing in Publication Data
Warner, Timothy
  Pop music–technology and creativity : Trevor Horn and the
  digital revolution. – (Ashgate popular and folk music
  series)
  1.Horn, Trevor 2.Sound recordings–Production and
  direction 3.Popular music–Great Britain
  I. Title
  782.4'2164'092

Library of Congress Cataloging-in-Publication Data
Warner, Timothy, 1954–
    Pop music–technology and creativity: Trevor Horn and the digital revolution/
  Timothy Warner.
        p. cm. – (Ashgate popular and folk music series)
    Includes bibliographical references, discography, and index.
        1.Popular music–20th century–History and criticism. 2.Music and technology. 3.
  Electronic music–History and criticism. 4.Creation (Literary, artistic, etc.) 5.Horn,
  Trevor. I.Title. II.Series

  ML3470 .W38 2002
  786.7'164–dc21

  2002074728

ISBN 0 7546 3131 1 (Hbk)
ISBN 0 7546 3132 X (Pbk)

Typeset by Manton Typesetters, Louth, Lincolnshire, UK.
Printed and bound in Great Britain by MPG Books Ltd, Bodmin, Cornwall.

Contents

List of Tables   viii
General Editor's Preface   ix
Acknowledgements   x
Introduction   xi

Part One: Pop Music   1

1   Characteristics of Pop Music   3
    Pop and rock   3
    Pop as a format: the single   5
    Short and sweet   6
    The art of the familiar   7
    Simplicity and repetition   9
    Round and round, like a record   10
    Machine aesthetics   11
    Pop and television   12
    Pop and commerce   13
    Pop and fashion   14
    Let's dance   14
    Image   15
    Mixed media   16

2   The Production of Pop Music   18
    An aural art   19
    The recording studio as resource   20
    From analogue to digital   20
    Using technology   22
    Multitrack recording   22
    Signal processing   23
    MIDI sequencing   24
    Sound synthesis and sampling   28
    Recording the voice   31
    The fade-out   32
    The record producer   33

Part Two: Technology and Creativity   39

3   'Video Killed the Radio Star' by The Buggles   41
    The ghost in the machine   41
    Music   43

Lyrics   44
Production and arrangement   45
Disco killed the radio star   47

4   'Buffalo Gals' by Malcolm McLaren   50
    A charismatic manager   50
    From manager to artist   52
    Applied cultural theory   52
    The anthropological connection   53
    Stylistic collage   54
    'Buffalo Gals'   55
    Structure   57
    Timbre   58
    Half-heard words   59

5   'Owner of a Lonely Heart' by Yes   62
    Yes: from progressive rock to chart pop   62
    90125   64
    A new image   64
    Live/recorded   65
    Chart pop music   66
    'Owner of a Lonely Heart'   66
    Form: repetition and suspension   67
    Timbre and gesture   69
    The artificial guitar   70
    The multitracked vocal   71
    Machine drums   72

6   'Relax' by Frankie Goes to Hollywood   75
    Zang Tuum Tumb   75
    Another band from Liverpool   76
    The image   78
    Too much, too young?   79
    The making of 'Relax'   80
    'Remix, Re Use It'   81
    Banned   82
    The sound of 'Relax'   83
    A novel approach to musical form   84
    What's the hook?   86
    Repetition in 'Relax'   87

7   *Who's Afraid of The Art of Noise?*   91
    What's in a name?   92
    Who's afraid of The Art of Noise?   93
    Cover imagery   94

Sampling 95
Recording records 96
Listening to samples 97
Sampling and The Art of Noise 98
Studio made 101
Timbre 101
Space 102

8   'Jewel', 'Duel' and 'Jewelled' by Propaganda 106
Recordings revisited 106
Propaganda 108
A Secret Wish: pretentious packaging 110
From engineer to producer 112
The music of *A Secret Wish* 113
'Jewel'/'Duel'/'Jewelled' 116
'Jewel'/'Duel'/'Jewelled' – the structure 116
'Jewel'/'Duel'/'Jewelled' – the sound 118
Technology and Propaganda 120

9   *Slave to the Rhythm* by Grace Jones 123
Slave to the fashion 123
Slave to the image 124
Slave to the cliché 126
Slave to the Rhythm 127
'Re-written by machine' 128
Concerto for Synclavier 129
Slave to the sampler 131
Space 132
Spatial orchestration 133
Words 134
Slave to the remix 135

Conclusion 139

Appendix 1: Interview with Trevor Horn 143

Appendix 2: Trevor Horn Discography 157

Discography 160

Bibliography 162

Index 167

List of Tables

4.1	The structure of 'Buffalo Gals'	57
6.1	The structure of 'Relax'	85
6.2	Repetition in 'Relax'	89
8.1	The structure of 'Jewel'	117
8.2	The structure of 'Duel'	118
8.3	The structure of 'Jewelled'	119
9.1	Musical repetition in *Slave to the Rhythm*	128
9.2	Verbal repetition in *Slave to the Rhythm*	129
9.3	Sampled phrases in 'Operattack'	130
9.4	Space in 'Don't Cry – It's Only the Rhythm'	134
C.1	Horn's recordings and the pop charts	141

General Editor's Preface

The upheaval that occurred in musicology during the last two decades of the twentieth century has created a new urgency for the study of popular music alongside the development of new critical and theoretical models. A relativistic outlook has replaced the universal perspective of modernism (the international ambitions of the 12-note style); the grand narrative of the evolution and dissolution of tonality has been challenged, and emphasis has shifted to cultural context, reception and subject position. Together, these have conspired to eat away at the status of canonical composers and categories of high and low in music. A need has arisen, also, to recognize and address the emergence of crossovers, mixed and new genres, to engage in debates concerning the vexed problem of what constitutes authenticity in music and to offer a critique of music practice as the product of free, individual expression.

Popular musicology is now a vital and exciting area of scholarship, and the Ashgate Popular and Folk Music series aims to present the best research in the field. Authors will be concerned with locating musical practices, values and meanings in cultural context, and may draw upon methodologies and theories developed in cultural studies, semiotics, post-structuralism, psychology and sociology. The series will focus on popular musics of the twentieth and twenty-first centuries. It is designed to embrace the world's popular musics from Acid Jazz to Zydeco, whether high-tech or low-tech, commercial or non-commercial, contemporary or traditional.

Professor Derek B. Scott
Chair of Music
University of Salford

Visit Project Pop: http://www.salford.ac.uk/FDTLpop/welcome.htm

Acknowledgements

I wish to thank all the friends and colleagues who have generously commented on my work. I am indebted to Trevor Horn who has kindly given permission to reproduce the interview included at the end of this book.

Introduction

This book is intended for all those – students and teachers, specialists and non-specialists alike – who wish to approach pop music as an artistic, and not primarily as a social, cultural or historical phenomenon. Its main argument is that musical creativity in pop music is inextricably bound to developments in audio technology and the working practices which ensue. Because of the strength of this relationship, pop music differs in a number of important and significant ways from other kinds of popular music. This aspect is exemplified in this study through analysis of several recordings by Trevor Horn, who is widely acknowledged as the most important, innovative and successful British pop record producer of the early 1980s.

The book provides a definition of pop as distinct from rock music in the British context, highlights the key role of the record producer, shows the impact of the transition from analogue to digital technologies on the creative process, develops appropriate means of analysing pop music by focusing on the record as the central artefact, and seeks to promote a better understanding and appreciation of pop music from this perspective.

In this respect this study is at odds with dominant trends, which tend to explain pop music essentially as a sociocultural phenomenon. The current situation is largely the result of four interconnected factors: the nineteenth-century aesthetics and elitist prejudices against pop music of many musicologists; seminal, and largely negative texts by Marxist thinkers like Theodore Adorno (1903–69) – whose influence is still felt in cultural studies; the rejection of 'textual' analysis, that is, close readings – as an ahistorical approach by the leading exponents of cultural studies; the fact that, within the broad umbrella of cultural studies, media or popular culture studies play down the specificity of each medium to concentrate on their common characteristics and functions in the consumer society and mass culture.

Musicology as an academic discipline was developed during the nineteenth century specifically in order to study works of Western European art music. As a consequence, any music that was outside this canon was firstly ignored and later studied through, and in relation to, established musicological methodology and terminology.

Adorno's thought largely evolves from the same aesthetic stance as traditional musicology. His text 'On Popular Music', written over 50 years ago (Adorno, 1990), remains profoundly influential. Adorno produces compelling arguments for viewing popular music as a force of social stasis, and the examples with which he supports his thesis are persuasive: popular music employs standard forms in which the parts seem almost interchangeable; popular music emphasizes regular metre; popular music does not aspire to create the same kind of artistic response as serious music; and popular music largely shuns the development of musical material. However, although the characteristics of popular music clearly differ from those of serious music, these differences only become weaknesses if one accepts a priori that the latter is some kind of ideal form to which all other musical artefacts should aspire. Adorno's prejudices are apparent in the misleading musical classifications he adopts when he contrasts 'serious' music with 'popular' music.

The emerging discipline of cultural studies was sympathetic to Adorno's view that the popular music produced by the culture industry was 'conformist and mind numbing, enforcing ... general acceptance of the capitalist order' (Strinati, 1995, p. 63). However, the view of the consumer as an entirely disempowered and hoodwinked automaton, with a rather gross and brutal aesthetic, has come to appear both patronizing and unsupportable:

> Studies have shown how audiences for popular culture are more discriminating and critical in terms of what they consume than the theories of mass culture or the culture industry allow ... Audiences appear to be able to engage in active interpretations of what they consume which are not adequately described by Adorno's notion of the regressive listener. (Ibid., p. 78)

The experience of many music teachers suggests, moreover, that young people with little or no formal musical training can often show a highly developed level of musical perception, grasping and even reproducing the subtlest nuances and inflections of pop music.

Cultural studies' socio-centric stance led to a broad rejection of textual analysis as ahistorical, discouraging further investigation of the specificity of the artefacts of popular music – notably records and videos. Even in those areas of study where one might expect closer individual readings and analyses, the emphasis has instead been on identifying commonalities between related media.

Unlike literature or film, pop music occupied a low artistic and academic status during the period when textual analysis was the dominant method of approaching artistic phenomena. The rise in importance of cultural studies from the 1970s onwards, meant that the specific elements of pop music were left largely unexplored. Although, as will become clear in several of the analyses presented in this book, pop music is a mixed medium, the way the various elements interact is specific.

For the purpose of this study, the insights of Walter Benjamin (1892–1940), a thinker associated, like Adorno, with the Frankfurt School and often quoted, seem more appropriate. Although Benjamin's 'The Work of Art in the Age of Mechanical Reproduction' was specifically concerned with film and the changes in art brought about by modern technology, his basic thesis is entirely applicable to audio recording and pop music. The relationship between technology and pop music is both important and significant. Specifically, the means used to realize musical ideas and give them substance can have a major impact on the resulting artefact. Benjamin hints at such a transformation at the very beginning of his article with a quote by Valéry: 'We must expect great innovations to transform the entire technique of the arts, thereby affecting artistic invention itself and perhaps even bringing about an amazing change in our very notion of art' (Benjamin, 1970, p. 211). Benjamin goes on to suggest that mechanical reproduction tends to undermine the authenticity and 'aura' of a work of art. Time is fragmented through the use of editing and dubbing techniques, and the audience is confronted by new, intimate perspectives in new environments: 'the choral production, performed in an auditorium ... resounds in the drawing room' (ibid., p. 215).

It is well over 50 years since Benjamin wrote his essay on mechanical reproduction and, in the mean time, the pace of technological change has continued and accelerated relentlessly. Nowadays, the experience and appreciation of music largely occurs through listening to often highly manipulated recordings, and the relationship between live performance and recording grows ever more tenuous. Since technological mediation is a fundamental aspect of pop music, comparisons with more traditional arts highlight irreconcilable differences and are largely inappropriate.

The first part of this book is a general investigation into the nature of pop music as an artistic phenomenon. Chapter 1, 'Characteristics of Pop Music', identifies some of the most important features of pop, largely through comparison with rock and through the ways in which pop is represented on television. Chapter 2, 'The Production of Pop Music', argues that the central pop music artefact is the record. It considers the equipment and working practices that inform the specific sound characteristics of pop recordings, and leads to an overview of the role of the record producer, who is the key figure in the relationship between technology and creativity.

The second part of the book consists of seven analyses of recordings produced between 1979 and 1985 by the British record producer, Trevor Horn. During the six years under investigation, the initial transition from analogue to digital technology in the recording studio occurred. These changes enabled new ways of working with sound and gave rise to new approaches to creativity. As the analyses show, Horn, more than any other successful producer of the time, was able to exploit the possibilities offered by the emerging digital audio technologies. The sheer creative momentum that he achieved during these six years as a record producer is remarkable. While the commercial success of the records themselves ensured his future as a 'world player', these records also remain much admired and emulated in professional circles. They were, at least partly, responsible for fundamental changes in the ways pop recordings were made, as well as introducing new musical and sonic characteristics to the world of pop.

Although these analyses are presented separately and their presentation suggests a historical time line, in fact their order has been defined by when they entered the UK singles chart. Chapter 3 focuses on The Buggles hit single 'Video Killed the Radio Star' which Horn co-wrote, performed on and produced. Chapter 4 is an analysis of Malcolm McLaren's 'Buffalo Gals' from the album *Duck Rock* – the recording that introduced scratching and hip hop to the UK. Chapter 5 reviews the Yes single 'Owner of a Lonely Heart', the group's most successful single; while Chapter 6 analyses 'Relax' by Frankie Goes to Hollywood, Horn's most memorable pop production of the 1980s. Chapter 7 is concerned with The Art of Noise, which was co-founded by Horn and was one of the first groups to exploit sampling as a creative device. Chapter 8 focuses on the German pop group Propaganda and explores the ways in which musical material can be reused in the pop recording studio. The final chapter is devoted to Grace Jones's *Slave to the Rhythm*, regarded by many as one of the finest pop productions of the 1980s.

Throughout the emphasis is on the record as an artefact: a combination of a variety of elements, including music and sound, lyrics, cover design and artists' persona. Although the analyses focus primarily on the production of the recording, some attention is devoted to the other elements where these elucidate, support or contrast specific aural aspects.

While the emphasis in this book is placed firmly on musical considerations, the use of notation to support the analyses has been avoided. This is not intended to imply that music notation and the theoretical stance that underpins it have no place or value in the study of pop music. Indeed, many pop musicians rely on notation in a variety of situations. However, in Western European art music notation plays a central role – the score is usually the fundamental creative product and is the focus for most subsequent analysis – whereas in pop music it is the audio recording which is more often the primary artefact and the basic term of reference. The absence of notation reflects this difference in emphasis, as well as the author's reluctance to adopt a technique so strongly associated with traditional musicology, a concern that Middleton has already raised (Middleton, 1990, p. 105). Moreover, the technology used to make pop music recordings – a central element in this book – usually involves little reference to notation and instead encourages musicians to work directly with sound. Finally, it was felt that the book would be accessible to a wider audience if the use of notation were avoided.

To summarize, the study of pop music as an art form represents a largely uncharted area of music research. The scarcity of work in this field results in confusion over terminology, methodology, aesthetic principles and the nature of creativity. The scope of the present study is to provide, through the analysis of a specific body of work, an initial exploration of the relationship between technology and creativity in pop music.

PART ONE
Pop Music

Chapter 1

Characteristics of Pop Music

Pop music is a slippery concept. (Frith, Straw and Street, 2001, p. 94)

In the past 40 years the phrase 'pop music' has come to refer to a particular branch of popular music. Although pop music might be regarded as a relatively recent phenomenon, few elements have remained constant during its short history. As a result, providing a simple, straightforward definition of pop is problematic. *The New Grove Dictionary of Music and Musicians* defines pop as 'a term that from the late 1950s has been applied to the central and most widely circulated kinds of popular music (analogously with "pop art"), in particular rock and roll, reggae etc.'. For Hardy and Laing, on the other hand, it is 'a broad term normally used for the softer, even more teenage-oriented, sounds that emerged as Rock 'n' Roll waned in the early 1960s. It is often contrasted with the tougher or more serious-minded Rock' (Hardy and Laing, 1990, p. x).

Yet comparing pop with rock raises new problems. While British writers[1] seem able to make clear distinctions between pop and rock, their American counterparts – as several important studies suggest[2] – do not perceive such marked contrasts between the two. This tends to suggest that any definition of pop music is not only historically but also geographically determined. The present study which, as we shall see, clearly differentiates between pop and rock, must therefore be viewed as the reflection of a culture that is, at least in part, fundamentally British (or even English).[3]

Pop and rock

The comparison between pop and rock has often been used to suggest that pop music is less worthy of serious consideration. For example:

> The Monkees reached their peak in 1967 … the year pop music seemed to split into two distinct camps, leaving on the one hand the music of the underground, incorporating acid-rock and head music, and on the other, mundane bubblegum, pop at its most blatantly commercial and at its most hideously banal. Bubblegum was tots' music, literally, distinguished by its crude, pip-squeak rhythm and nursery-rhyme lyrics, conveyor-belt music at its lowest level ever. (Stephen Barnard, in Gillett and Frith, 1996, p. 126)

It must therefore be stressed that for the purposes of this study pop music will simply be compared to rock in order to highlight, rather than make value judgements upon, the significant features that emerge.

In the past 15 years the elements that characterize rock have grown increasingly diverse and fragmented: the days of rock as a vibrant and cohesive artistic form seem to have passed. As Martin Cloonan has noted: 'If 1967 saw the beginning of rock as art, 1992 saw rock as nostalgia' (Cloonan, 1996, p. 7). Hence, the rock under discussion here is largely confined to that style of popular music which flourished during the period 1967–87.

Adopting such a qualified and circumspect approach enables several clear distinctions to be made between pop and rock. These might be summarized as follows:

Pop	*Rock*
Singles	Albums
Emphasis on recording	Emphasis on performance
Emphasis on technology	Emphasis on musicianship
Artificial	Real ('authentic')
Trivial	Serious
Ephemeral	Lasting
Successive	Progressive

These distinctions include factors as diverse as record format, performance, featured sounds, musical technique, social make-up, and historical development. The preferred audio format for pop is the single – the 7-inch, 45 rpm vinyl disc, the compact disc (CD) or cassette single – while rock tends to rely to a greater extent on the album format; the Top 20 which charts the commercial success of individual singles is dominated by pop music. In comparison to other kinds of popular music, pop places very little emphasis on 'live' performance; indeed, much of the pop music produced in recording studios cannot be reproduced live convincingly. On the other hand, live performance is regarded as a fundamental aspect of rock and one of the characteristics that confers 'authenticity'.[4] Pop music features the voice and most pop stars are singers, rather than instrumentalists, while rock often places greater emphasis on the electric guitar. Unlike rock, pop often makes greater use of modern electronic technology: pop music is usually not only realized but *created* in the recording studio. Traditional musical skills, especially flamboyant manual dexterity on a conventional musical instrument, are rarely stressed on pop recordings. Finally, like fashion, pop music goes through cyclical patterns of change instead of following a linear development, while rock has some sense of its own historical development.[5]

As Simon Frith points out: 'Rock was something more than pop, more than rock 'n' roll. Rock musicians combined an emphasis on skill and technique with the romantic concept of art as individual expression, original and sincere' (Frith, in Martin, 1983, p. 36). As early as 1970 Andrew Chester was writing of a rock aesthetic[6] and in academic circles rock has established a musical credibility which pop has been denied. Allan Moore writes of 'progressive' (that is, rock) musicians developing 'an ideology of artistic freedom and self-expression ... within what was considered a freedom from the constraint of an immediate, dancing audience' (Moore, 1993, p. 57) and, later, 'a concern with aesthetic and individual rather than immediate and communal qualities' (ibid.). Rock involves the creative, artistic pursuits of the individual, while pop is an immediate, communal form.

Keith Negus builds on this distinction and suggests two kinds of 'ideology of creativity': the organic and the synthetic. 'The organic ideology of creativity is a naturalistic approach to artists ... The synthetic ideology of creativity is a combinatorial approach to both acts and material ... These ... distinctions ... found expression in a rigid distinction between rock and pop' (Negus, 1992, p. 54).

Although a number of artists have produced work that simultaneously draws on elements of both pop and rock, the general distinctions outlined above remain valid.

Pop as a format: the single

In the past 50 years, consumer formats for recorded music have become smaller. Simultaneously the amount and quality of recorded sound on each successive format have increased. Yet throughout this period, and in spite of several important technological developments, the 'single' has persisted. When CBS introduced the 33⅓ rpm, 12-inch, long-playing (LP), microgroove disc in 1948, RCA countered with the 45 rpm, 7-inch, extended play disc a year later; and this quickly 'established itself as the format for popular hits' (Gronow and Saunio, 1999, p. 98).

With the development of the compact cassette and the CD, record companies started releasing versions of these formats as singles for pop music, and this principle continues to the present day. Like many other kinds of modern popular music, pop is technologically mediated but, unlike these, it consistently tends to adopt recorded formats that do not fully exploit the technological resources available. Moreover, accepting the single as the main vehicle of delivery for pop music also suggests that, unlike many other kinds of music, pop music is largely purchased and consumed on a piece-by-piece basis, and those pieces are highly distinctive musically: diatonic, strophic songs of three to five minutes duration.

The idea of a 'hit parade' – a weekly list of the best-selling records – was established in the early days of radio when only one consumer format for recorded sound was available: the 78 rpm disc. The consistency of musical duration in pop music, as well as the emphasis on a single piece of music rather than a collection, enable and encourage the continuation of this tradition across several formats.

The arrival of online music distribution, while having the potential to bring about enormous changes in the record industry as we know it, nevertheless continues to favour the single piece as the basic unit of recorded sound. Hence MP3.com, the Internet-based company that typifies this latest form of recorded music dissemination, offers downloads of MP3 files on a piece-by-piece basis. Moreover, MP3.com has 'Top 10' charts in a variety of genres, indicating which are the week's most often downloaded recordings.

The continued importance of the single in pop music is also evident in the newer contracts that some pop stars are signing. Hence George Michael 'wants to see how well the new record [a single] is marketed before giving the company enough material for a full LP' (Morrison, 2002).

The single, then, is the preferred format for pop music but, in spite of the continued support that it receives from record companies, is rarely financially viable. In recent years the costs of production, distribution and retailing of most singles are only covered through the sale of albums. Record companies use the single as a showcase for the artist in the hope that consumers will then purchase the album. For pop music, record companies often employ record producers to provide an album's worth of recorded material. Hence, the pop record producer will usually simultaneously concentrate on producing one or more pieces which will be suitable for release as singles, while also achieving a similar level of musical and technological manipulation for the rest of the material on the album.

Short and sweet

Most pop songs last less than five minutes. Before the introduction of the long-playing record, it made sense for one pop song to fit on one side of a 78 rpm record: there was a technological reason why pop songs were short. Nowadays there are no such technological constraints but pop albums continue to be collections of five-minute songs. This suggests that single songs of short duration are a fundamental musical characteristic of pop.

Inevitably, listening to a four-minute pop single is quite different from listening to a recording of a whole opera by Wagner, for instance. The pop listener has to be drawn into the music quickly, and no ambiguity is really possible (unless, of course, the fundamental character of the piece is ambiguity). It is perhaps for this reason that pop music has generated so many qualifying classifications: a pop recording tends to state its classification within the first 20 seconds or so, enabling the listener to decide whether to carry on listening or not. Simon Frith wrote that as a critic he received '20 to 30 LPs to listen to each week and the only way through the ever growing pile is instant classification' (Frith, 1983,

p. 18). Similarly, for the artistes and repertoire (A & R) departments of large record companies the sheer number of demonstration recordings that are received each week demand that only the first few seconds can be listened to: if the recording does not attract attention almost immediately then it is rejected. This seemingly rather ruthless approach, also adopted by disc jockeys (DJs) and many pop music listeners, highlights another characteristic of pop music: the first few seconds of a pop record must be both immediate and compelling. At times, the start of a recording is so impressive that the rest of the song disappoints: as an example one might cite the beginning of Jerry Rafferty's 'Baker Street',[7] a memorable saxophone solo followed by a somewhat less memorable song. The brevity of most pop songs demands a structure which will, first, capture the listener's attention, second, sustain and nurture that attention through some sense of progression and change, and, finally, tease the listener by ending at the point of maximum attention and interest. Songs that do not follow this plan are rare and will require some other element(s) to enable them to sustain the listener's interest.

The art of the familiar

Pop songs are designed ... to sound familiar. (Frith, Straw and Street, 2001, p. 97)

In order to capture a listener's interest immediately, a pop record must simultaneously present something that is both familiar and yet distinctive enough to differentiate it from its competitors. Hence, every pop record will have several musical characteristics that have appeared, in similar guises, on earlier records. As a result, inexperienced listeners will often find it difficult to differentiate one record from another, giving rise to the criticism that 'they all sound the same'.

Similarly, a number of already known musical elements, originally developed and associated with other kinds of popular music (Gospel or rap, for example), may appear on pop records, and this aspect of pop music has become increasingly prevalent in recent years as a result of sampling. These elements can take many forms: a vocal inflection (for example, breaking to falsetto at the end of a phrase); a vocal interjection (for example, 'come on' or 'yeah'); a particular chord pattern (for example I–flatVII–IV); a guitar gesture (for example, chugging power chords); a rhythmic motive (for example, a distinctive shuffle beat); or a particular synthesizer figure (for example, the 'pad' keyboard).

As a result, individual pop recordings often contain a number of elements that at least partially make reference to other records and, consequently, hardly seem original. This derivative quality in much pop music is an important characteristic, offering potential for musical analysis (see Tagg, 1991, for example). It also makes pop music markedly different from 'serious' music. Instead of trying to produce innovative, different or unusual works, pop musicians clearly favour relatively minor modifications to existing musical parameters. Indeed, part of the delight of popular music lies in the recognition of elements that echo previous pieces and, here again, sampling is important (see Chapter 7 on The Art of Noise). The role of these elements may be related to the notion of 'Signifyin(g)', first posited by Gates Jr. (1988) and described by Potter as follows:

> Simply put, Signifyin(g) is repetition *with a difference*; the same and yet not the same. When, in a jazz riff, a horn player substitutes one arpeggio for another in moving from key to key, or shifts a melody to what would be a harmony note, or 'cuts up' a well-known solo by altering its tempo, phrasing or accents, s/he is Signifyin(g) on all previous versions. (Potter, 1995, p. 27)

This common stock of musical ideas means that each new pop recording will have a number of elements which are already familiar to the audience. This sense of the familiar is a recurrent aspect of pop music generally and is evident in several areas, including musical ideas, lyrical themes and iconography. It also inevitably has a historical dimension: pop music plays with collective cultural memory. This has become a feature of many television documentaries in which images of the past are accompanied by pop music recordings of the same period. This facet of pop music to evoke a sense of the past is also evident in a number of popular films (such as *American Graffiti*, *Goodfellas* or *Platoon*) and in television advertising (Levi's jeans advertisements, for example). However, there is something of an idealized quality in many of these evocations: it is not 'how it was' but rather 'how it should have been', an odd kind of fantasized nostalgia. In recent years, some of the pop recordings used in popular films and advertising have been re-released and been successful in the Top 20. While this may be, and often is, interpreted as pop music's inability to renew itself as a form, it may also be viewed in a somewhat different light: the people who buy these records often have no memory of the original release and instead are fascinated by evocations of a past which has been reinterpreted *in the light of the present*. This aesthetic of the past is evident in new recordings, too. For example, the use of musical clichés associated with early rock 'n' roll from the early 1970s onwards (Mud and Shakin' Stevens, for example) ensures that rock 'n' roll will never (quite) die; similarly, in the 1960s groups like The Temperance Seven aped 1930s British dance bands, and in the 1990s The Beatles found powerful imitators in Oasis. The timbre of the lead vocal in 'Video Killed the Radio Star' by The Buggles (see Chapter 3) provides another example of this aspect of pop music.

Hence, pop music can be both 'the unofficial chronicle of its times' (Hennion, 1990, p. 205) and an evocation of an idealized sense of an imagined, collective past. This at times contrived sense of the familiar also inevitably brings a sense of accessibility: the record does not alienate listeners by confronting them with too many new ideas. Accessibility is, in turn, further enhanced by the simplicity of much pop music – an insistent simplicity that is supported by a high level of repetition. Hence pop music would appear to emphasize familiarity, accessibility, simplicity and repetition – qualities that, from the Western art music perspective, tend to imply a passive and undiscriminating audience. Yet these apparently predictable and undemanding artefacts are listened to again and again by both producers and fans with great intensity and pleasure. Since these aspects are fundamental to an understanding of pop music, they will be explored in a little more detail in the following sections.

Simplicity and repetition

The simplicity of much pop music is evident musically and lyrically. First, the short phrases, regular phrase lengths, simple time signatures and mostly step-wise diatonic melodies that characterize pop music result in simple musical ideas that are easily memorized by the listener. Second, the restricted harmonic palette and movement, uncluttered textures and clearly defined instrumental roles all support and encourage the perception of this melodic simplicity. Finally, highly sectionalized, non-developmental forms with short, concise, well-defined sections deliver the content in small, easily followed portions. Similarly, the lyrics of pop music display a fondness for simplicity with limited vocabulary, short sentences, much use of cliché and straightforward narrative themes. Simplicity is a major characteristic of pop music and, unlike the tendency in many other kinds of music to become more musically complex over time, the simplicity of pop persists to the present day.

Repetition is also a vitally important characteristic of pop music. The artefacts of pop – the record and video – are themselves infinitely repeatable and, consequently, the appreciation of pop music is founded on the ability to listen or view again and again. The promotion of a pop record on the radio involves multiple playings of that record. This is partly so that as many people as possible hear it, but also implicitly highlights the characteristic that pleasure is derived from listening to the same musical artefact several times: a pop record that does not continue to delight after several hearings is unlikely to be successful.

There is also a high level of internal repetition within individual pieces of pop music. Siegmund Levarie and Ernst Levy describe repetition as 'the basic mode of idiogenesis'[8] and point out that, 'In music it can never be quite so mechanical as in visual decoration, because the passing of time always modifies the repetition in its relation to the original. Of two apparently identical musical statements, the second contains irreversibly the memory of the first' (Levarie and Levy, 1983, p. 237).

In pop music, the fact that few songs are through-composed tends to give a prominent role to repetition of musical material. Repetition appears at several different levels: first, the repetition of a hi-hat cymbal or bass drum sample, for instance, over and over again, several times per bar; second, the repetition of a short musical idea within a section (a bass line or guitar figure, for example);

third, the repetition of whole sections within pop songs, like the ubiquitous repeated chorus. (For a more detailed analysis of repetition within a piece of pop music see Chapter 6 on 'Relax' by Frankie Goes to Hollywood.)

As mentioned, the repetitive simplicity of much of pop's musical material belies another vitally important quality: these musical ideas must be immediately likeable (or interesting, or intriguing) and remain so after numerous listenings. Making a pop record takes a surprisingly long time given that many pop records aspire to a sense of freshness and spontaneity. It also requires highly focused concentration. A simple musical idea may well have to be listened to literally thousands of times in the process of production. Certain ideas simply cannot sustain the listener's interest for such long periods, and these are usually rejected at the production or even pre-production stage. The process of pop music production provides an invaluable testing ground for the viability of musical ideas since fundamental to a successful production is the continued enthusiasm and belief of the composers, musicians, technical staff and producer throughout the process.

Clearly repetition permeates pop music and, one would imagine, contributes to the pleasure it gives. However, repetition rarely appears as a valued musical characteristic for most commentators: Boulez, for example, describes repetition as '"sedating" … with memory',[9] suggesting repetition appears contrary to reasoned thought. Yet this is perhaps the essential pleasure of repetition in pop music – it excites by its very lack of demand on mental activity, and enables an unreasoned, yet no less involved, response from the listener. The Hegelian linear view of time (as often represented by through-composed music), fundamental to Western notions of history and logic, is, at least momentarily, replaced with a cyclic one. As Blaukopf writes: 'Historical perspective springs from a way of thinking that is tied to the linear concept of time: the sequence of events is no longer viewed as cyclical activity but rather as linear history' (Blaukopf, 1992, p. 32). In repetitive pop music significance comes about rather like a religious mantra instead of through reasoned argument.[10] Cyclic notions of time are more closely aligned with the natural world, while the linear view of time is that which humanity attempts to impose on nature (and itself): it is progress, a sense of development and an ordered future. As such, the enjoyment of this aspect of pop music might be regarded as somewhat subversive and socially threatening.

Round and round, like a record

As mentioned, the repetition found in so much pop music also occurs at a higher level through the often modified repetition of musical ideas between pieces. Through sampling and scratching, portions of earlier records are used as the basis of new recordings (see Chapter 4 on Malcolm McLaren and Chapter 7 on The Art of Noise). Similarly, remixes rely on using sounds from existing multitrack recordings which are then rearranged and modified to create new, and often radically different, versions of the same piece (see Chapter 8 on Propaganda). Finally, pop records from the back catalogues of record companies can be re-released and gain further commercial success, often following their use as part of a film soundtrack or in a television advertisement.

Some writers interpret the notion that pop, unlike rock or 'serious' music, does not develop in a demonstrably linear way, negatively:

> The history of *pop* ... is more usually one of successive, not progressive, styles and performers ... In pop there are always stars serving out chunks of disposable music which will be forgotten as soon as they have left the charts. Succeeding generations of pop stars merely do the same things. If you think of history in the European sense of continuous progressive development, then pop is outside history. (Blake, 1992, p. 20)

Yet it is a mistake to suggest that pop music does not undergo periods of rapid stylistic change: a hit single from the 1970s will often sound very different from one of the 1980s, for example. The elements which many music commentators use as a yardstick to illustrate change in 'serious' music are often the ones that remain most constant in pop: changes in structural organization; changes in harmonic language; changes in melodic writing; and changes in instrumental ensemble. Instead pop tends to change rhythmically, change in timbral qualities (particularly vocal, with all the implications of phrasing, accent and microphone placement, as well as tone), in visual impact, in stylistic message, in how pre-existing musical ideas are assembled and in iconography.

Machine aesthetics

While the musical characteristics of pop music might be said to simply change rather than develop in any discernible, linear way, and so give little sense of historical progression, when it comes to technology, a clear sense of progress emerges. Pop music is inextricably linked to technology: it is realized with technology (the wide range of devices that constitutes the modern recording studio) and perceived through technology (television, radio, CD player, etc.). Perhaps more importantly, the artefacts of pop music – audio and video recordings – could *only* exist as a result of the mass production techniques that modern manufacturing technology has made possible. As audio technology develops, so pop music changes, yet the ways in which technology permeates pop music have received relatively scant attention. Hence the readiness of some commentators to assert questionable views:

> Technology is seen to threaten not creative status but creative practice or what Peter Fuller once called the 'joy of labour': 'I think we may have to accept that

William Morris was right; machines may be useful to us for all sorts of things. They are, however, fundamentally incompatible with true aesthetic production'. (Frith and Horne, 1987, p. 173)

Certainly, for much contemporary popular music the use of technology has blurred distinctions between '"live" and recorded sound, between musicians and engineers, between composition and performance, between natural and unnatural noise' (ibid., p. 174). Therefore, given its dominant and pervasive role, it would be surprising if technology did not have some impact on pop music. As shall become evident later in this study, certain technologies channel the creative energy of artists and give rise to particular kinds of artefact. Moreover, the image of the machine as an object of power and beauty recurs again and again in twentieth-century popular art generally, and pop music in particular (see Chapter 8 on Propaganda). Thus not only are the production and reception processes of pop dominated by technology, but often also the semantic content: pop music exists through technology and is often *about* it too (see Chapter 3).[11]

Pop and television

While comparing rock and pop may be useful in highlighting some of pop's most important characteristics, it does not account for several others that cannot be altogether ignored. These are perhaps most easily elucidated by the ways in which pop music is presented and represented on television, pop's largest and most important public arena.

While there have been many different programmes devoted to popular music, one should be considered central to any discussion of British pop music: BBC Television's *Top of the Pops*. It has been running, at peak viewing times each week, for over 35 years and, as its name suggests, presents several current, commercially successful, pop records in each programme. The continuing success of this show demonstrates an important characteristic of pop music that is often ignored by commentators: it appeals to a large, non-expert audience.

Over the years there have been a number of minor changes in the style of presentation of *Top of the Pops*, however, for the purposes of this study, it is useful to highlight a few important elements which have remained constant throughout the programme's long history. First, instead of attempting to present a seamless flow of music, each record or 'performance' (for many years the performers would mime rather than actually perform) is introduced, often in the manner of a radio DJ. Indeed, many of the presenters on the programme have also been DJs from Radio 1, the BBC's popular music radio station. And, like radio presentations of pop music, this method of delivery again tends to emphasize the basic creative unit in pop: the single. The focus on a particular recorded format is further supported by the second regular element in *Top of the Pops*: the 'Top 20' countdown, culminating in a playing of the week's best-selling single. The final unchanging aspect of the programme is the inclusion of a young, and fashionably dressed, standing audience that is seen to dance or at least move to each of the records.

Top of the Pops tends to draw upon several presentational characteristics originally established by radio but, as television, adds further elements which are central characteristics of pop: the idea of image and the notion of a mixed-media art form. These aspects are most evident in a secondary, but no less important, artefact of pop music: the promotional video. The pop video evolved during the 1960s to enable musicians with an international following to promote their recordings without necessarily having to actually take part in specific television shows. The success of the promotional video as television was such that specific channels, devoted entirely to their presentation, were quickly established (for example, MTV).[12]

The recent ITV series *Pop Stars* and *Pop Idol* have provided a different, but no less potent, view of pop music. The furore and polarity of opinions which these series attracted, once again illustrate pop music's ability to provoke: that so many people seem to want to involve themselves in debates on the value of pop music suggests that pop continues to raise certain fundamental questions about art and society. While this is no place to evaluate the merits or otherwise of such programmes, they have attracted high viewing (and voting) figures and, for the purposes of this study, illustrate some of those characteristics which the general viewing public value and appreciate in pop music performers.

Pop and commerce

Like much television, pop music – also sometimes known as 'commercial' music – functions within a relatively free market economy. This has enabled certain companies and individuals to become extremely wealthy and, consequently, the successful pop musician is often regarded as a glamorous individual, empowered financially as well as socially. A further consequence is that pop music has gained a somewhat tainted and ambiguous reputation. The question of whether pop music is motivated by artistic endeavour or the lure of 'easy money' has generated a great deal of debate over the years. Artistic pursuits and financial gain are often mistakenly regarded as mutually exclusive, yet all artistic institutions, as well as the artists themselves, not only need money to survive but may also, perhaps wrongly, come to consider financial status as some kind of measure of artistic success. Furthermore, the system whereby certain kinds of art require state subsidy tends to inadvertently perpetuate the notion that art should somehow be above financial considerations. As should be evident, a hint of naive romantic idealism often clouds discussions on this complex issue.[13]

In fact, this view of art as a market-based commodity has enticed a number of budding artists to actively take up pop music. Dieter Meier of Yello, for example, said 'I was attracted to pop music precisely because "it turned the elitist morality of art on its head, as a form where the market is dominated by the consumer"' (Frith and Horne, 1987, p. 109).

Pop and fashion

As a market-based, inessential commodity, pop music invites comparison with the fashion industry. It is not simply that pop records seem to become fashionable rather like items of clothing, but also because, like pop music, fashion clothes are often regarded as a frivolous luxury, a childish fad, an irrelevance which nevertheless appears to generate almost obsessive enthusiasm. Like pop music, fashion clothing is designed, manufactured and marketed, like any other consumer product, by an industry which must persuade people to spend more money than necessary for their physical well-being on something of often little or no superior functional benefit. Brian Eno observes that 'all products gradually assume the status of paper money (that is, all products become objects in which confidence is the biggest source of value)' (Eno, 1996, p. 54).

Moreover, like fashion, pop often presents a brash, flashy, flaunting image: a similar courage seems to permeate displays on the fashion catwalks and presentations on *Top of the Pops*, for example. Frith and Horne feel that Andy Warhol made a significant contribution when he suggested that 'Culture is Advertising, Advertising creates Fashion, and now Fashion was Art – his aim was to complete the circle that make the innovatory imagery of the twentieth-century avant-garde a part of the High Fashion discourse' (Frith and Horne, 1987, p. 64).

Noteworthy here is the idea that pop music is *unashamedly* fashion-conscious, addressing the perfidious whims of an ever-changing, largely uninformed and historically unaware youth audience, rather than offering the rigorous sense of historicism to which most 'high' art forms seem to aspire.[14]

Let's dance

As mentioned, the *Top of the Pops* 'audience' is not only fashionably dressed but also dances to the music. A close relationship between dance and music has always existed. However, at some point in their development, musical genres have a tendency to dissociate themselves from bodily movement: Blaukopf notes this with regard to religious music,[15] but the same applies to the transition in the Baroque from dance forms to stylized dance forms, the change from swing to bebop in jazz, perhaps even the transition from rock 'n' roll to progressive rock. This is a recurrent pattern: a popular musical style, explicitly linked to dancing, makes the transition to 'listening music'. Dance music, perhaps because it is designed primarily to evoke a physical rather than a mental response, is rarely considered worthy of serious study and, instead, is often regarded as a lesser and more ephemeral form. Contrary to many other forms of music, pop has included musical elements intended to encourage dancing throughout its history.

For at least the past 30 years there has been a thriving dance music culture in the UK giving rise to a plethora of genres. Each genre is characterized by specific tempos, recurrent rhythmic motifs, particular timbral emphases and musical arrangements. Once such a genre becomes established and has achieved a sufficiently large following, it is taken up by pop musicians, and those musical characteristics begin to appear in pieces of pop.

That much pop music is either intended to encourage dancing, or exhibits musical characteristics associated with dance music, results in certain rhythmic patterns, tempi and timbres recurring in a range of pieces. These common elements change as dance styles evolve, often aping the changes occurring in clubs. Over the past 30 years styles of dancing have tended to be physically angular and energetic. The music intended to invite and accompany these movements has been generally staccato in character with as much contrast as possible between sound and silence. This contrast, emphasized by repetition and by the kind of powerful sound systems found in clubs, makes the music relentlessly insistent, evoking a bodily rather than a mental response.[16] Hence, like most other kinds of music created to encourage dancing, most pop dance music keeps to a constant tempo, employs short and predictable phrase lengths, and is structured in such a way as to keep the dancers dancing throughout the piece. While some of the elements of pop dance music are predictable and common to many pieces, each piece will also strive to assert some kind of musical individuality. Even so, as mentioned before, the borrowing of several of the musical characteristics of a particular style once it has established a certain level of commercial success, is a recurrent feature of pop music.

Image

In addition to fashion and dancing, *Top of the Pops* highlights another major aspect of pop music: the notion of image. Although there are notable exceptions (see Chapter 7 on The Art of Noise), in most cases, a pop group's image will largely be articulated through the lead singer. 'As singers became the dominant pop stars, so the meaning of the pop song changed. The song ... was now a vehicle to display the singer's personality rather than being the object of the music itself' (Frith in Martin, 1983, p. 21).

While pop music generally shuns extreme musical originality, it does place great emphasis on personality. Each recording, each video, each performance attempts to convey a special sense of individuality through distinctive performance characteristics: timbre and phrasing of voices and instruments; physical movement, etc. Instead of aiming for purity and consistency of tone and delivery, timbre and phrasing are expected to be idiosyncratic: pop music has no performance ideals to which all individual performers aspire. Rather than follow standardized movements, pop performers develop and exhibit particular characteristics of physical behaviour which support their distinctive, and often entirely premeditated, persona. These personae range from the natural and complex to the theatrical and absurd, the entirely believable to the utterly fantastic. Pop musicians construct and promote their own particular image and then consistently present it in their work, and in this sense a high level of originality is often evident.

An attractive or interesting personality and a sense of individuality are vital attributes of any successful pop musician's image, while a high level of musical ability is far less important. A consequence of this is that fans are charmed rather than alienated: the new, young pop star (and the new ones are almost invariably young) is talented rather than gifted, and human rather than superhuman. The image of a pop star or group is not only articulated visually in promotional videos and appearances on the television, but in a variety of media.

Mixed media

'Pop has always involved a mélange of *at least* the following: melodies, sounds, language, clothes, fashions, lifestyle, attitudes to age, authority, relationships, the body and sex, dancing, visual imagery and the reassessments of value in all these things' (Eno, 1996, p. 393).

As the above quote suggests, a primary characteristic of pop music is that it is a mixed art form which includes a diverse range of artistic elements such as music, poetry, movement, drama and visual imagery.[17] It is not accidental that pop music as we know it today developed with the growth of television, which provides sound *and image*. Although the promotional video and the newer interactive CD have tended to be less commercially successful than the audio recording, each recording has its own specially designed, and usually highly evocative, cover, often with the lyrics included on the inner sleeve or booklet. Visual and verbal elements are offered to the buyer before the recording is purchased. From an aesthetic perspective the interaction between audience and artefact is obviously multiple and complex. For a full appreciation of the artefact, the perceiver must relate diverse elements, first, to each other (the relationship between clothes/movement/sound, for example), then, through the process of contextualization, to other, similar works.

The approach adopted in this book largely concentrates on the musical and technological characteristics of certain pop records. However, references to (and interpretations of) lyrics, image and packaging are included in the analyses which make up the second part of this study, where they are considered pertinent to a fuller understanding of the pop artefact: pop music is not only a slippery concept but a complex one, too.

Notes

1. Negus (1992), Frith and Horne (1987) and Frith, Straw and Street (2001).
2. Jones (1992), Zak (2001) and Gracyk (1996) for example.
3. See Bracewell (1998).
4. For a discussion on authenticity in rock see Keightley in Frith, Straw and Street (2001, pp. 131–9).
5. It is perhaps worth mentioning at this point that pop musicians and pop consumers are neither gender, nor race specific, but tend to be younger than the stars and fans of rock who are predominantly male and white.
6. 'Second thoughts on a rock aesthetic: The Band', *New Left Review*, No. 62 (1970), partially reprinted in Frith and Goodwin (1990, pp. 315–20).
7. UP 36346.
8. 'Musical growth can be accomplished only by either idiogenesis or heterogenesis. To continue a given musical unit, one can repeat it exactly or varied, or one can juxtapose a contrasting musical unit. There are no other possibilities of growth' (Levarie and Levy, 1983, p. 237).
9. Boulez (1990, p. 93). Also quoted by Middleton.
10. Richard Middleton has written extensively on repetition in popular music: see Middleton (1990); his paper given at the IASPM conference, July 1995; and the article 'Over and Over' (http://www2.rz.hu-berlin.de/fpm/texte/middle.htm.).
11. Machine aesthetics have even permeated the dance floor: during the period 1979–85 a dance popular with British teenagers was called 'The Robot' and involved machine-like movements of one's head, arms and legs.
12. For a full exploration of the pop promotional video see Goodwin (1993).
13. See Frith and Horne (1987, pp. 108–10) for an overview of Andy Warhol's contribution to the debate on art and commerce.
14. See Chapter 9 on Grace Jones for further exploration of the links between fashion and pop.
15. 'It was precisely Christianity's ideological "hostility to the body" that provided the basis for the subsequent autonomy of music' (Blaukopf, 1992, p. 147).
16. In particular, the bass and 'sub-bass' frequencies included in much modern dance music, when played over a large and powerful sound system, are quite literally felt rather than heard.
17. In this sense, pop music might be regarded as a kind of popular *Gesamtkunstwerk*.

Chapter 2

The Production of Pop Music

By studying how pop records are made one begins to appreciate the level of creativity involved. The technologies used to produce pop records are both hugely varied and in a state of almost continuous development and refinement. Moreover, the ways in which these technologies may be, and often are, combined and manipulated offer the potential for a high level of innovation and creativity. While the development of those elements traditionally associated with creativity in music – melodic, harmonic, rhythmic and structural manipulation/innovation – often may be derivative in pop recordings, the ways in which technology is used are often highly innovative. The result is a vast body of work characterized by variety and startling innovation in sound and sound manipulation. And it is at this level that the study of pop music becomes truly worth while.

While the traditional musical characteristics of pop often tend towards the simple (and in some cases simplistic) and straightforward, the procedure from conception to finished product is long and complex. In this respect pop is similar to other types of popular music. A brief comparison with the production practices of rock reveals, however, a few important differences. First, the emphasis placed on synthesizers and samplers in pop music not only results in a greater timbral range but also firmly links it to a technology that has been developing rapidly in the past 30 years or so. In contrast, rock continues to be dominated by electric guitars, bass guitar and drum kit – instruments whose basic timbral characteristics were fixed, at least in terms of production, in the 1970s, and whose design characteristics go back to the 1950s.[1] Second, in pop music the use of sequencers to control synthesizers and samplers removes much of the emphasis that rock places on individual instrumental dexterity. Third, pop tends to involve more people in the production process as evidenced in the credits for songwriters, arrangers/orchestrators, sampler operators, keyboard and sequencer programmers, and an array of session musicians which often feature on pop album covers. Rock production, on the other hand, appears to be rather more self-contained and to result primarily from collaboration between a record producer and the members of the band.

The strong link between pop music and an ever-developing technology ensures a continually evolving 'sound' in pop, while the presence of an often extensive team behind the production of a pop record undermines the notion of a single artist/creator, and hints at the range of procedures involved in the production process. This chapter will look at some of these procedures in more detail.

An aural art

The act of listening underlies the entire pop music production process: the melodic and harmonic characteristics of a pop song will tend to evolve through improvisation; arrangements will often be composed using a musical instrument digital interface (MIDI) based sequencer controlling synthesizers and samplers; the record will be constructed timbre by timbre through the multitrack overdub technique; and, finally, it will be mixed (or remixed) over a variety of audio systems, using an array of signal processing devices. Throughout this often lengthy and complex procedure the piece is *heard* – pop musicians tend to work directly with sound rather than any form of notation or other mediating system. Perhaps the only exception to this rule is the visual information imparted by the computer screens and displays used in digital editing, sequencing, sound synthesis and mixing-desk automation.

While an understanding of music theory may be useful to pop musicians, it is significant that many successful pop musicians have never learnt how to read music notation. Pop music is rarely transcribed or published in the form of a full score. Although this absence of notation is not unique to pop music, it is a significant factor in the way songs are conceived and realized. Blaukopf distinguishes between 'prescriptive' notation (that is, the contemporary use of notation), which determines how something is to sound, and 'descriptive' notation (the original function of notation), which records how something sounded (Blaukopf, 1992, p. 160). Modern technology might be regarded as providing resources (recording and sequencing) which enable the pop musician to bypass both these functions of notation. Moreover, unlike the direct and particular relationship to sound that every musician evolves over time with their instrument, orthodox Western music notation tends to merely suggest a standardized response which takes no account of the numerous idiosyncratic and idiomatic gestures that make each performer and performance unique. Furthermore, traditional notation is often limited to the depiction of certain kinds of pitch organization (the chromatic scale tuned to equal temperament) and rhythmic gesture (simple subdivisions of periodic pulses) over all other sound parameters. Pop musicians, by working directly with sound, are able to bypass these notational constraints and, similarly, aspiring pop musicians often learn by listening to recordings rather than by reading notation. The absence of a score and the importance of the record as the central artefact of pop music also encourage those who study popular music to address sound recordings as the definitive 'text'. However, traditional musicology, which tends to prioritize the score, is ill-equipped to deal with music in this way.

This emphasis on listening and the absence of notation enable pop musicians to explore and exploit parameters like timbral change, and treat frequency and time as continua rather than elements to be divided in simple mathematical ratios as 'pitch' and 'rhythm'. And the ability of pop musicians to work in this way is supported and enhanced through the use of modern electronic technology.

The recording studio as resource

In the past 40 years the resources and working practices of pop musicians have changed considerably. Stereo analogue tape recorders have been replaced by digital multitrack machines with far superior audio specifications, operational characteristics and editing facilities. The four- and eight-channel, valve-driven mixing desks of the 1960s have been superseded by 48- or 60-channel mixers with highly resourceful equalization controls, extremely flexible signal routing and 'total recall' automation. With the growing numbers of digital mixing desks the modern recording studio is often entirely digital, reserving analogue signals purely for the initial and final points in the recording chain (that is, microphones, amplifiers and loudspeakers). Similarly, signal processing devices offer vastly improved performance and diversity of control through the development of digital technology. However, it is the use of new technologies as providers of sound sources which have resulted in some of the most important changes in the production of pop music: synthesizers and samplers now supply many, and in some cases all, of the sounds heard on pop recordings. These new resources, now often appearing as software programmes within an integrated digital audio system, offer a very high degree of flexibility, as well as enormous control to the pop musician when working with sound. Furthermore, many of these devices or programmes have become extremely accessible, and relatively inexpensive, because of the huge demand. Much of the music that may finally be recorded and mixed in costly studios will have been created initially using digital systems in a less expensive environment – the now ubiquitous 'home studio', which has become virtually a prerequisite for any aspiring pop musician. One result of this has been a breakdown of amateur/professional status in the production process. And this breakdown is also evident in the equipment itself: manufacturers now rarely distinguish between 'professional' and 'domestic' products.

From analogue to digital

The transition from analogue to digital audio technology has had a profound impact on all aspects of pop music production and is one of the key issues in this book. Indeed, the impact of digital technology is such that many of the products themselves are not separate devices but computer programmes, designed to work within an integrated digital audio system. This transition to digital technology has not only brought about a revolution in working practices but has also played an important role in determining how pop music as an art form has evolved in the past 25 years. This is because digital technology has not merely improved sound quality but has fundamentally altered the ways in which musical gestures are created, manipulated and interact with one another.

In fact, apart from improvements in sound quality, the advantages that digital audio technology provides over analogue technology initially appear relatively minor: infinite copying with no deterioration of quality; non-destructive, software-based editing; and the eradication of distortion (that is, unwanted 'deformation of the signal or recording medium at any point' as defined by Capel, 1991, p. 63). However, each of these features has precipitated important changes not only in how pop music is made but also in what it sounds like. Moreover, the transition from analogue to digital technology also affected how pop music is consumed with the introduction of the digital compact disc in 1982.

Each time an analogue recording is copied, the audio quality of the copy will always be less than that of the original, while it is possible to copy a digital recording infinitely without any deterioration of audio quality. Assuming that the same standards are retained throughout the process, this means that the audio data available to a listener on a compact disc is precisely the same as that produced at the mastering stage of the production – an exact, flawless copy. Hence sound, as audio data, can be transferred within any production system and also between any number of production systems without any degradation in quality.[2] For the pop musician this enables a much more flexible approach to working directly with sound: single sounds, parts and even whole sections of pieces can be arranged and rearranged within the whole until the ideal settings are found.

Once a sound has been digitally recorded it can be manipulated in a wide variety of ways within a digital editing programme, and these manipulations are non-destructive. As a result, pop musicians can extensively explore the musical potential of recorded sounds without ever losing the original recording. It is possible to edit the tuning, timing and timbre of any sound either globally or in part. And since so much is possible with digital editing systems, it is the creative imagination of the pop musician that becomes the determining factor in pop music production, rather than any physical limitations.

The eradication of distortion in digital recording systems has had a rather different but no less profound impact on pop music. Up until around 1980 all pop recordings were made using analogue recording equipment, and specific working practices had evolved over the years, originally to minimize some of the limitations of analogue tape recording. Consequently, balance engineers in recording studios learned to record at as high a level as possible (that is, before the effects of distortion became unacceptable) to ensure that the omnipresent system noise (usually known as 'tape hiss') was largely masked by the high level of the required signal. Yet this process had an impact on the sound of the recording: signals recorded at high levels were always subject to some dynamic compression and harmonic distortion. Over the years this audible distinction between recorded sound and natural, acoustic sound became not only an accepted convention of pop music production, but also a sonic characteristic associated by listeners with pop music records.

With the introduction of digital recording systems, such recording practices not only became redundant but had to be consciously avoided: when too high an audio signal overloads a digital system, the sound is usually unacceptably distorted. Hence one of the most basic techniques of a balance engineer's art had to be discarded. As a consequence working practices within the studio changed radically and, in turn, the actual sound of pop music records evolved. The distortion that had, over the years, become a sonic characteristic of pop music was replaced by a new and audibly different clarity. Fans and producers of certain kinds of popular music had difficulty accommodating this new-found clarity. Many rock musicians and producers, in particular, were reluctant to embrace the new digital technologies, as their use resulted in sonic characteristics that were radically different from, and uncharacteristic of, the established genre.

Producers of pop music records, on the other hand, were among the first to champion the new digital technologies. Consequently, it was largely pop musicians who were responsible for evolving and developing specific working practices associated with these new technologies, and these practices have now largely become established throughout the record industry. The period 1979–85 was a particularly important time in this regard and, at least in part, explains the choice of recordings analysed in the second part of this book. However, one should bear in mind that even today, the transition from analogue to digital audio technology is far from complete and remains an ongoing process.

Using technology

> The technologies we now use have tended to make creative jobs do-able by many different people: new technologies have the tendency to replace skills with judgement – it's not what you *can* do that counts, but what you *choose* to do, and this invites everyone to start crossing boundaries. (Eno, 1996, p. 394)

Multitrack recording, signal processing, MIDI sequencing, and sound synthesis and sampling are the four essential techniques which dominate the creative processes involved in the production of pop music. The impact of these techniques is evident both in how pop music is made and in what it actually sounds like. The following sections will look at these technologies, the techniques which have evolved with their use and their implications for the ways in which pop music has developed, in a little more detail.

Multitrack recording

Multitrack recording involves the use of a tape recorder or other storage device, either analogue or digital, which allows the user to record each distinct instrument or voice separately and in series – a process known as 'overdubbing' – for a single piece of music. Each instrument or voice that is recorded is stored on a separate 'track' of the tape recorder (standard formats range from four to 96 tracks) and, once recorded, returns as a separate signal to a particular channel on the mixer. The multichannel mixer, an essential and central element in any multitrack studio, allows the user to 'balance' the signal from each track in relation to all the others. 'Balancing' involves the modification of the signal in a variety of ways including volume, timbre, and spatial position in relation to the other tracks.

Analogue tape recorders convert audio signals to magnetic patterns and store them on magnetic tape while digital recorders convert audio signals to digital information, which is then stored in a variety of formats. As outlined above, digital recording differs in several important ways from analogue recording, offering increased flexibility and resourcefulness to the musician. Yet in spite of the limitations of analogue recording, it provided a 'warmth' (that is, distortion) that many musicians were reluctant to lose. As well as greater flexibility, digital recording systems offer better specifications in terms of frequency response and signal-to-noise ratio. As should be evident, digital recording is a rather more transparent process that tends to neither add to nor subtract from the signal, while analogue recording is a more intrusive and sonically defining process.

Artistically, whether using digital or analogue systems, the rewards of multitrack overdub recording are enormous: first, recording each track separately enables the user to attain a much higher level of musical accuracy, specifically timing and tuning; second, each track can be recorded in minute sections, bit by bit and, as a consequence, levels of performance are achieved which would be impossible 'live'; third, the complete separation of each track offers control of volume, timbre and spatial positioning of the signal on that track *in relation to the other tracks*; and, finally, decisions as to suitability of virtually all the separate sounds need only be made at the mixdown stage – that is, when the multitrack tape is 'mixed down' to the stereo format that will be the final product. However, while multitrack overdub recording offers great artistic control and flexibility, it also channels (both literally and metaphorically) creativity into particular patterns of working, emphasizes certain musical parameters over others and is time-consuming. As will be seen, these factors influence creativity and affect the nature of the final art work.

Signal processing

The complete separation of each track offered by multitrack recording is attractive to artists partially because of the access and control of each sonic detail that it offers. Signal processors are designed to modify and enhance one or several of these sonic details. These modifications can range from clearly audible and often dramatic changes in the signal to extremely subtle changes that are barely perceivable by the listener. The startling changes, often known as 'effects' (or even 'FX'), most notably include artificial reverberation, delay, chorus, flanging, phasing, radical equalization, compression and frequency specific compression, auto-panning, pitch shifting and even emulation of analogue distortion. The subtle changes may include slight timbral modification through equalization, 'psychoacoustic enhancement' and gentle reductions in a single part or the entire mix of the dynamic range through the use of compression.

Signal processing not only ranges from the dramatic to the barely audible but also from the 'natural' to the utterly artificial.[3] A modern digital signal processor designed to imitate reverberation, for example, is capable of producing anything from a relatively convincing emulation of a 'typical' room ambience to a completely 'impossible', and hence highly unrealistic, environment – 99 seconds of reverberation time, for example. The use of effects is often the result of musical convention rather than the depiction of some natural acoustic phenomenon. Hence, a certain process may be applied to a particular signal, in the first instance, as one way of differentiating it from other recordings. However, a successful recording of this sort will spawn many imitators and as a result may establish new conventions of signal processing. Obvious examples of this trend include the slapback tape echo associated with rock 'n' roll in the 1950s, or the use of gated reverberation on drums established by Hugh Padgham on the recordings of Phil Collins in the early 1980s.

Signal processing offers the pop musician a wide range of facilities which enhance audio signals in a variety of ways, producing sounds that are fundamentally more interesting because they are more varied and complex. Pure, stable, unchanging timbres, especially when subject to a great deal of repetition in a recording, tend to lack character, provoke little interest in the listener[4] and are consequently rarely found in pop music.[5] At the same time, the persistent use of certain kinds of particular signal processor setting on several different recordings can result in a sense of tired cliché.

MIDI sequencing[6]

The development of MIDI as a universally recognized code by Dave Smith and others in 1982 was both a remarkable and significant achievement.[7] While other microprocessor-based technologies continued to be dogged by company-led diversity, the synthesizers, samplers, signal processors, mixing desks and computers used to make music could operate together through a single interface and code – MIDI. With companies as numerous, diverse and competitive as Yamaha, Roland, Sequential Circuits, Casio, Akai, Korg, E-Mu and Kawai among others, the successful establishment of MIDI in the early 1980s was all the more impressive.

At the simplest level, MIDI enables one keyboard to control another device: the musical information (pitches, rhythms, articulation, phrasing, sometimes called 'performance information') played on one keyboard is transmitted along a MIDI cable to another device whose sound producing circuits respond without any physical contact with the player. The information transmitted along a MIDI cable can also be stored and manipulated in a variety of ways by a computer using a program or a dedicated device – a 'MIDI sequencer'. Once recorded as data, this information can be edited in terms of pitch, rhythmic position/accuracy/ duration, articulation, etc. and then combined with similar information on other channels (there are 16 MIDI channels but modern systems can enable many more) to build up complex musical arrangements, often involving several synthesizers and samplers, each producing a number of different timbres, and all controlled and synchronized with each other via MIDI.

Most modern synthesizers, tone modules (synthesizers without keyboards developed as a direct result of MIDI), samplers and computer sound cards are 'multitimbral' – capable of producing several different timbres at the same time – and can often receive MIDI data via all 16 channels simultaneously. The MIDI studio (often a 'home studio') may contain several synthesizers, samplers and tone modules, a multichannel mixer, a controller keyboard, a personal computer (usually Atari, Macintosh or PC) with MIDI sequencing software (for example, Steinberg *Cubase* and C-Lab *Notator*, which tended to dominate the British market during the 1990s), a monitor system and a two-track mastering device. A multitrack tape recorder is not always part of a MIDI home studio since the sequencing programme often replaces it – offering multiple separate tracks which can be used to 'record' MIDI performance data for any of the MIDI compatible devices.[8] When used in conjunction with a multitrack tape recorder, it is possible to synchronize the running of the MIDI arrangement with the tape recorder, without actually recording any of the MIDI sequence, by recording a synchronization tone on one of the tracks of the tape recorder. Although several formats exist concurrently at the moment (MIDI sequencer and multitrack tape recorder, MIDI/audio recorder, MIDI sequencer and hard disk recorder, etc.) it is increasingly the case that all digital processes are handled within a single, multi-tasking computer environment.

While MIDI sequencing programmes often have the visual aspects and operating procedures associated with multitrack tape recording (specifically a number of tracks and tape recorder transport controls: play, rewind, record, counter, etc.), the facilities for editing and manipulating recorded MIDI data are somewhat greater. Tracks may be transposed, made more rhythmically accurate (to a very fine resolution) and changed in terms of note duration or keyboard touch velocity; pitch and modulation wheel data can be recorded and modified; synthesizer patch change data may be included and edited; and notes can be added or deleted at will. This level of flexibility (which offers so many parameters that can be addressed creatively) combined with the fact that the MIDI studio tends to be operated by a single person, results in finely wrought music arrangements painstakingly assembled over many hours of work.

In spite of the highly editable nature of MIDI information, MIDI does impose certain constraints. The accurate imitation of traditional acoustic instruments via MIDI, for example, remains problematic. Furthermore, digital synthesizers often lack the distortion, limited bandwidth and dynamic range of many of the 'interesting' sounds associated with pop music. Another area of constraint is the human interface. For several years it has been possible to make relatively cheap, reliable instruments, like MIDI guitars and wind instruments, which 'play' like traditional acoustic instruments and transmit MIDI data to synthesizers and tone modules. One would imagine that the physical instrumental technique built up by the player over a number of years – the level of competence and expression – could be harnessed, recorded and edited if necessary, to produce remarkably convincing results. However, the further away in terms of spectrum and envelope the timbre is, the more difficult it is to make the physical technique of the particular instrument work in relation to that timbre.

A further limitation of MIDI is the present lack of accurate voice tracking devices. Various microphone-plus-processor devices do exist but tend to be inadequate for anything but the simplest musical gestures. Clearly, the voice is the most human of musical instruments and the ability to convert the vast range of vocal utterances into MIDI data would offer enormous expressive power. However, the sheer amount of data that would have to be generated by such a device would be large and consequently difficult to handle in real time. For many modern applications MIDI is beginning to show its age and its background in keyboard-driven synthesizer technology: MIDI was developed at a time when the fast processors necessary to deal with digital audio (as opposed to MIDI performance data), as well as storage media, were very expensive. The past 20 years have seen huge advances in the power, speed and cost of digital technology, and the modern home studio increasingly emphasizes audio rather than MIDI data.

The considerable flexibility of some of the musical parameters offered by MIDI sequencers, and the few but distinct limitations of MIDI, result in the generation of music showing the following characteristics: all the sounds tend to be in tune and in time with each other (except when a sampler is used[9]) since minute fluctuations in pitch and rhythm, typical of a 'live' situation are very hard to produce convincingly on a sequencer; there is rarely any attempt to produce a sequence that could be mistaken for a 'human-played', 'live' piece; the visual nature of the computer screen presents musical material as simple blocks and, as a result, encourages the production of pieces with additive, rather than organic structures. Musically, the sequenced piece tends to be faster than the 'human' equivalent and lacking in many of the subtle performance elements (essentially deviations in pitch, rhythm, timbre, loudness, tempo and any combination of these) that 'give life' to a piece. On the other hand, the sequencer replaces these elements with technically perfect precision, a sense of balance that would be unlikely outside the mixdown environment of the recording studio, and a blatantly mechanical effect, particularly evident in the rhythm section of pieces of dance music from the 1970s onwards.

A review of MIDI reveals a system and approach largely dominated by the synthesizer keyboard – this, after all, was the original reason why MIDI was developed. MIDI allows for 128 pitches with middle C (C3) placed at number 60. This, like several other parameters, was established as a standard and any new user of MIDI is immediately confronted by a 'normal' configuration that is difficult to bypass. This specific pitch configuration stresses the Western chromatic scale tuned in equal temperament and is reinforced with the use of the key set-up found on any MIDI keyboard. Hence any MIDI system will support a particular approach to pitch organization not only through its protocols but also through the physical actuality of its input device: the MIDI keyboard. Although controllers such as MIDI guitars and MIDI wind instruments are available, they are the exception in sequencing and tend to be limited to real-time performance use. It is significant that computer-based MIDI sequencers should often define pitch through a visual representation of the keyboard, thus encouraging the MIDI user to adopt this particular notion of pitch organization. Similarly, program change, pitch and modulation wheel data are all derived from synthesizer technology and do not appear on other musical instruments. Hence MIDI reflects its background and reinforces the particular parameters associated with that background: MIDI developed as a result of the demands of keyboard players and keyboard manufacturers, and both of these were often directly associated with the production of pop music.

Yet MIDI has also had a profound effect on the way traditional musicians perform when making recordings. As mentioned previously multitrack overdubbing enables individual musicians to record 'performances' that are in reality collages of the best parts of several performances. When a recording is underpinned by some kind of MIDI controlled sequence, and this is the case with most pop records, then an extremely high level of accuracy for rhythm and pitch is established at the beginning of the recording process. Musicians overdubbing their parts onto such sequences are expected to achieve a similar level of musical accuracy. In other words, musicians are expected to play with machine-like precision, and such requirements inevitably prioritize accuracy over individual expressive gesture. Hence, the unique expressive performance qualities audible on many of the recordings of great musicians up to the 1970s have increasingly been replaced by a less personalized style of musical performance. It is only singers who have managed largely to avoid this trend and, as a consequence, they have become increasingly responsible for the 'human' elements of the recording.[10]

Another effect of the rise of MIDI has been a change in the expressive impact of the rhythm section in pop music. When a drummer and bass player record their parts – usually the initial stage of an overdub recording – a certain kind of concentration and effort is involved, and this results in a particular sense of striving which is actually audible in the performance itself. When similar parts are generated with a MIDI sequencer, this sense of human striving can be absent.[11] Often, in order to compensate for this, the MIDI sequenced rhythm section has to be played at a faster tempo than the human equivalent. It is perhaps as a result of this that the tempos used for dance music have been increasing in the last 20 years.[12]

Hence the impact of MIDI has been profound and far-reaching. It has not only changed the ways in which pop music is made, but also, in many cases, who is making it: increasingly pop songs begin as ideas generated on MIDI sequencers in home studios by people using computers, rather than playing musical instruments. Moreover, the performance styles of musicians working in pop music studios have had to evolve in order to accommodate the exacting demands of machine-generated musical precision. And, finally, the human, gestural elements which were such a feature of the rhythmic underpinning of pop music up to around 1975, have been steadily replaced by a more 'automated', machine-driven sound which requires ever faster tempos in order to compensate for the absence of the sense of human effort.

Sound synthesis and sampling

The idea of creating interesting sounds by using electronic machines to generate signals, which can be converted into acoustic energy through the use of an amplifier and loudspeaker, is confined to the twentieth century. Indeed, affordable (at least to the relatively wealthy consumers of the West), mass-produced synthesizers only began to appear in the late 1960s, as a direct result of the development of transistor technology and the principle of voltage control. The transition from analogue synthesis, in which continuous electrical fluctuations 'correspond in a one-to-one fashion with the audio output' (Armbruster, 1984, p. 306), to digital synthesis, in which 'potentially continuous fluctuations in value (such as amplitude)' are divided 'into discrete quantized steps' (ibid., p. 307), heralded significant changes in both sound and practice. While digital synthesis may appear to be a step backwards, by denying the continuous fluctuations that more faithfully represent the acoustic characteristics of sound, the practical and financial advantages are numerous. Typically, a modern synthesizer will be MIDI controllable, 64-note polyphonic and at least 16-part multitimbral; it will have hundreds of 'preset' sounds which will be extremely diverse in character and on-board signal processing including digital reverberation, chorus and delay; it will offer extensive editing features and may also have built-in sequencing capabilities. These facilities are only financially feasible with the use of microprocessors and, as a result, virtually all modern synthesizers are either separate digital devices or software programs within a digital system.

While modern synthesizers offer an extremely wide range of possibilities for the production of sound, they are also subject to a series of inevitable limitations and constraints. First, as the number of editable parameters on any synthesizer defines its potential for creating new sounds, it also defines its complexity. The greater the complexity, the longer and more difficult it becomes to create new sounds. Hence, paradoxically, the greater the potential, the less likely that potential is to be realized by synthesizer players. Second, the imitation of acoustic instruments remains a yardstick by which many synthesizers are judged – perhaps wrongly since such imitations are rarely convincing. While the source might even be a digital recording of a particular 'real' instrument, the expressive capabilities and variety of articulations that characterize that acoustic instrument cannot easily (or, perhaps, feasibly) be convincingly re-created on a synthesizer. Partially convincing imitations are only possible if the musical ideas are themselves generated directly in conjunction with the limitations that the synthesizer voice inevitably imposes. In other words, the limited qualities of the synthesizer sound allow only a limited musical potential. Third, and as mentioned above, the keyboard, with all its obvious expressive limitations, remains the dominant user interface. Fourth, while the development of digital synthesizers has greatly enhanced the possibilities of sound synthesis and timbral simultaneity, they have the reputation of producing sounds that lack 'warmth' and 'drive', and, as a result, in recent years, there has been something of a renaissance of the use of the older analogue synthesizers of the 1970s. Moreover, in an effort to give character to digital synthesizers and compensate for their reputation for coldness, manufacturers have produced instruments with highly distinctive sounds as presets. While these sounds immediately attract potential buyers, they quickly become clichéd through overuse and lack of adaptability on pop recordings. Paradoxically, then, the digital synthesizers with the most character are those which become dated most quickly. Finally, many modern digital synthesizers are defined by the qualities of the samples that are the source waveforms within the system, and the modifications in signal by the on-board signal processor(s). The presets, which are used to sell the synthesizer to the musician, are often the best possible configuration of those samples, with appropriately impressive signal processing. Now, in spite of the wide variety of sounds that most synthesizers can produce, these waveforms and the specific signal processing give the synthesizer a particular aural character. This character can be rather difficult to define but is often easily recognizable. For example, the analogue synthesizers of the 1970s all tended to work in the same way (that is, subtractive synthesis based on voltage control using discrete electronic components); however, the richness and depth associated with Moog synthesizers (defined largely by the quality of the filters) was different from the 'sparkle' of Arp synthesizers. Today, the aural differences between synthesizers are often more pronounced because the samples that lie at the heart of their sound-generating capabilities have more distinctive characteristics. Furthermore, on-board signal processing tends to level out differences between separate sounds on a synthesizer, providing a 'wash' of pseudo-presence that is partly impressive because of its very artificiality. The fundamental point here is that a particular synthesizer, regardless of its resourcefulness in terms of programmability, will tend always to have a certain distinctive tonal character whatever particular timbre is actually being sounded.

Sampling will be dealt with in much greater detail in the chapter dealing with The Art of Noise. However, a number of points are relevant here. First, it should be noted that the use of sampling in pop introduced new ways of using pre-recorded material. These sonic manipulations owe something to the way vinyl records are used rhythmically by DJs ('scratching'), as first developed by hip hop musicians during the late 1970s. Specifically, the ways that samples are used in pop often tend to emphasize the rhythmic characteristics of the music. Second, much pop sampling relies on identification of specific samples on the part of the listener. As we shall see later, there are various levels of sample identification which affect the way the sample functions within the piece. The important point to note here is that the identification of each sample is only relevant *in relation to* the rest of the piece: meaning is often generated through the interaction between an identified single sample and its context (and often not on a purely musical level). Third, while many of the manipulations offered by samplers directly relate to the techniques developed in *musique concrète*, they also tend to offer many of the characteristics of synthesizers rather than tape recorders: polyphonic and multitimbral, and controlled by a MIDI keyboard with facilities for filtering and manipulating the envelopes.[13] Finally, samplers enable musicians to introduce sounds that are acoustically impure (often with limited bandwidth and dynamic range) and use them rather like sonic *objets trouvés*: their imperfections provide their aesthetic significance. The grainy, distorted nature of many samples also provide a useful foil to the 'sanitized' quality of the sounds produced by many modern digital synthesizers, and as a result give a greater range and depth of sound palette. Once again, it is the *interaction* between samples and synthesized sounds which generates the listeners' interest. Moreover, because samplers can record rhythmic phrases as well as single timbres, those human elements mentioned in relation to MIDI sequencing can be reintroduced into the arrangement of a pop recording by sampling breakbeats, for instance, from records of live musicians.

It is for these reasons that sampling has become so important and significant in recent years: sampling, in spite of its background in digital technology, offers ways of countering the sonic impact of purely machine-driven and machine-generated music, and reintroducing sounds (albeit digital recordings) of human-made sound.

Clearly, the technological resources used in the creation of pop music offer great flexibility and control yet, at the same time, tend to impose certain constraints and encourage particular working methods. All these factors have a direct impact on the musical characteristics of pop records. The following section will look at a few of the specific creative/technological situations which arise in the modern recording studio in a little more detail, in order to illustrate how modern audio technology and artistic creativity interact.

Recording the voice

The lead vocal is an extremely important element in most pop music: it commands the listeners' attention not only because it is a human voice – *it speaks* – but also because it carries the lyrics of the song – it communicates the song's 'message'. Moreover, the emphasis pop musicians place on accessibility, familiarity and personality is especially evident in the lead vocal through idiosyncratic phrasing, pitching, timbre and regional accent. Pop musicians have long recognized the importance of the lead vocal – prior to multitrack recording, the quality of a 'take' was often judged by the success of the lead vocal – and have developed a number of techniques in the recording studio designed to enhance certain aspects of it. The first is the careful and close positioning of the microphone in relation to the singer, which gives the recording, and hence the listener, a sense of intimate closeness.[14] The effect of this is to imply an 'intimate, personal relationship with fans' (Chanan, 1995, p. 128), which paradoxically emerges from a machine. As Michael Chanan writes, specifically of the Walkman: 'This is perhaps the final coup in the negation that recording perpetrates on musica practica, where instead of music coming from bodies in front of the listener, it is reduced to an unreal and intangible space enveloping the isolated head' (ibid., p. 155).

The second technique developed in the recording studio to enhance the lead vocal is the 'drop in'. Multitrack tape recorders not only allow each timbre to be recorded separately but also enable musicians to record and edit their particular contribution, a section at a time, by dropping the track in and out of record mode. For the lead vocalist, this means that each phrase, each word even, can be dropped in several times until it is judged suitable. One consequence is the greatly increased amount of time required to record a lead vocal. A more significant consequence is the sheer intensity of expression and musical accuracy that can be obtained from this process and it is here that the judgement of pop musicians referred to by Brian Eno (Eno, 1996, p. 394) is clearly so vital.

A further technique is to ensure a relatively constant dynamic level, regardless of the actual dynamic fluctuations inherent in the singer's performance in the studio, either by the practice of 'riding the fader'[15] or subjecting the signal of the lead vocal to dynamic compression during recording. This enables the level of the lead vocal to always balance and hence be intelligible in relation to the other sounds on the recording. Once again, however, it results in the illusion of a performance that would be impossible to achieve naturally.

These three techniques are not confined to the recording of the lead vocal, although the latter often receives the greatest attention in the recording of pop music. They illustrate both the level of sound control that is possible in the modern recording studio and also the level of competence necessary to produce a convincing musical artefact. While traditional musical skills are often required to generate the initial acoustic events, the sensitive manipulation of technology can greatly enhance the final artistic product.

The above techniques are rarely employed in the recording of classical music and illustrate fundamental differences in intention between the two genres. Classical music was conceived with live performance in mind, while pop is usually created *as a recording*. Hence, classical music recordings seek to evoke the illusion of live, purely acoustic performance, while pop music is free of such constraints. Moreover, being conceived in the recorded medium, the creation of pop music involves the exploitation of all those elements which are characteristic of that medium, and as such provides a huge market for the development of technology which further extends the creative possibilities.

The fade-out

The fade-out is an obvious example of a sound characteristic of pop music that bears no relation to acoustic reality. Many pop songs have no definite ending but simply decrease in volume to silence. This characteristic has no real parallel in any genre of acoustic music: in 'live' performances of pop music, for example, the song often ends with some kind of traditional cadence producing a strong sense of finality. Another perplexing aspect of the fade-out is that it clearly does not have any spatial connotation: using slightly different techniques (that is, decreasing the volume of the higher frequencies more quickly and increasing the relative level of the reverberation in relation to the direct sound), could imply that the music was simply receding or going away from the listener. Instead, the music as a whole simply gets quieter. Strangely enough, a successful fade-out is, in reality, quite difficult to achieve: it needs to start at a particular point (neither too early nor too late), be over at a particular point, and usually follows a non-linear pattern of volume decrease (decreasing more quickly at the end). It is worth noting that the fade-out usually begins in the chorus of a pop song, often at the point where the arrangement is at its fullest ('chorus to fade' is a standard phrase in sheet music). It is as if the whole of the song aspires to this point and the fade-out, by denying the listener the sense of success and achievement implied by multiple repetitions of the final chorus, acts as a kind of goad encouraging the listener to listen to the record again – and consequently might be regarded as a purchase incentive. Furthermore, the fade-out, which produces a final effect that is acoustically impossible, can be seen as an assertion of the technological nature of recording and also 'echoes' the radio DJ's technique. Finally, the fade-out also functions as a way of ending a repeated musical pattern which should not be brought to an abrupt end since the musical effect of the repetition would then be destroyed. In effect, there is nowhere else to go, the chorus representing the high point of the song, and the music is forced to die away.

Recording the lead vocal and the fade-out are two relatively straightforward examples of how pop music production relies on the technology of the recording studio in order to achieve specific sonic results which have no parallel in the acoustic domain. Their ubiquity in pop music also illustrates the importance of the recorded medium within the genre and highlights the central role played by recording studio technology. Moreover, the ways in which this technology is used are often inseparable from the creative impulse, rather than a product of it: the pop record is conceived, as well as realized, through the manipulation of technology. Yet, as mentioned above, the production of pop music is usually the work of several different people, each with their own particular musical or technological expertise. Typically, a single overseer is required to marshal and guide this team to ensure that a uniquely focused, aesthetically cohesive artefact – the recording – emerges from all this diverse artistic and technological activity: the record producer.

The record producer

> When the disco sound originated in Munich, a new star was born, the Producer. Regarding the future, I would predict that the predominance of the producer and the role of the sound, will remain. (Wallis and Malm, 1984, p. 160)

> They're not playing, they're just having adventures in modern recording.[16]

While the changes in music brought about by modern technology have evidently had a profound effect, musicological studies and analyses which explicitly address these issues are surprisingly scarce. This partly stems from the pace of change and the complexity of the technology. Gaining intimate, practical knowledge of specific pieces of equipment is highly time-consuming, and often quickly becomes redundant as new products and techniques are developed. Furthermore, the traditional analytical parameters of music (pitch, tonality, rhythm, arrangement, etc.), those with which academics are most familiar, continue to demand attention. However, modern pop music is clearly bound to this technology both creatively and perceptually, and appropriate analytical methods need to be developed which not only take this relationship into account but also illustrate its pervasive influence.

A fundamental aspect of the relationship between technology and pop music is embodied in the record producer, who oversees the production process in the recording studio. However, the role of the record producer 'can often be very enigmatic and unclear' (Gillett, 1980, p. 93):

> Is it the guy who sits in the corner of the control room grinning encouragingly and chopping cocaine, or is it Phil Spector, who writes the music, hires the musicians, grooms the vocalist, invents the sound, designs the image and then marries the lead singer? Somewhere between these extremes is a vague cloud of activities that get credited on record covers 'produced by …'. (Eno, 1996, p. 394)

Like film, pop music recordings come about as a direct result of the work of a number of different people – each with specific tasks to accomplish. Typically, the film director tends to be the person who oversees the range of work required to produce a film and also makes the important artistic decisions. The pop music producer plays a similar role. Since the nature of the producer's work is fundamental to this study, it is necessary to examine it in more detail.

In directing the production of recordings, the pop record producer fulfils a number of different functions. First, the producer negotiates a budget with the record company with which to produce the recording(s). This budget will include the cost of studio time to record and mix the recordings, hiring extra equipment, payments to session musicians, engineers' fees, personal expenses and all other costs incurred in the making of the recording(s). Hence, producers must be competent managers of money, able to fully cost a complex business venture. Keith Negus writes:

> At the beginning of the 1990s a major record company in Britain anticipated having to spend between £250,000–£330,000 over the first 12–18 months of an average deal for a new act; roughly broken down into £100,000 for advances to the artists, £150,000 for recording costs and £80,000 for basic promotional expenses. (Negus, 1992, p. 40)

Second, the particularly large sums of money involved in pop record production inevitably result in contracts that are legally binding. Hence, the record producer must be aware of the legally enforceable obligations inherent in the contract and have some grasp of this extremely complex area of law. Third, producers must be able managers of people. This is perhaps the most demanding aspect of their work because the number and variety of people involved in pop record production is high: the artist(s) with the recording contract, the recording studio staff, balance engineers, session musicians, specific operators of complex technology (synthesizer, sampler and sequencer operators), arrangers, managers and record company staff all make claims on producers' time and usually require an appropriate personal response. Hence, an astute understanding of social and psychological skills is also a prerequisite.

The range of abilities listed above, while vital, is not in any way related to the producer's musical judgement, which will be the primary reason why they are employed by a record company. The producer's success, measured by the number of records sold, ensures future contracts with other artists. Astute and ambitious producers have to assess which of the recording projects they are offered are most likely to be commercially successful. Success is not just vital for a producer's reputation but has a direct bearing on the amount of income they will receive from royalties and on the budgets available for future projects. As Keith Negus points out: 'The artist is "giving" some of their "creative" royalty points to the producer. Hence, the producer's musical significance is inscribed in these financial arrangements' (Negus, 1992, p. 83). Producers must estimate the creative and financial potential of artists within the constraints of a given budget. With pop music this is extremely difficult: only a small percentage of records released manage to sell in sufficient quantities to cover their production costs.

While the ability to manage money, understand legal documents, work successfully with a range of people and predict potential success is a prerequisite of the record producer, their work mostly takes place in the recording studio and is predominantly of an artistic and creative nature. Here the producer must have an overall conception of what needs to be achieved creatively as the process itself progresses, and they must guide and direct the personnel involved in order to realize this vision. Although, in practice, decisions often come about through consensus, the final responsibility for the artefact rests with the producer. Paradoxically, although record producers wield great artistic power in the recording studio, they are rarely credited with physically producing any of the recorded sounds, nor do they necessarily manipulate any of the audio equipment. Walter Legge, the classical record producer, described himself as 'a midwife to music' (Schwarzkopf, 1982, p. v). Charlie Gillett probably best sums up what a record producer does as follows:

> The essence of the producer's role is to be the catalyst for the other participants in the studio, the person who sparks them off into delivering their best, together. In some cases, the producer is doubling up some other role, as songwriter, arranger, recording engineer, or performing musician, in which case he (producers are rarely women) can lead by example and physically control what happens. But more often, the producer is there strictly as a producer, and has to coax or bully the team into an inspirational performance. (Gillett and Frith, 1996, p. 111)

In the popular imagination the recording studio is, somewhat unfortunately, regarded as a mysterious place – a fiercely guarded environment full of expensive, complex technology, arcane processes and riddled with jargon. The record producer, who retains a relatively low profile in the high-profile world of pop music, is a central figure in this forbidden realm.[17] The recording studio is also perplexing because, being a closed environment, assigning specific artistic responsibility for each element of the finished product is virtually impossible. A recording may be attributed to Kylie Minogue, for instance, but it is readily acknowledged that she was not entirely responsible for every aspect of it. The transposition of the Romantic notion of the artist as inspired individual into popular culture is undermined by the reality of pop music production, which is almost invariably the result of teamwork. And it is in the recording studio, the very crucible of creativity in pop music, that the team works. This team comprises not only the stars but also shadowy, often nameless figures – such as session musicians, arrangers and balance engineers – directed by the record producer. Hence, ascribing artistic responsibility for specific musical gestures is largely inappropriate in the analysis of recordings of pop music. The record producer, who carries the financial and artistic responsibility for the recording, must ultimately rely on the rest of the team.

Although record producers have become an established element of pop record production, the working practices that they adopt and the artistic power that they wield remain somewhat vague and less clearly delineated. Obviously this whole area will, to a certain extent, be dependent on individual personalities, the demands of specific projects and the kind of technology that is adopted or available. Furthermore, the popular perception of record producers will be coloured by those figures that have established international reputations in the past: Phil Spector, Joe Meek and George Martin, among others.[18] As Angilette points out, 'recordings should not be compared with live performances. Each is an art to be valued separately' (Angilette, 1992, p. 27). Unlike cinema, which quickly became established as a form of art separate and distinct from theatre, recording remains more closely linked, at least linguistically, with other kinds of musical activity. This has often led to fierce debate as to the precise nature of music itself, and has resulted in suggestions for the use of new phrases to distinguish between traditional musical activity and the manipulation of sound using recording studio technology (see Wishart, 1985).

The importance of recording is evident in the effect that it has had on the notion of music as an art form. Music recording has a relationship to music similar to that of cinema to drama. Yet there has been surprisingly little reflection on the aesthetic impact of this transformation. In the field of classical music, the ideas of Glenn Gould[19] while being extremely influential have not resulted in new generations of purely studio-based performers. And although the transformation from 'live' musician to studio musician has already taken place in pop music, few have drawn attention to it and its impact on the art of music.[20]

The analyses that follow attempt to address this issue through a study of seven recordings attributed to the British pop record producer, Trevor Horn. One of the reasons why these particular recordings have been chosen is that, while they feature a highly diverse range of artists with often markedly different musical characteristics, they present to a lesser or greater extent many of the aspects summarized in Chapter 1. Moreover, these records were all produced between 1979 and 1985: a time when recording studio technology was changing rapidly with the transition from analogue to digital technologies. The choice of this particular producer is also significant: Horn, perhaps more than any other pop record producer of the time, embraced these new digital technologies and developed working methods with them which later became established practice in the pop recording studio. Finally, these records were all relatively successful in the pop charts. While this factor is no guarantee of artistic worth, their very success did ensure that these records were highly influential on the work of many subsequent pop musicians and hence often imitated.

Unlike many film directors, record producers rarely receive critical acclaim for their work and tend to be largely ignored in academic circles. While they may be awarded accolades within the record industry – Trevor Horn has received several 'Grammy' awards for his work – in a wider cultural context they remain largely anonymous. As Charlie Gillett perceptively notes:

> I still think that record producers achieve a miracle every time they capture the spirit of a song or an idea, when they make it 'work' for the rest of us who listen to the record; and that they will eventually be recognised as having been more important than many of the artists who received all the attention at the time. (Gillett and Frith, 1996, p. 119)

Notes

1. The sense of a timbral convention in rock is often compounded by gestural conventions. For example, the lead vocal in rock is often characterized by a certain kind of vocal delivery that includes not only timbre but also accent and phrasing.
2. The transference of digital recordings over the Internet has been a major issue facing the record industry in recent years and raises problems of copyright enforcement, as well as offering new possibilities regarding production, distribution and consumption.
3. For a discussion of the question of fidelity versus definition see Chion (1994, pp. 98–99).
4. This at least partly explains why most musicians employ vibrato and even the early monophonic analogue synthesizers had a low frequency oscillator (LFO) to provide modulation of the oscillator, filter and/or amplifier.
5. Hence, the eighth and sixteenth note hi-hat patterns found in much pop music of the 1990s, usually derived from a single sample, were often treated by a flanger to ensure that each individual sound had a slightly different timbre.
6. For a detailed technical overview of MIDI see Rumsey (1990).
7. MIDI was provisionally agreed as an acceptable standard by all the major manufacturers of electronic instruments at the exhibition of the US National Association of Music Merchants (NAMM) in 1982.
8. Modern MIDI sequencer programmes (for example, *Cubase VST*) offer the user the possibility of recording and editing several audio tracks in the manner of a multitrack recorder, as well as MIDI.
9. Samplers often use parts of existing recordings as their sound source. If the source recordings are of human performances then fluctuations in pitch and rhythm are usually present. Moreover, several samples taken from different recordings, played together, can result in further deviations in pitch and rhythm. This has become a feature of many hip hop records, as well as pop recordings influenced by hip hop.
10. This is something of a simplification since it is usually the case that pop musicians in the recording studio will generally try to ensure that some 'human' element is present in every recording. While this is often provided by the lead vocal, the use

of sampling, particularly the use of samples taken from pre-MIDI recordings, has become another way of introducing such elements.

11. Compare, for example, the difference in impact between the rhythm section on Grace Jones's album, *Nightclubbing* (played by Sly Dunbar and Robbie Shakespeare), and that on the track 'Jones the Rhythm' on *Slave to the Rhythm*.

12. The standard *circa* 120 beats per minute (bpm) associated with 1970s disco is a good deal slower than the *circa* 175 bpm now found in much modern drum and bass.

13. With a tape recorder one physically manipulates magnetic tape while with a sampler the digital recording is manipulated as part of a software program, rather like a word processor. Because the way one may manipulate recordings with a sampler are so varied and convenient, and any manipulation can be 'undone', a much more exploratory approach to collage-based composition is possible.

14. This effect goes back to the radio 'crooners' of the 1930s. It can also be used to create a more aggressive and immediate effect too – giving the listener the impression that someone is shouting in their face – and is often used as such in rap and punk.

15. Here the recording engineer monitors the signal coming from the singer's microphone and controls the signal level that is sent to tape by manually changing the position of the output fader.

16. From *Adventures In Modern Recording* (T. Horn/B. Woolley/S. Darlow) by The Buggles, copyright 1981 Island Music Ltd, Carlin Music Corp. and Perfect Songs.

17. This mysterious, creative quality sometimes gives the record producer a Svengali-like image. See Mackay (1981, p. 90).

18. See Cunningham (1996), which charts the work of these important producers as artists.

19. See Gould (1987) and Payzant (1978).

20. Jones (1992) and Zak (2001) remain exceptional in this regard.

PART TWO
Technology and Creativity

Chapter 3

'Video Killed the Radio Star' by The Buggles

The Buggles was a relatively short-lived duo (1979–81) comprising Trevor Horn and Geoff Downes. Downes was a keyboard player who, like Horn, began his career in the 1970s as a session musician. As is the case with many singles chart groups, The Buggles never performed live, and existed for their fans purely through recorded media: vinyl, magnetic tape and video. This chapter will analyse certain aspects of The Buggles' greatest chart success, 'Video Killed the Radio Star',[1] but the analysis of this single will be preceded by discussion of a more general issue which lies at the heart of the study of modern technology and artistic creativity.

The ghost in the machine

Artistic presentation through the media of modern technology characterizes much twentieth-century popular art: photography, cinema, radio, television and audio recording are all the result of relatively recent technological developments, and are entirely dependent on the exploration, use and support of that technology. While these technological inventions have transformed the whole nature of popular art, attitudes towards them remain mixed. For example, Sousa – one of the first musicians to profit from the phonograph – predicted 'a marked deterioration in American music and musical taste, an interruption in the musical development of the country, and a host of other injuries to music in its artistic manifestations, by virtue – or rather by vice – of the manipulation of the various music-reproducing machines' (Gelatt, 1984, pp. 146–7). The expression of similar worries concerning the artistic consequences of new media permeates the twentieth century. Mechanized reproduction, as commented upon by Benjamin,[2] is evidently one aspect of this concern. Since the artefacts of much popular art are both created and perceived through the intervention of modern technology, the human elements can often seem rather subsumed, indeed almost buried. Hence, the creative and perceptual potential inherent in these relatively new technologies can at the same time excite and disturb.

While reluctance to accept change is perhaps a natural human reaction, there is also often a sense of alienation evoked by these technologically generated and technologically perceived artefacts of popular culture. The aesthetic experiences of viewing films and listening to records are clearly fundamentally different from those of their more traditional counterparts: theatre and 'live' music. Notions of 'live' music and drama came about with the advent of modern technology. The very idea of 'live' music only evolved as a result of the radio: broadcasters needed to differentiate between recordings and 'live' performances for listeners. Implicit in the notion of 'live' popular art is the view that films and records are not live, but 'dead'. Photography, film and audio recordings present sounds and images created by (and often representing) human beings entirely through the media of machines. These sounds and images, stored traces of real human actions and capable of infinite duplication, are often intended to be highly believable, producing illusions of naturalness and life. At the same time, after the initial production process (that is, the physical creation of the sounds and images) it is technology that stores and 'replays' these illusions of human reality. This singular quality of technologically mediated art has been highlighted by a number of commentators. Claudia Gorbman, for example, notes that one of the functions of 'live' music for silent films was 'to mediate between live audience and "dead" mechanically-produced shadows on the screen' (Gorbman, 1987, p. 43). Similarly, Hans Eisler and Theodor W. Adorno noted that:

> The pure cinema must have had a ghostly effect like that of the shadow play ... . The need was felt to spare the spectator the unpleasantness involved in seeing effigies of living, acting, and even speaking persons, who were at the same time silent. The fact that they are living and nonliving at the same time is what constitutes their ghostly character. (Eisler and Adorno, 1947, p. 75)

Roland Barthes writes of 'that faint uneasiness' (Barthes, 1982, p. 13) which seizes him when he looks at his image on a piece of paper, and later describes photography as 'a kind of primitive theatre, a kind of *Tableau Vivant*, a figuration of the motionless and the made-up face beneath which we see the dead' (ibid., p. 32).

Specifically referring to recording, Evan Eisenberg describes listening to records as 'a séance where we get to choose our ghosts' (Eisenberg, 1988, p. 46). He later writes at some length on Francis Barraud's famous painting, *His Master's Voice* (ibid., pp. 51–3), which was first popularized by the Consolidated Talking Machine Company and remains a much used image to this day. In all these cases the machine carries implications of both life and death. As we know, the phonograph[3] and the camera can record sounds and images of living people, and these traces continue to exist after those people have died: some element of them is preserved, rather like ghosts. Michel Chion, referring to both cinema and work by Merleau-Ponty, defines a ghost as 'the kind of perception made by only one sense' (Chion, 1994, p. 125). Such a definition encapsulates this particular aspect of the phonographic experience.

Moreover, there is a fascination, among artists and audiences of popular culture, with the narrative potential of the situations that such machines are able to create. At one level, it is the whole area of artifice that allows the audience to 'see' or 'hear' something that is not and could never be a 'record' of a single, linear performance. In this instance the performer becomes superhuman, and the machine enables them to transcend their actual performing capabilities. Similarly, the use of unusual camera angles, such as close-ups, or microphone placements, such as close miking, offer the viewer or listener a privileged physical proximity to the performer. This aspect produces some unusual situations: a film actor's body may be known in detail by an audience who have never met him in the flesh; a recording of a small vocal ensemble allows, through close-miking every singer, both a clarity and separation that would be impossible to achieve acoustically. Finally, the machine can also have a detrimental effect on artists' careers. The analogy with manual workers facing redundancy through the rise of automation should be apparent. In the arts, various technologies have emerged which alter the relationships between artists and audience: in music, for instance, the phonograph, electrical recording, radio, the tape recorder, stereo, multitrack recording, sound synthesis, the cassette recorder, digital sampling and television have all precipitated change both in the production of the art work and its reception. The notion of the human casualty of technological change has itself provided an interesting theme in a number of works.

This chapter will now explore some of aspects of the relationship between audio technology, the creative process and the aesthetic response to popular music through an analysis of 'Video Killed the Radio Star' by The Buggles.

Music

'Video Killed the Radio Star' (and the album *The Age of Plastic*) was made without any drum machines or sequencers, even though it sounds like that. (Cunningham, 1996, p. 270)[4]

Like so many of the hit singles of this period 'Video Killed the Radio Star' has the basic rhythmic characteristics associated with disco: an insistent, indeed almost constant, reiteration of the four beats of each 4/4 bar at 132 bpm on either bass drum, or bass and snare drums alternating. Altogether the arrangement consists of drum kit, electric bass guitar, piano, synthesized strings and brass, electric guitar, synthesized sounds, and voices. Generally speaking, the timbres of the instruments are not unusual, while the voices, and particularly the lead vocal, are most distinctive. In common with much pop music, the harmonic language of this song is not complex: it employs a maximum of six basic chords. However, individual chords are often enhanced through the use of unresolved suspensions, particularly fourths and ninths. These chords retain their harmonic functionality while introducing a piquant dissonance. The song is, on the whole, melodically unpretentious with relatively restricted ranges, while the complete absence of any blues-based inflections (that is, modified thirds, fifths and flattened sevenths) is particularly noticeable. There is liberal use of syncopation in the instrumental lines, while the vocal melodies tend to be more rhythmically restrained. Indeed, the vocal line of the verse comprises simply a string of quavers.

Structurally the song is an intelligent adaptation of a typical pop song form. The inclusion of two separate middle eight sections – a truly musically different middle eight followed by a modified final verse – subtly disturbs expectations: it would be more usual for the fade-out to begin in the chorus following the first middle eight. The instantly recognizable, strongly tonal chorus with the 'sing-along' factor, is never repeated more than once at a time before the end, thus providing an excellent 'hook'.

Lyrics

The lyrics are conceptually both adventurous and unusual, yet couched in the simple, conversational language associated with the genre of pop music.[5] The verse presents a first person male narrator reminiscing about his admiration for a radio star ('back in '52') who was unable to make the transition to the audio-visual medium ('Pictures came and broke your heart'). Some 30 years later they (narrator and radio star) meet and acknowledge that the progress of technology and the passing of time make a return to the 'Golden Age of Radio' and, presumably, the youth of the narrator, impossible. The female voices of the chorus merely reiterate the phrase 'Video killed the radio star', harshly reinforcing the implications of the verse narrative. This line, which is also the title of the song, manages to evoke a range of images, from philosophical/political slogan to 'whodunit', and, as neither the gender nor the particular nature of the radio star's talent are ever made explicit, the lyrics shrewdly offer the listener's imagination the widest range of possibilities.[6]

Nostalgia is inherent in the lyrics of the verse: regret for the passing of years, a fond memory of adolescent infatuation ('You were the first one'). We shall see later, however, that this is a far more complex issue than first appears. It is worth noting in passing that nostalgia for a time long past is a surprising, but hardly unusual, topic for a pop single apparently intended for adolescent consumers.[7] The victim of technological change is, particularly in the popular arts, a recurrent image of the twentieth century – the silent film stars who did not manage the transition to the talkies, for example. However, also implicit here is the complex transition from a purely aural performance on radio to a pre-recorded (and highly manipulated) visual illusion of performance on video: perhaps one of the most radical developments in recent music history.

The lyrics raise a further series of issues relating to the ambiguous relationship between human beings and machines: first, the strong association between mind and machine ('In my mind and in my car/ We can't rewind we've gone too far'); second, the problems of mechanical copyright and intellectual property ('They took the credit for your Second Symphony'); and, finally, the apparent erosion of traditional musical skills by modern audio technology ('Re-written by machine on new technology'). The strongly self-referential quality in these lines, dealing explicitly with music technology, is evident.

Production and arrangement

Trevor Horn spent three months on the Buggles single 'Video Killed the Radio Star'. (Zak, 2001, p. 136)

Accepting that much popular music, and particularly pop music, only exists as a direct result of technological manipulation by artists in the recording studio, necessarily leads the analyst to consider specifically the relationship between technological processes and the artistic product itself. As in many pop records, the influence of recording studio technology and the working practices that it engenders, as opposed to the practical limitations imposed by live performance, are evident in several aspects of 'Video Killed the Radio Star'. For example, the multi-track and multichannel procedure, which separates every timbre, results in a final arrangement dominated by the technique of channel muting: individual timbres are either present or absent (*off* or *on*) and singly possess very little dynamic range. As a result most change is produced by addition or subtraction of timbres, not through organic growth or musical development. Furthermore, the sheer diversity of sounds, the level of accuracy of pitch and rhythm, and the high definition of each timbre achieved on this recording, are only feasible with the multi-tracking process.

During the relatively quiet introduction to 'Video Killed the Radio Star' one can detect quite high levels of system noise (or 'tape hiss' as it is more generally known) generated through the use of analogue tape recorders. The presence of this phenomenon indicates the use of analogue multitrack tape recording at the heart of the production process.[8] The audio quality perceived by the listener not only provides an indication of the technological means used to produce the recording, but also implies a particular period in time for its production.

Similarly, the timbres of the synthesized sounds – 'piano', 'strings' and 'brass' – have the sonic characteristics associated with analogue synthesis: standard voltage controlled waveforms as the basis of the sound; the slightly muted quality resulting from low pass filtering; relatively simplistic envelopes due to the use of four stage envelope shapers; and, especially evident with the 'brass' and 'string' sounds, the adoption of musical ideas which require minimal polyphony (most of the synthesizers available at the time were monophonic). Hence, regardless of any musical or lyrical elements, the specific technology used to create this recording gives the listener an aural indication of when it was produced.[9]

Initially, the most striking aspect of the production of 'Video Killed the Radio Star' is the extreme use of compression and radical equalization settings on the male vocal, which result in a highly reduced dynamic and frequency range. The resultant sound is reminiscent of an early radio broadcast[10] and is in marked contrast to the 'contemporary' clarity of the female voices that interject in the verse and sing the chorus.[11] The differentiation is strengthened by the use of different accents: the male voice has a mid-Atlantic accent, reminiscent of British radio singers of the 1940s and 1950s, while the female voices have a strong American – and specifically New York – accent. These elements provide timbral contrast but also imply historical contrast: the male voice sounds old-fashioned, whereas the female voices sound modern, through timbre, accent and implied (but illusory) variations in recording techniques. It is not surprising, then, that the verse text expresses nostalgic sentiments while the chorus does not.

A less striking but no less significant aspect of this production concerns the separate female voice that first appears in the third verse as a long wordless melisma backing the lead vocal. This voice has an operatic quality that is further enhanced by extensive use of reverberation, implying the kind of distant microphone placement and ambience traditionally associated with recordings of classical music. This voice reappears during the second middle eight section, with the words 'You are a radio star'. When this line is repeated, the balance between direct signal and reverberation shifts, suggesting that the singer, like a distant memory, is getting closer. Significantly this gesture is preceded by a perceptible increase in reverberation on the very last line of the male voice in the song, giving the impression of it receding into the distance. Once more, a strong contrast is established between the close, pop-like chorus voices, with their syncopated melodies and staccato phrasing, and the distant 'classical' voice, marked by predominantly down-beat melodies and legato phrasing.

There is an apparent reconciliation between these two contrasting voices when they appear together in the final fade-out, with the chant-like chorus voices accompanied by the classical voice. However, on the album version of the song,[12] there is an added coda, derived from the music of the verse. This appears in a serenely classical arrangement (albeit played by synthesized instruments) with no hint of disco beat.[13] This serenity is undermined by the appearance of a repeated recorded phrase: 'owa owa', from the female chorus voices, in marked conflict with the prevailing pulse and feel. A quick fade-out leaves one in no doubt that these two elements (which perhaps represent two opposing forces – old and new, then and now, classical and popular, radio and video, stasis and change, etc.) cannot in the end be reconciled.

Finally, the use of traditional word painting techniques is also evident in this production. For example, following the phrase 'You remember the jingles used to go', a synthesized sound, with many of the attributes of a jingle stick, is introduced. A more complex example is the synthesized brass line that follows the words 'Second Symphony'. Although reminiscent of a solo Baroque trumpet figure, its synthetic timbre is only justified by the line that follows: 'Re-written by machine on new technology'.

Hence, a variety of production and arrangement techniques are used to reinforce the ideas evoked by the lyrics. Nostalgia is repeatedly implied through the numerous contrasts between the old and the new, while the relationship between musicians and machines is firmly established both by word-painting and by the audible influences of the equipment used in the recording process.

Disco killed the radio star

In spite of the sense of common intent presented by the separate elements of 'Video Killed the Radio Star', its real fascination derives from a fundamental paradox: nostalgia for live music presented on a disco record. Disco was one of the first pop genres that was never intended to be performed live. The rise of disco in the 1970s was regarded with dismay by many musicians and the 'Keep Music Live' campaign, instigated by the Musicians Union in the UK, was a direct response to the perceived threat that it posed. First, disco, by being an infinitely reproducible product of the machine-dominated pop recording studio, was viewed as simply another manifestation of the pitiless advance of industrialized processes. Second, the popularity and the increasing number of discotheques, which dispensed with musicians by playing records, resulted in fewer live venues and less work. Finally, and perhaps most disturbing of all to the members of the union, disco seemed to celebrate its mechanical and repetitive characteristics: short, repeated phrases either played by sequencers and drum machines, or by musicians with machine-like precision, was intrinsic to the disco aesthetic. For example, consider the classic bass sequence of 'I Feel Love' by Donna Summer[14] with its utterly regular semiquaver pattern made possible by the arpeggiator of an analogue synthesizer.

Interestingly, these three characteristics have remained fundamental to debates about dance music up to the present time, although arguments are complicated by the emergence of the DJ – a live 'musician' who uses record decks and samplers to create new dance music in venues. While 'Video Killed the Radio Star' was in the first instance a chart single rather than a disco record,[15] it contains the vital elements necessary for a dance record of the time. The irony, then, is that a record apparently concerned with the adverse effect of technological change on human beings represents an ideal example of that very process.

'Video Killed the Radio Star' was extremely successful: it was Island Records' first number one single and, perhaps the ultimate irony, 'the innovative promotional video was later used to launch the MTV music channel in the USA' (Larkin, 1993, p. 207). Considering the subtle complexities and rich paradoxes that an analysis of 'Video Killed the Radio Star' reveals, dismissing it as a 'novelty song' (Hardy and Laing, 1990, p. 368), as one commentator has done, would seem inappropriate. It certainly has a number of musical elements in common with many of the other pop songs of the time, however, as explained in Chapter 1, the visible pursuit of originality for its own sake has never played a strong part in the aesthetics of pop music. Much pop music is rightly regarded as ephemera, intended to satisfy the transitory whims of adolescents, with no pretensions to lasting greatness. However, the apparent simplicity of many chart singles implies neither a simplistic message nor a simplistic response.

Notes

1. Island Records (1979), WIP 6524. Entered the UK singles chart on 22 September 1979.
2. Benjamin (1970).
3. Remember, Edison's original cylinder phonograph was able to record as well as playback.
4. Of the production of 'Video Killed the Radio Star', Horn is quoted as saying: 'We made Richard Burgess [the drummer] sound like a Linn [drum]. If there was a single buzz, if we even suspected he'd slowed down on one beat of a take, if it wasn't perfect – we wouldn't keep it.' (http://home.t-online.de/home/fisonic/tchmusin.html).
5. Trevor Horn has stated (http://home.t-online.de/home/fisonic/tchmostw.html) that the idea for the lyrics of 'Video Killed the Radio Star' was derived from a short story by J.G. Ballard, 'The Sound Sweep'.
6. In the video for 'Video Killed the Radio Star' there is a shot of a small girl tuning in to the radio which further complicates the interpretation of the narrator's gender.
7. In a different but clearly related context, Joseph Lanza writes of a music that 'celebrates a nostalgia for the future as it paradoxically looks ahead toward unsolved childhood mysteries' (Lanza, 1995, p. 190).
8. When 'Video Killed the Radio Star' was made the standard formats for the production of pop music were analogue multitrack and mastering tape recorders.
9. Of course, such indications are only fully appreciated years later by listeners accustomed to relatively noise-free digital recordings, and the brightness and clarity associated with digital synthesizers.
10. This sense of an early radio broadcast for the lead vocal is strongly supported by the imagery of the video, which shows Horn singing into a large and old-fashioned microphone. Similarly, the timbre of the voice is reflected in the use of black and white film for this image while the rest of the video is in colour.
11. In fact, these female voices were performed by Tina Charles with whom both Horn and Downes had worked as session musicians during the 1970s.
12. *The Age of Plastic* (Island Records, 1980).

13. In conversation Trevor Horn has referred to this coda as the 'Symphony', linking this section directly with the 'Second Symphony' of the verse.
14. GTO GT 100 (1977).
15. Real disco records tended to be longer (the 12-inch 45 rpm was the standard format) with a much more mixer-led structure and a more insistent use of repetition than the chart singles that aped their characteristics.

Chapter 4

'Buffalo Gals'
by Malcolm McLaren

After 'Video Killed the Radio Star', Trevor Horn produced several singles for the pop duo Dollar[1] and the ABC album *The Lexicon of Love* (1982).[2] He performed as a singer and bass player with Yes on the 1980 album *Drama*[3] and also produced two albums as part of The Buggles: *The Age of Plastic* (1980)[4] and *Adventures in Modern Recording* (1981).[5] The diversity and extent of his work during this period is staggering, particularly since the standards of performance, arrangement, and technological invention and manipulation on all these recordings are very high.[6] For the purposes of this study, however, the next important achievement, in Horn's career as a record producer is *Duck Rock*[7] with Malcolm McLaren, which undoubtedly influenced his subsequent work, as he readily acknowledged: 'for a few years, we had it all sewn up and going around the world working with Malcolm McLaren put me in a very strong position for a considerable time' (Cunningham, 1996, p. 272). *Duck Rock* entered the album charts on 4 June 1983, climbed to number 18, and included two Top 10 hit singles: 'Buffalo Gals' and 'Double Dutch'.[8] It was both an innovative and controversial album, not least because it represented a considerable creative departure for the already notorious McLaren, who until this point had largely been concerned with pop music management.

A charismatic manager

> [McLaren] is not the star who became a svengali, but the svengali who became a star. (Rogan, 1989, p. 352)

If the creative role of the record producer tends to be ambiguous in relation to the creation of the final 'product', then the influence of the manager on a pop group is even more so. Like record producers, managers are rarely known to the public. Exceptions to this rule, such as Colonel Tom Parker and Brian Epstein, achieve a certain degree of notoriety simply because the artists whom they managed became so famous that they were illuminated in some of the reflected limelight. Pop management is generally extremely diverse in nature ranging from the highly organized, financially astute and industry conscious business managers (Gordon Mills, for example) to the hugely charismatic, often manipulative, and artistically proactive svengali figures like Larry Parnes.[9] Malcolm McLaren, while showing some of the qualities of the former, is usually regarded as one of the most important exponents of the latter managerial style.

Together with his collaborators at Glitterbest – the management company that he established with fashion designer Vivienne Westwood and graphic artist Jamie Reid – McLaren was probably the most famous, or perhaps most infamous, pop group manager of the 1970s. As the manager of the proto-punk New York Dolls and, more importantly, The Sex Pistols, he is regarded as one of the most influential figures in the British Punk Rock movement, which had such a significant impact on popular music in the late 1970s. Like so many pop musicians, McLaren's interest in pop developed while he was a student of fine art (at Harrow, Croydon and Goldsmiths' College) during the 1960s. Influenced by the ideas of Andy Warhol and the situationist movement,[10] 'he realized the significance of fashion and style as a blank cultural canvas on which political ideas could be stencilled: "It's very important because I work with human beings. That's the only difference. Instead of using the canvas, I have to use human beings"' (Frith and Horne, 1987, p. 60).

McLaren's influence on British pop continued with the management of later groups such as Adam and the Ants and Bow Wow Wow. These groups are now rightly regarded as being seminal in the transition from Punk to New Romantic which occurred in the early 1980s and McLaren himself is sometimes viewed as 'the spider at the centre of the web which binds the seventies to the eighties' (ibid., p. 130). He certainly took a highly intrusive stance as a manager, dressing and generally defining the image of the groups he managed. He also actively promoted and documented his ideas through a variety of media including the film *The Great Rock 'n' Roll Swindle* (1980). This kind of documentation made punk 'a cultural form in which the theories all made sense! Within months of "God Save the Queen" punk had become the most theoretical (and theorized) music ever' (ibid., p. 133). This is perhaps rather surprising from an aesthetic standpoint, considering the elements which characterized punk rock: harmonic, melodic and rhythmic simplicity; limited timbres; structures highly reminiscent of early rock 'n' roll; chaotic delivery; and a general revelling in 'shoddiness'. As Johnny Rotten said, 'we want to be amateurs' (quoted in Hebdige, 1979, p. 109). These characteristics are quite contrary to the traditional view of the artist as an expert obsessed with the manipulation of a specific medium, while going against the then prevalent view of the pop star as an attractive and charismatic individual blessed with an innate talent to compose and perform. It is, however, possible to regard punk as a reaction to some of the rather overblown artistic pretensions of popular music of the mid-1970s, and particularly progressive rock, in much the same way as Dadaism sought to question high art in the early part of the twentieth century. It is perhaps no coincidence that 'punk should [have been] absorbed into high fashion at the same time as the first major exhibition of Dada and surrealism in Britain was being launched' (ibid., p. 159).

Like Dada, punk as a movement managed to overturn the prevalent pop aesthetic and also precipitate a period in which popular culture took on a more socially active role. As such, its importance as a movement is profound and McLaren's influence on it remains seminal.

From manager to artist

Having established himself as a major figure in punk rock, McLaren decided to 'transform himself into a recording star, despite the fact that he could not sing' (Larkin, 1993, p. 774). With Trevor Horn as record producer, he recorded, under the title *Duck Rock*, 'a collection of songs based on "field recordings" made in Africa and America, which led to McLaren being attacked for plagiarism' (Hardy and Laing, 1990, p. 511).

As a pop product, *Duck Rock* is a fascinating artefact, which raises a whole series of questions. First, the contribution that McLaren makes in terms of sound on the album is relatively slight: the credits are detailed yet ambiguous, so who exactly is responsible for what we hear?[11] This raises further questions of ownership in terms of creativity. Second, the inclusion of music from Africa, South America and New York reveals an interest in World Music which was relatively absent from the punk aesthetic: how did such a radical change in direction come about? Third, there are a wide range of disparate and seemingly unconnected elements both in the music and the record sleeve imagery – punk rock, Zulu singing and dancing, New York radio stations, 'scratching' and skipping, Hispanic New York culture, Afro-American religious ritual, Tennessee square dancing, etc. – and the question arises as to whether it is possible to create any artistically unified whole from such diversity. Fourth, why is the album entitled *Duck Rock*, although 'Duck for the Oyster' is one of the tracks, there is otherwise no reference to this phrase?[12] Finally, where is the star image? Record companies normally insist that 'an artist's identity is articulated and mediated to the public' (Negus, 1992, p. 66) as a fundamental part of the marketing of new artists. One could argue that McLaren already had a perfectly adequate public persona through his part in *The Great Rock 'n' Roll Swindle*: he plays a kind of Fagin character. However, the photographs of McLaren on the cover and the sleeve notes of *Duck Rock* do little to support this particular image: as suggested below, the pictures and text tend to baffle rather than explain.

Applied cultural theory

The front cover has a photograph of a wildly decorated portable radio cassette player of the kind associated with early hip hop.[13] It has cow horns, a leopard skin handle and several extended aerials, as well as the words 'duck' on the left speaker cover and 'rock' on the right (in a typical, multi-coloured hip hop graffiti font). Above the radio 'MALCOLM McLAREN!' is printed in Day-Glo lime and orange. The whole cover has a backdrop of what looks like symbolic 'ethnic' art with snakes and human figures. On the front this appears in two shades of pink while on the back it is in two shades of blue. These backdrop paintings are by the American artist, Keith Haring, whose 'graffiti-like work became a familiar motif in pop and specifically in hip hop culture in the 1980s, featuring as it did a striking blend of the primitive and modern: cave paintings for the urban age' (Warner, 1996, p. 98).

The back cover continues this theme with a variety of photographs: African American schoolgirls skipping; a Zulu family sitting outside with the same radio as that on the front cover (enclosed within an extremely simplified line drawing representing a television set); a black woman in traditional African dress carrying the radio on her head; a young man break-dancing; and McLaren himself wearing a bizarre hat and headphones, turning the dial of the radio.[14] As well as the list of tracks included on each side of the record, a range of words and phrases from the album appear in a variety of fonts, usually in the same Day-Glo colours, reminiscent of hip hop graffiti. Once again the implication that there are links between tribal culture and the youth culture of New York is evident. This recalls the work of Marshall McLuhan who wrote of 'the tribal drum of radio' (McLuhan, 1964, p. 298) in his assessment of the impact of new technology on human perception.

The startling and distinctive imagery of the cover, which posits links between tribal culture and the youth culture of New York, appears as some kind of concrete representation of cultural theory. Certainly the use and manipulation of cultural theory is a characteristic of much of McLaren's work. As Simon Frith and Howard Horne remark: 'Punk, McLaren-style, "drew attention to its own construction", and all over the country cultural studies students grappling with Barthes and Derrida (many of them in art college classrooms) were aghast – here was a cultural form in which the theories all made sense!' (Frith and Horne, 1987, p. 133).

The anthropological connection

The album also contains extensive inner-sleeve notes, illustrated with several monochrome photographs and a variety of drawings. The notes include the lyrics of the songs and descriptions of the musical sources with some background information, much in the manner of ethnomusicological field recordings. For example, the notes for the track 'Legba' state that 'People in New York are beginning to Smurf to this song. The Smurf is a dance adapted from the movements of the cartoon characters', while for 'El San Juanera' a diagram of the basic dance steps is provided. This world dance connection is further supported by a full-page photograph in the inner-sleeve notes. It depicts McLaren, a black girl (wearing a T-shirt with 'Zulus on a Time Bomb') and a dark-haired girl (Latin?) dancing against a backdrop of cut-outs in the shape of Africa and South America.

In addition to pictures like these, which directly relate in one way or another with the tracks, the inner sleeve is illustrated with photographs of the instruments used on the album (including a record deck), and others which seem to defy classification such as a still from a Marilyn Monroe film, a publicity shot of Brigitte Bardot and the first photograph of The Sex Pistols. The line drawings, mostly of people and anthropomorphic creatures, are clearly in imitation of the ritualistic and religious art.

The point here is that the artwork of the album directly reflects the complex and varied sources of the music and clearly attempts to support the overall 'concept' which underlies it. *Duck Rock* – through its sounds, texts and images – suggests a cultural, and specifically anthropological, connection between hip hop, modern technology and those other cultures represented on the album. This sense of combining elements associated with social anthropology with pop music is present in some of McLaren's other projects at this time: the group Bow Wow Wow, which he managed, and their album *See Jungle! See Jungle! Go Join Your Gang Yeah, City All Over! Go Ape Crazy!*,[15] for example.[16] Specifically referring to this group, Simon Frith has commented that 'McLaren (who with The Sex Pistols drew loosely on Situationism) is drawing loosely now on autonomism – the concept of the young as an American Indian tribe … developed by the youth movement in Zurich' (Frith, 1988, p. 179).

Stylistic collage

As suggested in Chapter 1, pop music often tends to rely on the use of known material as an intrinsic part of its message and to exploit the cultural connotations of this material. The music of *Duck Rock* combines five different types of musical element: hip hop ('Buffalo Gals', 'World's Famous'); square dances ('Buffalo Gals', 'Duck for the Oyster'); Black South African pop music ('Double Dutch', 'Punk it Up', 'Jive My Baby Jive', 'Soweto'); Latin American music ('El San Juanera', 'Merengue'); and Afro-American music of the Lucumi cult ('Obatala', 'Legba' and 'Song for Chango').[17] Each track combines two disparate elements which both clash and resonate culturally: 'Obatala' has Afro-Cuban ritualistic and trance-inducing drums contrasting with sentimental, highly diatonic melodies, reminiscent of Easy Listening music, on synthesizers; 'Buffalo Gals' has New York hip hop contrasting with square dancing; 'El San Juanera' has traditional Colombian folk dance contrasting with modern New York radio; 'Punk it Up' has African pop and

British punk rock; 'Living on the road in Soweto' has African pop with Bluegrass fiddle; and 'Duck for the Oyster' has square dance with hip hop scratching and samples. In each case a modern Western element is combined with a folk-like or World Music element.

The nature of the individual elements themselves further accentuates the disquieting effect of the oxymoronic devices present in each track. The music from 'foreign' sources, mainly South Africa and South America, tends to be rich in known and expected musical ideas – Zulu choirs, predictable African pop rhythms, melodies, harmonies and timbres – while the music from New York, which should be more familiar to a British audience, is full of unknown elements – record scratching; bizarre Soul music samples; excerpts from radio programmes, particularly phone-ins that are, at times, difficult to understand; phrases from square dances (e.g. 'Duck for the Oyster'); and hip hop rhythms.[18] In many of the tracks, the 'foreign', yet easily recognizable, musical ideas are juxtaposed with 'closer to home', yet unfamiliar, elements, thus accentuating the unsettling effect produced by the juxtaposition of diverse cultural elements.

The extensive sleeve notes do not offer any explanation as to why these disparate elements are combined on this album, ostensibly a pop music album.[19] On the face of it, there seems to be little geographically, culturally or linguistically to connect the five different types of recurring elements. However, a number of links, already implicit in the imagery and the accompanying notes, clearly emerge through the music, notably dance and radio.

While 'dance' is a common characteristic of the composite tracks, the 'radio' element is most forcefully felt in the links between the tracks of this album. The World Famous Supreme Team are radio presenters, and extracts from their shows (particularly phone-ins) are included between each track. At times the listener has the impression of tuning between stations on a radio. Clearly the suggestion here is that radio, which provides the continuity link between each track, is a medium capable of linking diverse cultures. The radio links are also perhaps a reminder of the significance of radio for pop music both as a means of communication and a marketing tool.[20]

'Buffalo Gals'

> Whatever reservations one may have about McLaren's methods and the shortcomings of his music, his imagination deserves respect. (Rogan, 1989, p. 352)

The most successful track on the album, 'Buffalo Gals', combines elements of New York hip hop and Tennessee square dancing, two cultural forms which would appear to be in complete opposition:

Hip hop	*Square dancing*
Black	White
Urban	Rural
Modern technology	Traditional technology
New	Old

In 1982 hip hop was regarded as a very modern genre involving innovative uses of technology (scratching) and unusual vocal delivery techniques (rap), while square dancing was part of a much older tradition. In fact, the track has direct links with some of the earliest forms of popular music, as Simon Frith points out:

> In the 1984 issue of his magazine *Old Time Music*, Tony Russell has an entertaining account of the making of Malcolm McLaren's hit version of 'Buffalo Gals'. Russell had put McLaren in touch with the East Tennessee Hilltoppers, an 'old-timey' family string band, and band-member Joel Birchfield's fiddling duly took its place in the mix, together with McLaren's own square dance spiel, lifted directly from the work of the New York caller Piute Pete (as recorded on a 1949/50 Folkways LP). What McLaren did not mention in his gleeful appropriation of American 'roots' music for his own eclectic ends, was that back in the 1850s there were already men and women wandering London's streets in pursuit of a similar livelihood from mixed-up American sounds. These 'Ethiopian Serenaders' had switched from glee songs to minstrel songs under the influence of the visiting Afro-American dancer, Juba. They learnt the latest transatlantic tunes from the barrel organists, and, as one performer told Henry Mayhew, their favourite was 'Buffalo Gals', originally written as a minstrel number in 1844. (Frith, 1988, pp. 47–8)

Nevertheless, there are some elements that link hip hop and square dances. First, in spite of their obvious differences, they are both part of the culture of the USA and reveal some of the cultural richness and variety that can develop in a country originally formed of different peoples. Second, both forms are intended for dancing. As noted, dance and movement is a recurrent element on this album, however, on 'Buffalo Gals' dancing is explicitly mentioned in connection with both square dancing (McLaren's lyrics are the steps to a specific square dance) and hip hop ('She's only dancing just to be friendly'). Finally, there are some similarities in the language and the vocal delivery. The lyrics to rap and square dances are both in English, although the codes are particular and restricted: square dances include words like 'dossido' and 'promenade' to refer to various dance steps, for example, while hip hop uses the vocabulary of black urban American youth in rap lyrics. Similarly, the vocal delivery of these two genres tends towards the spoken rather than the sung.

Structure

The structure of 'Buffalo Gals', although based on clearly delineated sections, does not follow the verse/bridge/chorus form so typical of many pop songs (see Table 4.1).[21] The absence of a bass line for much of the record, combined with a general sense of tonal ambiguity, result in a structure that works through timbral and rhythmic repetition, rather than pitch organization. This is a characteristic of a great deal of hip hop of the 1980s and may be seen as a direct result of the use of digital sampling and scratching, both of which encourage the use of short samples from a variety of records which rarely share the same tonality.[22]

One could regard the structure of 'Buffalo Gals' as an elaborated ABA form, the A section being McLaren's 'calls' and the B the sung Soul part. The differing

Table 4.1   The structure of 'Buffalo Gals'

Bars	Characteristics
Introduction	Radio link, 'Brown-Brown-sville' stutter sample Zulu chant sample
1–4 (4 bars)	Reverb. from chant continues through + drums; 'Ahh' sample on beat 2
5–8 (4 bars)	Drums + scratching Synth. chords with reverb.
9–16 (7 bars + 2 beats)	'b-b-b' + 'ha', 'ha', 'oo' + drum fill samples 'Boy, that scratching is making me itch' sample
17–20 (4 bars)	'duck-duck-duck' sample
21–24 (4 bars)	'b-b-b' + 'duck-duck-duck' alternating
25–40 (16 bars)	Call 1 (M.M.) – synth. chords + 'You know it' sample 'Ahh', scratching
41–49 (1 + 8 bars)	Bass, sustained chords, repeated rhythmic scratch + 'She's looking …'
50–57 (8 bars)	'Looking like a hobo' + 'Three Buffalo Gals' samples
58–69 (12 bars)	Sung 'soul' section: 'It's a pity that you're so dirty …' Bass line, sustained chords + 'Ahh' 'Looking like a hobo'
70–73 (4 bars)	'Promenade/Hominy' sample + scratching
74–89 (16 bars)	Call 2 (M.M.) – synth. chords + 'Ah ha' 'Ah ha' 'You know it'
90–98 (8 + 1 bars)	Bass, scratching + 'Buffalo' + 'Looking like a hobo' Synth. chords to end

musical aspects of these two reinforce the contrast between black and white American popular music that permeates much of the album. Meanwhile, the other sections of the piece are characterized by the alternation and repetition of a few samples and scratching gestures, which are again derived from the two contrasting musical sources. However, the minimal ways in which pitch is featured in 'Buffalo Gals' provide very little sense of structure or direction; instead, it is through textural and timbral manipulation that the structure becomes apparent. Once again, such an approach suggests the influence of recording studio technology, which generally tends to offer far more opportunities in these areas.

Timbre

'Buffalo Gals' has a relatively restricted timbral palette: drums; samples taken from the radio (for example, 'You know it' and 'Ah ha'); samples from square dances (for example, 'Three Buffalo gals' and 'Promenade/hominy'); samples of a Zulu choir (for example, wail at the beginning and 'She's looking like a hobo'); record scratching; synthesizer sounds (bass and chords); and vocals (McLaren's square dance calls and the Soul-like sung section). While the record is attributed to Malcolm McLaren, it should be evident that his contribution in terms of actual sound is quite small. As many of the timbres that appear on 'Buffalo Gals' come about through the use of scratching and sampling – sounds derived from other recordings – lack of tonal cohesion is perhaps inevitable. Instead the rather limited palette of 'Buffalo Gals' ensures that the record has timbral cohesion. This is supported through the multiple repetitions of many of these sounds.

The manipulation of records on record decks is a fundamental technique of hip hop and has subsequently become a feature of the DJ's art. Scratching not only appears on recordings but also is often featured in 'live' performance. As Simon Warner notes: 'using two turntables, the DJ would feed one record into another, and by moving one disc back and forth on the deck by hand, create a distorted yet infectious new rhythm line' (Warner, 1996, p. 296). As such, scratching enables a similar kind of creative use of pre-recorded sound as *musique concrète* and sampling. In spite of the limitations of scratching in terms of sonic manipulation and the demanding level of manual dexterity required, it has become a feature of many pop music records and performances. Scratching not only utilizes pre-existing records for timbral effect but also tends to emphasize their rhythmic qualities within the new recording. Again, a similar emphasis is clearly audible in the use of digital sampling. Hence, scratching is an interesting example of the innovative use of a cheap, old-fashioned technology influencing the use of a more expensive modern technology. It also demonstrates the influence of musical experimentation by relatively deprived social groups (young Black Americans) on the pop music industry. In spite of the enormous decreases in price and improvements in quality and capability of digital samplers, scratching techniques continue to be used in pop music. Ironically, the price of high-quality turntables suitable for scratching now exceeds that of many digital samplers and expensive CD 'turntables', designed explicitly for scratching, have been developed.

However, certain sampler techniques are impossible to re-create using record decks: rhythmic stutter effects and distinct pitch changes, for example. These are both clearly audible with the 'Brownsville' sample with which 'Buffalo Gals' begins. 'Stuttering' became something of a cliché in many pop records following the enormous success of 'Nineteen' by Paul Hardcastle,[23] although 'Buffalo Gals' pre-dates this by over two years.

Half-heard words

Both scratching and sampling of spoken or sung words can give rise to intentional and unintentional changes in meaning. In 'Buffalo Gals', for example, the repeated scratch of the beginning of 'She's looking like a hobo' at bar 49 sounds like 'She's itching'. This is entirely appropriate since it links neatly with the radio sample 'All that scratching is making me itch'. Similarly, the repeated sample between bars 70 and 73 which appears as 'Promenade' in the printed lyrics of the inner sleeve, actually sounds like the word 'hominy';[24] both words are evocative of square dancing. This technique highlights one of the ways that ambiguity can be created through the creative manipulation of sampling and scratching: simple words or phrases of pre-recorded material can carry complex messages. A more detailed investigation of sampling appears in Chapter 7 of this study.

Duck Rock, Malcolm McLaren's first album as a musician/performer/composer, is a thought-provoking artefact. Its diverse range of musical sources simultaneously perplex and hint at some underlying socio-philosophical stance. As such, it reveals a desire to present both a complete pop artefact (music, image, text, etc.) and to utilize the format of the pop album as a vehicle for a different kind of discourse: that of 'high art'. This combination of pop and 'high art' became something of a feature of Trevor Horn's productions in the next few years (see Chapters 6, 7 and 8). Clearly working with McLaren was an important creative experience for Trevor Horn (see Appendix 1). Yet while the cultural stance and use of collage strongly reflect McLaren's background, Horn's contribution tends to be felt in the sonic and musical characteristics, and the ways in which these are achieved through technology.

McLaren may well have provided the ideas for this record but he is personally responsible for few of the sounds, raising questions of both copyright and authorship, which are becoming increasingly relevant to contemporary pop music – again largely as a result of technology. Many of the sounds on *Duck Rock* are the result of the manipulation of pre-recorded musical material, and the album is characterized not only by the sounds of that material but also by its technological manipulation. The sounds of sampling, scratching and more piecemeal 'borrowings' dominate this record. *Duck Rock* is a montage in which technology enables parts to fit precisely. This precision is as important an aspect as the original sounds themselves. In this sense it could be seen as a recording produced from other recordings, made possible by the technology available in a modern recording studio: an artefact uniquely defined by its medium.

Notes

1.   Most notably 'Hand Held in Black and White' (WEA BUCK 1), 'Mirror, Mirror (Mon Amour)' (WEA BUCK 2), 'Give Me Back My Heart' (WEA BUCK 3) and 'Videotheque' (WEA BUCK 4), all produced 1981–82.
2.   Neutron NTRS 1.
3.   Atlantic K 50736.
4.   Island ILPS 9585.
5.   Jimco JICK-89266.
6.   Horn's work with these different artists certainly reflect differing approaches to the use of technology during this period. For instance, the song 'Into the Lens' on the album *Drama*, reappears as 'I am a Camera' on *Adventures in Modern Recording*. Although melodically, harmonically and lyrically the two versions are virtually identical, the Yes recording has an extended and diversifying structure, and is dominated by the timbres of electric guitar and 'real' drums; while the Buggles version is structurally much less diverse and is largely made up of synthesized timbres, including those of the drum kit.
7.   Charisma MMLP 1.
8.   'Buffalo Gals' (Charisma MALC 1) entered the UK singles chart on 4 December 1982 and reached number 9, while 'Double Dutch' (Charisma MALC 3) reached number 3 (entering on 2 July 1983).
9.   For a general overview of pop managers see Rogan (1989).
10.   'The *Internationale Situationniste* was founded in Italy in the summer of 1957. Combining Marxist and Dadaist thought, the fellowship sought to enlighten the proletariat by attacking the passivity of consumerism, deriding the mindlessness of work and exploiting the creative possibilities of enforced unemployment and increased leisure time' (Rogan, 1989, p. 328). Its work consisted of 'perpetrating "situations" conceived to pervert established codes and values and make the individual aware of the repressive politics of the modern technological world' (ibid.).
11.   The credits include string arrangements (Anne Dudley), additional keyboards (Tom Dolby), additional guitars (David Birch), engineering (Gary Langan), and cover design (Nick Egan). Anne Dudley continued to be a regular contributor to Trevor Horn's productions in the years to come and was a member of The Art of Noise, Tom Dolby (as Thomas Dolby) pursued a successful solo career and Gary Langan appeared on several other projects associated with Trevor Horn and was credited as producer on The Art of Noise recordings. The presence of Dudley (Art of Noise)

and Langan (Yes/Art of Noise) on McLaren's *Duck Rock* is another instance of musicians working on several projects at the same time in the recording studio.

12. One possible explanation for the title is that McLaren is being ironic: the album avoids all the aspects of rock identified earlier under 'Pop and Rock' in Chapter 1 entitled 'Characteristics of Pop Music'.

13. The appearance of a radio cassette is perhaps not accidental: McLaren had only recently appeared to be championing the idea of copying recordings – a process which record companies felt was an infringement of copyright – in the lyrics of Bow Wow Wow's 1980 single 'C30, C60, C90, Go' (EMI 5088).

14. While McLaren is not credited with playing any of the instruments on *Duck Rock*, sounds associated with the radio appear throughout the album. The cover photograph suggests that McLaren is 'playing' the radio in the same way as DJs now use scratching. Hence, the image of McLaren controlling the dials of the radio suggests that his relationship to the recording is similar to that of a DJ with their audience on a particular night at a dance venue.

15. RCA LP 3000 released in 1981.

16. Similarly, McLaren had combined Red Indian and pirate imagery with Adam Ant.

17. Obatala, Legba and Chango are oreishas (gods/saints) of Santeria, which combines the religious beliefs of the Yoruba with Roman Catholicism. It has existed on the islands of the Caribbean and in South America since the first Africans were brought as slaves. Subsequently Cuban immigrants took it to New York where it still thrives.

18. *Duck Rock* is generally regarded as 'the first British record to feature scratching' (Hardy and Laing, 1990, p. 511). However, it also includes sampling, rap and graffiti, which are central to the hip hop culture of New York. As such, these elements were unfamiliar to a British audience in 1982.

19. The only hint is provided in the credits: 'I'd like to thank ... Trevor Horn who through all the madness, soldiered on to rediscover the origins of Rock 'n' Roll.'

20. 'Radio fanfares a record's release' and 'if a record isn't heard, it won't sell' (Barnard, 1989, p. 94). For a discussion of the role of the radio in the history of pop music, and the way it is marketed, see the sections entitled 'The ghost in the machine' in Chapter 3 and 'Banned' in Chapter 6. McLaren was certainly aware of the power and significance of the radio as a means of marketing tool. As manager of The Sex Pistols he enjoyed the added publicity of having a record banned on the radio. 'Certain records could be banned outright, on the grounds of offensiveness; The Sex Pistols' 'God Save the Queen' was the obvious example, particularly because its release was deliberately timed to coincide with British royalty's Silver Jubilee celebrations' (Barnard, 1989, p. 122).

21. The remix version, 'Buffalo Gals II' on *Malcolm McLaren Presents The World Famous Supreme Team Show – Round The Outside! Round The Outside!* (Virgin CDV 2646), follows the structure of the original very closely.

22. This absence of an identifiable tonality is particularly evident in the recordings of the New York rap group Public Enemy, for example, which also often avoid the use of bass lines that might provide a tonal root.

23. Chrysalis CHS 2860.

24. 'Hominy' is '*Chiefly* U.S. coarsely ground maize prepared as a food by boiling in milk or water. [C17: probably of Alonquian origin]' (Hanks, 1986, p. 733).

Chapter 5

'Owner of a Lonely Heart' by Yes

The ability to collaborate with a diverse range of musicians on a variety of often concurrent projects is a prerequisite for all successful record producers. Having achieved some success with The Buggles, Trevor Horn and Geoff Downes, in a surprising career move, joined the archetypal progressive rock band, Yes, in 1980. Although the album *Drama*[1] was produced, their role was primarily that of performing musicians: Horn was the lead vocalist and bass player, and Downes played the keyboards. This 'bizarre marriage' (Larkin, 1993, p. 1217) lasted a year before the band split up to pursue solo careers. In 1983 the band reformed and recorded their thirteenth album, *90125*,[2] this time produced by Trevor Horn. The album was a radical departure for the band and gave rise to success in the singles chart with 'Owner of a Lonely Heart',[3] which was a number one hit in the USA.

Yes: from progressive rock to chart pop

The notion of the popular music art work as the product of a team rather than an individual is well illustrated by the examples in this study. However, the individual members of a team and their particular contributions to a series of recording projects may change considerably over a number of years; in other words, the team rarely remains an entirely fixed entity. The group Yes has been in existence for over 30 years but the number of changes in the members of the group that have occurred in that time show that it has had very few permanent musicians. The group was formed in 1968 by vocalist Jon Anderson and bass guitarist Chris Squire. The drummer Bill Bruford, guitarist Pete Banks and keyboard player Tony Kaye completed this first line-up. By 1970, Banks was replaced by 'guitar virtuoso' Steve Howe (*The Yes Album*[4]) and in 1971 Tony Kaye was replaced by the extrovert Rick Wakeman (*Fragile*[5]). As a result, the group underwent a marked stylistic change with greater emphasis on complexity and instrumental improvisation. By 1972 Bruford had left the band and was replaced by Alan White (*Close to the Edge*[6]), and two years later Wakeman was replaced by Patrick Moraz (*Yessongs*[7]). Later Wakeman returned. During 1980, Wakeman and Anderson left, being replaced by Trevor Horn and Geoff Downes (*Drama*). Yes then broke up in 1981 only to be reformed in 1983 with Anderson, Squire, White, Kaye and Trevor Rabin (guitars, keyboards and vocals) to record *90125* and the single 'Owner of a Lonely Heart', both produced by Trevor Horn. In

1987 *Big Generator*[8] was released with the same members, this time co-produced by Trevor Horn. By 1989 a legal wrangle had developed around the right by Anderson, Bruford, Wakeman and Howe to call themselves 'Yes'. This was finally solved in 1991 and the band released a new album that was highly successful in the US charts (*Union*[9]). This brief history clearly shows that the individual musicians who play a part in defining a band can differ from the actual members involved in any single recording project.

For many commentators, Yes represent the quintessential exponents of British progressive rock – a genre of popular music most strongly associated with the early 1970s. Progressive rock is generally characterized by extended song forms with unusual and at times disparate sections; a tendency to release albums, often based on unifying and 'serious' themes, rather than singles; instrumental rather than vocal dominance; and long improvisatory solos, usually for guitar or keyboards. These characteristics are represented most successfully in Yes's album, *Close to the Edge*, which is considered by many to be their finest work.[10] Other groups associated with progressive rock include Pink Floyd, Emmerson, Lake and Palmer, and the early Genesis. Progressive rock musicians evidently had aspirations to create 'high art', in contrast to the singles chart pop music of the period. As Allan Moore points out:

> Few progressive (rock) musicians may have been trained in the techniques of art music, but many were touched by a not unrelated drive towards the self-conscious attempt to validate rock as art, thereby apparently raising the status of the product. This may have been done by disguising the self-containedness of three minute song structures, and employing more advanced harmonies (often imported from jazz and late nineteenth-century European art music), rhythmic patterns (borrowed from twentieth-century Eastern European composers) and electronic sounds (copied from the European avant-garde, especially Stockhausen and Berio). (Moore, 1993, p. 81)

Obviously these characteristics make it more appropriate for assimilation into a traditional musicological approach, and the emergence of punk rock around 1976 is often interpreted as a populist, 'low art' reaction to the excessive, pseudo-Romantic posturing of progressive rock. Caroline Coon wrote at the time: 'There is a growing, almost desperate, feeling that rock music should be stripped down to its bare bones again. It needs to be taken by the scruff of its bloated neck and given a good shaking, bringing it back to its sources and traditions' (Heylin, 1993, p. 195). Punk is frequently regarded as failing to achieve one of its fundamental aims – to produce a form of popular music that successfully countered domination of the music scene by international, major record companies. However, this was secondary to punk's other purpose which was to counter the aesthetic of progressive rock, and in this it was entirely successful: with very few exceptions, progressive rock has generally been consigned to a place in the history of popular music and no major revivals of the genre seem imminent. Naturally, progressive rock groups, like the representatives of so many other kinds of popular music who manage to retain their fan base, still persist in creating music and releasing records; however, since the 1970s they have been unable to re-establish their aesthetic as a major force in popular music.

90125

> 'Owner' [of a Lonely Heart] was Yes's only number one and *90125* was their most successful album. (Morse, 1996, p. 76)

The relative success of the Yes album, *90125*, in 1983, and especially the chart-topping single 'Owner of a Lonely Heart', is surprising: that a band so firmly associated with progressive rock should produce a successful recording in a post-punk and anti-progressive rock climate; and that it should achieve success in the singles chart, which had traditionally been perceived as inappropriate to the group's musical aspirations. The success of the album and single may stem from the fact that both contain a number of elements that appear quite contrary to the typical work of the band. The fact that *90125* is quite atypical of progressive rock generally seems to reflect the influence of Trevor Rabin (guitars, keyboards, vocals) and record producer, Trevor Horn. Rabin had formed a band called Cinema with Kaye, Squire and White, and worked on the music that became *90125*. When Anderson agreed to sing on the album it seemed logical to call the band Yes. Horn spent nine months working on *90125* 'working virtually every day of every week at a variety of studios' (Gary Langan, quoted in Cunningham, 1996, p. 278).

A new image

The title of the album – *90125* – is enigmatic rather than dramatic and quite out of keeping with Yes's earlier work (for example, *Time and a Word*, *Tales from the Topographic Oceans*). Initially there is a certain sense of mystery – is it a telephone number or a secret code? – but this is quickly dispelled as the derivation of the number is fully explained on the back cover: 90125 is 'the album's number in the Atlantic Records catalog'. The title is in stark contrast to the themes traditionally associated with progressive rock: fantasy, science fiction, mysticism or often rather naive social comment (for example, *The Wall* by Pink Floyd). Since the album was released in 1983, a change from earlier work would seem overdue. However, the choice of a five digit number as a title is significant, indicating a move away from escapist fantasy and personal expression: the album, particularly when one reads the back cover, is about nothing in particular and can be represented simply by a string of numbers, which themselves stand for a measuring system instituted by the record company to 'record' its output.

In the same way as the album title points towards a change in direction, the cover design of *90125* is also unusual. Yes, perhaps more than any other progressive rock group, established a tradition for their album covers in the early 1970s based around several of the fantasy-inspired landscapes of Roger Dean. By the time *Drama* was released (1980), Dean's work was considered an intrinsic part of the band's image. These paintings tend to be brightly coloured scenes reminiscent of the artwork found on the covers of fantasy books. Some of Dean's album cover designs for Yes were so successful that they were sold as posters, and as such graced many a young person's bedroom wall during the early 1970s. In contrast to Dean's work, the cover of *90125* is a simple design in few colours with no representational elements. The centre of the design is taken up by a stylized letter 'Y', reminiscent of the logo of a large company. This sense of corporate identity is reinforced by the use of silver as the fundamental colour of the design, implying metal with both its industrial and badge-like allusions. Yes had introduced recurrent visual motifs on covers before: on previous albums the group's name would always appear in the same 'swinging sixties' fat-lettered font. This motif does not appear on the cover of *90125*. In the same way as we are informed of the source of the album's title, we are told that the cover was 'PRODUCED ON ROBOGRAPH 1000 SYSTEM UTILISING APPLE IIE 64K RAM MICRO-COMPUTER AND BITSTICK CONTROLLER'. It would seem that Roger Dean's work and the pre-industrial mysticism it evoked was inappropriate to the new mechanized and scientific image that the band were trying to put across.

As already noted, the recording, its format and the playback devices necessary to realize it as sound, are all the result of industrial processes. Art has always relied on technology to offer new means of expression, but with the advent of the Industrial Revolution a growing fascination with technology is visible in art. The title of the album and its cover perhaps evoke a little of this fascination.

Live/recorded

Another interesting addition on the album is the presence of a single track that was 'recorded live at Air Studios, London'. The mention of this in the sleeve notes is of interest because it draws attention to the recording process, making a distinction between one product of a recording studio and another. For the listener it could simply be just another album track with a different sound; however, the band wants to inform the listener why it sounds different: this track was produced using the more traditional technique of musicians performing together simultaneously, while all the other tracks were the result of the processes afforded by overdubbing, and hence performing serially, in the multitrack recording studio. This emphasis on multitrack overdubbing and serial performance is visible in several aspects of this record. Furthermore, if the listener were to find the 'live' track the weakest and least fulfilling on the album (it is certainly the shortest and least defined in terms of timbre), they may well conclude that the best of the album is largely due to the realization by the band of the creative potential of the recording studio: the most successful aspects of the recording are the result of resourceful manipulation of modern audio technology, rather than the traditional practical skills of the musician, and this would seem contrary to the ethos of progressive rock in general, and Yes in particular.

Chart pop music

Turning to the music on *90125*, one finds further evidence of radical changes in the group's aesthetic: there is a greater emphasis on simplicity and repetition than in much of their earlier work. First, the songs follow structural patterns similar to those found in typical chart pop songs. These structures are quite different from Yes's earlier approach. On *Close to the Edge*, for example, there are only three pieces – 'Close to the Edge' (18 minutes and 50 seconds long), 'And You And I' (10 minutes and 9 seconds long) and 'Siberian Khatru' (8 minutes and 57 seconds long) – each with complex and somewhat rambling structures.[11] Second, many of the bass lines and other melodic ideas on *90125* are extremely simple and repetitive. The bass line on the verse of 'It Can Happen', for example, is simply a single pitch played as quavers on the first beat of the bar and preceded by a semiquaver. Third, the harmonic language and harmonic relationships are remarkably basic both within phrases and between sections. This harmonic simplicity is evident on the song 'Changes', for example, which is made up of just a few simple chords, all firmly in the same tonality. Fourth, there are no long improvisatory sections for guitar or keyboards. Finally, there is a great deal more internal repetition than one would normally find in songs by Yes. The listener is inevitably drawn to the conclusion that at least some of the work on *90125* has closer affinities to chart pop music than progressive rock. Bill Bruford drew attention to this aspect of the album when he said: 'It's very good pop. I don't have any other associations or feeling for it. I think they were a very good pop group at the time' (Morse, 1996, p. 76).

'Owner of a Lonely Heart'

> I wrote the bass line and came up with the lyric 'Owner of a Lonely Heart'. It just developed from there. (Trevor Rabin, quoted in Morse, 1996, p. 77)

Turning to the first track on the album, 'Owner of a Lonely Heart', one notices several important points. The song is credited to 'Rabin/Anderson/Squire/Horn' on the cover, which implies that several people had a creative role in the song and once more supports the notion of pop music being produced by a team rather than an individual. Moreover, the songwriting credits go to three members of the band – Rabin (guitar), Anderson (vocals) and Squire (bass) – but do not include Tony Kaye (keyboards) and Alan White (drums). Evidently, although the song was created by a team, not everyone in the band merited full inclusion in that team. Significantly, Trevor Horn is included in the songwriting credits which supports the view that record producers are creatively important in the recording studio. Naturally, the credits give no indication of the exact creative input of each of the four named, except that following convention, earlier names are likely to refer to the lyric writers while the later names refer to composers, strengthening the view that Horn's input was mostly, if not exclusively, musical.

Form: repetition and suspension

The second point of interest with 'Owner of a Lonely Heart' concerns its structure. The song is constructed as follows:

$$A - B - A - B - C - A - D - B - C$$

Taking the A section as the verse, the B section as the bridge, the C section as the chorus and the D section as the middle eight, the form is that of a fairly standard pop song structure. Moreover, some of these sections are more related than would first appear. The B section, for example, has the same bass line as the A section, while the D section could easily accommodate the same A section bass line. In effect then, apart from short transitional sections (for example, between the first section C and the A section that follows), the song is made up of just two contrasting ideas: A and C.

The contrasting elements between these two sections include the bass line, guitar/keyboard accompaniment and tonality. The sparse bass/guitar riff of the verse is countered by a fuller, quaver-dominated figure in the chorus, while the single plucked guitar strings of the verse and the varied keyboard gestures of the bridge are replaced by plectrum strummed chords in the chorus. The contrast in tonality is marked by the verse and bridge in the tonic minor whereas the chorus is firmly in the tonic major. This sense of minor followed by major is strongly supported by the bass, which has the respective minor and major thirds early on within both lines.

A more unusual structural element of the song is the surprising change of key within the final chorus: although the musical ideas remain the same, the key suddenly drops from A major down to F major, and then the song fades out in this new key. In terms of classical tonality this would be something of an absurdity and one could well imagine the Schenkerian 'ersatz' which such a piece would generate. This unusual key change, however, sounds entirely natural within the framework of a pop record that lasts less than five minutes, and a structural move of this sort is not particularly rare in popular music.[12] In fact it highlights one of the fundamental differences between popular music and 'serious' music (see Chapter 1): unlike serious music, popular music, due to its recorded nature, is *designed* for multiple listenings – when the listener reaches the end of 'Owner of a Lonely Heart', they listen to it again and the new start of the record resolves the suspended tonality created by the fade-out. In terms of tonality, a cyclic form is created whereby resolution only occurs when the record is replayed. Hence, at a fundamental structural level (that is, tonality), the exploitation of the potential of recording would seem to enable new kinds of formal arrangement to develop and flourish, and musical aesthetics have been modified to make the most of this new potential.[13]

A further structural element worthy of note is the relatively small amounts of actual chorus material within the song: only 32 bars of an overall song length of 138 bars. Many pop songs save their most memorable and catchy material for the chorus, which often functions as the 'hook' – the element that most listeners find most interesting and fulfilling. It is possible to view the standard pop song structure as a process of expectation and resolution: introductions, verses, bridges and middle eights provide a sense of expectation in the listener that is only resolved by the chorus. This process is especially evident in 'Owner of a Lonely Heart'. Having heard the chorus once, one would expect the final bridge to be the same length as the two which have preceded it; however, this final bridge is extended to twice its normal length, suspending the moment of resolution when the final chorus begins. The key change in this final chorus seems a temporary contrast, yet the song fades out here, reinforcing this sense of the 'unfinished'.

A final point about the structure of this song concerns its unashamed emphasis on repetition. As we have noted, the song is mostly constructed from just two basic musical ideas (A and C), and the chorus material (C) is relatively understated. Consequently, the verse and bridge material, which comprise a two bar bass riff, dominate the song. In fact, disregarding sections where this riff is suggested rather than actually stated, it is played a total of 46 times within the song. Even by the standards of pop music intended for dancing, this is quite a high level of repetition and clearly goes against the precedents that Yes had spent several years establishing – musical pieces with relatively complex structures and little repetition rather than highly repetitive pop songs with closed structures intended for dancing.

This high level of repetition of the A material is also interesting because it may be viewed as acting rather like a pedal note over the longer sections of the song. In fact, the use of pedal notes and ideas that function rather like pedal notes, occur frequently in music produced by Trevor Horn (see Chapters 6 and 8).

Timbre and gesture

In terms of timbre the song is dominated by a few contrasting elements: guitar, bass and drums, the vocal lines and a number of samples. Although each of these timbres is relatively distinctive in its own right, these distinctions are strongly reinforced by a variety of production and arrangement techniques. Particularly noticeable is the use of artificial reverberation to distinguish between those timbres which function primarily in the rhythmic domain and those timbres which tend to have a melodic function. The drums, bass, samples and some of the more prominent guitar tracks (especially the guitar solo) are recorded with a minimum amount of artificial reverberation and provide the driving rhythmic energy of the song, while the vocals, synthesizer voices and some of the accompanying guitar tracks are given a richer sonority and, consequently, a greater pitch emphasis through the addition of artificial reverberation. Reverberation makes the sound 'ring on' and hence increases the duration of the pitch. The rhythmic elements appear closer to the listener, stressing both the rhythmic impact of the song and providing an uncluttered sound environment for the fast attacks and minimal releases of their envelopes: a clean, direct and immediate effect is achieved.

The keyboard sounds on 'Owner of a Lonely Heart' are extremely varied and have a range of functions: word painting (in the second verse particularly), fills (throughout) and accompaniments (strings in the chorus, for example). Although the whole notion of digital sampling will be dealt with in greater detail later in this study, it is vital that the rhythmic way in which these samples are employed is fully appreciated. Progressive rock at the height of its popularity used pre-recorded ambient sounds to evoke specific environments – Yes, for example, included the sounds of birdsong in their album *Close to the Edge* and Pink Floyd employed similar techniques on a number of their albums (for example, *Atom Heart Mother*). However, the samples used in 'Owner of a Lonely Heart' function in quite a different manner. First, they are very short in length (rarely longer than a second). This is perhaps partly due to early digital samplers, such as the Fairlight CMI for example, having very little memory with which to record sound; if a variety of sounds were required they had to be either short (that is, using as little as possible of the precious recording time) or recorded with such a low sample rate as to be timbrally indistinct. Second, their function is almost entirely rhythmic in nature. They appear as brass stabs or as substitutes for (or recordings of) drum fills. The use of pre-recorded sound to provide rhythmic emphasis and drive is extremely difficult to achieve when using the tape splicing techniques originally developed by the composers of *musique concrète*; however, the sampler, with its sophisticated editing facilities and its music keyboard control, is ideally suited to this kind of use.

The keyboard-dominated nature of digital sampling is particularly noticeable in the short break between the first chorus and the guitar solo. There are no other sounds present at this point (apart from some vocal doubling) and a stab-like sample, played with a crotchet triplet rhythm which goes against the prevalent pulse, rises in semitones from E to A – a typical keyboard based sampler figure. Significantly, Jonathan Jeczalik, one of the team that made up The Art of Noise, a group whose work is strongly associated with Trevor Horn and the use of the Fairlight, is credited with keyboard programming on the cover of *90125*.

The artificial guitar

Although the timbres of the guitar appear to dominate the song, there are few memorable melodic ideas which are carried by the guitar. The prominent, rich and distorted guitar sound at the beginning of the song which introduces the A material, is quickly reduced in both level and sustain, to be replaced in prominence by the bass. By the time the vocal of the first verse begins, the guitar has disappeared and will only reappear in the second verse. With a few notable exceptions, the guitar tracks merely provide arpeggiated or strummed chordal accompaniments: the timbres are present yet command little melodic attention – the listener perceives guitar timbres but would find it hard to recollect melodic ideas. The two exceptions to this are in the guitar solo, which replaces the vocal in verse three, and the short eight-bar break that follows it. The guitar solo itself is worthy of further consideration since it once again reinforces the idea that this song, and this album, reverse many of the musical precedents that Yes had established during the 1970s. First, it is remarkably gestural in character, relying on short, clipped phrases, with little reverberation, which lack any sense of melodic contour and appear to shun virtuosic display. Second, its interest is fundamentally based in its rhythmic/declamatory and timbral elements rather than in pitch, and particularly pitch manipulation. Where pitch is prominent, it tends to be sliding rather than simply sustained. Finally, the interest of this solo is partially maintained through the use of extreme panning between left and right. Panning is essentially a product of recording studio technology and is rarely employed in such an extreme manner in the 'live' concert domain. This may well be because the 'live' concert sound engineer will attempt to position the amplified sound of an instrument as close as possible to the physical position of the player, reconciling sound and the visible sound source – fast, extreme panning would be both disturbing and distracting. Hence the guitar solo in 'Owner of a Lonely Heart' contains elements which undermine the notion of the record as document and instead highlight the artificial nature of the medium. This sense of the artificial is further supported by the use of several separate guitar tracks during this solo.

The break that follows the solo has a quite different guitar timbre with no other sounds present. The transition between these two sections is achieved either by a splice on the master tape or complete channel muting of all tracks except the guitar on the mixer. Whichever process is employed here, the result is a little awkward and unconvincing due to its abruptness and lack of sense of continuity (tending to suggest a tape splice rather than channel muting).

The guitar line that follows the break has several interesting features. It is clearly derived from the guitar figure accompanying the verse, yet here it is completely unaccompanied for the first three and a half bars; although it is characterized by a continuous quaver flow, one tends to lose the sense of beat. This sense of confusion around the pulse is heightened since the line has been subjected to a kind of semi-double tracking effect. With normal double tracking the player tries to repeat the line as closely as possible on another track of the multitrack tape recorder in order to provide a richer and more resonant overall timbre. Here, however, the second line is appreciably different both melodically and timbrally from the first and the two lines are panned hard left and right. Both lines are timbrally rich and bright and are given a fuller sense of presence through the use of chorus effect. Moreover, they contrast sharply with the earlier guitar solo by having more reverberation and no trace of distortion. A further contrast to the normal instrumental roles is created by the bass, which enters after three and a half bars, since it plays a relatively high melodic line in a sustained and almost bel canto style. The drums enter without the bass riff for the final four bars of this break, providing a more solid sense of pulse but lacking the drive of the A section due to the absence of the bass line. For the last few beats of this break the reverberation is increased, pushing the music, through a sense of expectancy, into the bridge that follows. As mentioned, a similar effect was achieved in 'Video Killed the Radio Star'. The important point about this section is that it functions structurally as a pause within the song: rhythm, pulse, timbral variety and drive are restrained and quite contrary to the normal parameters that have been established. The listener is given a moment of repose, as well as something of a sense of loss, before the final push towards the inevitable last chorus and subsequent fade-out. In spite of some enormously impressive arrangements involving a huge range of timbres, melodic ideas, spatial placements and a battery of effects, Trevor Horn's productions are often characterized by this device of returning for a few moments to absolute simplicity which provides an excellent foil to the otherwise highly complex textures. And these contrasts are given greater emphasis through technological manipulation.

The multitracked vocal

A further element within the song that enhances the studio-produced quality is the vocal. Although there are a number of distinct and separate vocal tracks, they are mostly sung by Jon Anderson, a founding member of the group. Evidently, this is only possible with overdubbing and the multitrack tape recorder which enable a single musician to make a series of several different recordings which can be played back simultaneously during mixdown. The effect of this technique on the listener is somewhat difficult to assess. On one level the voice takes on the qualities of an ensemble-based musical instrument (like a violin in an orchestra) with rich chorus-like sonorities. On another level, however, the listener is being 'spoken to' by several voices, which clearly belong to the same singer, simultaneously, and this extremely artificial situation has the internalized, ethereal quality of thoughts or dreams: something which is both magical and outside reality. The incorporeal and acousmatic nature of recording generally is both disturbing and aesthetically significant and has been commented on by a number of writers. One of the possible uses for recording which Edison suggested, for example, was to capture the final words of loved ones who were literally about to cease to exist. The multiple vocal tracks on 'Owner of a Lonely Heart' while simply acting as a reminder to the listener of this fundamental characteristic of the recorded medium, also display the impressive and intentionally disturbing potential of modern audio technology – recordings placed upon earlier recordings and all united in a final recording.

Furthermore, these vocal tracks are cleverly differentiated from each other through the use of studio technology: different reverberation settings, volume levels and panning provide a diverse range of techniques to differentiate between the various tracks and the differing musical functions of each of the lines. With reverberation, for example, one finds that the lead vocal track in the verse has a rich, bright and sustained sound which contrasts well with the close, driving rhythm section. The use of panning is particularly noticeable in the bridge section with two vocal tracks for the phrase 'Owner of a lonely heart' panned left and right. Further differentiation is provided by the musical arrangement, which has some of the less important, accompanying vocal lines rendered in harmony in the manner of backing vocals. Once again, this is particularly noticeable in the bridge section of the piece.

Hence, multitrack overdubbing, artificial reverberation and panning on Anderson's voice give rise to an overall sound that dislocates both time and space.

Machine drums

The final production element worthy of attention in this overview of 'Owner of a Lonely Heart' is the drums. The basic patterns played are very simple and, more importantly, hardly deviate throughout the song: usually the drums either play one of these patterns or remain silent. As such, they are quite different from the usual drum parts found in progressive rock which tend to be full and constantly varying. In fact, here they have a machine-like regularity both of pulse and timbre, and as a result sound like a set of sequenced drum samples rather than a 'live' player.[14] This is particularly noticeable in the verses where a cymbal crash begins every two-bar phrase. Whether the drums on 'Owner of a Lonely Heart' are actually sequenced samples or played live is irrelevant, the important point here is that they give the *impression* of sequenced drums: they aspire to the aesthetic of a technology driven and generated sound. Once again modern audio technology is at the forefront of the aural experience of this song.

In summary, Yes's album, *90125*, and the first track of that album 'Owner of a Lonely Heart' in particular, can be seen as a radical departure from their earlier work. Until 1982 the group had tended to emphasize the more traditional musical skills associated with 'live' performance and musical creativity: individual virtuosity; accurate, balanced ensemble playing; rhythmic, melodic and harmonic innovation; and structural variety. These elements are much less evident on *90125*. Instead the album cover, title, song structure, musical material, level of repetition, use of samples and emphasis on recording technology all point towards a new direction for the band – a direction which places greater emphasis on modern technology. Moreover, technology not only plays a leading role in the realization of the album but also has an aesthetic presence, evident in the use of samples, manipulations of the vocal and the machine-like performance of the drums on 'Owner of a Lonely Heart'.

It is interesting to speculate on whether some or all of these changes might be attributed to the influence of Trevor Horn. *Drama*, the album Horn made as a performer with Yes, has very few of the important innovations found on *90125*. Furthermore, the influence of Trevor Rabin, the new musician to join Yes for *90125*, should not be underestimated. Rabin 'had written most of the *90125* album' (Morse, 1996, p. 75) prior to joining the band. Perhaps the traditional musical qualities of the songs – the rhythms, melodies, harmonies and structures – can be attributed to Rabin, while Horn was largely responsible for the elements associated with the realization – timbral quality, signal processing and gestures created through the manipulation of the techniques of overdubbing and the technology of the multitrack recording studio. Of 'Owner of a Lonely Heart', Trevor Horn is quoted as saying: 'That song was our best shot, so I made sure that it was as right as I could get it' (ibid., p. 79). Whatever the truth of the matter, *90125* is a finely made and exciting pop artefact and a radical aesthetic departure for a band associated with the album-based and adult-oriented progressive rock of the 1970s.

Notes

1. Atlantic K 50736.
2. Atco 7567-90125-2.

3. Atco B 9817. In the UK this single entered the charts on 12 November 1983, remained there for nine weeks and reached number 28.
4. Atlantic 2400-101.
5. Atlantic 2409-019.
6. Atlantic K 50012.
7. Atlantic K 60045.
8. Atco 7567-90522-2.
9. Arista 211558.
10. 'Later that year Yes released what now stands up as their finest work, *Close to the Edge*' (Larkin, 1993, p. 1217).
11. For an analysis of *Close to the Edge* see Covach and Boone (1997, pp. 3–32).
12. This tradition can be traced back a long way. 'Weeping Willow Blues' performed by Bessie Smith, for example, ends in the subdominant of the original key, while a more modern example – Tina Turner's 'What's Love Got to Do with It' – has verses in the tonic minor followed by choruses in the relative major, modulates up a whole tone in the middle eight and ends with the chorus in that key (the subdominant major).
13. One is reminded here of early recordings of da capo arias in which the listener was expected to play the first side containing the A section, the second side containing the B section, and end with a second playing of the first side.
14. A similar effect was noted on 'Video Killed the Radio Star' and Trevor Horn's production of *The Lexicon of Love*. Horn says: 'In 1977, I got Paul Robinson to play his kit one drum at a time – the snare, bass drum and the hi-hat – and I recorded them on separate tracks, then used the sounds like a drum machine, punching him in and out on the desk. Paul said, "That's [*sic*] sounds fucking awful, just like a machine." I said, "Great, that's exactly how I want it to sound"' (quoted in Cunningham, 1996, p. 271).

Chapter 6

'Relax'
by Frankie Goes to Hollywood

MM say: Frankie singles yes, double albums no! (Barber, 1984, p. 27)

Zang Tuum Tumb

In 1983 Trevor Horn set up his own record label called Zang Tuum Tumb, which quickly became known simply by the initials ZTT. Horn had already established something of a reputation for himself as a record producer, musician and composer, but through the creation of a record label he precipitated a new period in his career. Within the world of pop music, the record company wields a great deal of power: the record company searches out new talent through its Artist and Repertoire Department; record company executives define company policy and have the final say as to which recordings will be released; and it is the record company that designs and carries out the promotion strategy of the pop music product. Hence, by setting up his own record company, Trevor Horn would inevitably gain greater artistic and commercial control over not only the projects that he would be involved in, but also the presentation of those products to the public. It is significant that the first band to be signed to the new label, The Art of Noise, 'fell out with ZTT over their marketing strategies' (Larkin, 1993, p. 69) rather than artistic differences, in 1985.

From its inception, ZTT was a highly image-conscious company intent on selling a complete pop product: 'ZTT was very much a "hands on" operation for Horn and he conceived of his label in terms of corporate identity both for sound and image. To the latter end he hired rock journalist Paul Morley, darling of the *NME* and *Face* set' (Beadle, 1993, p. 45). In the image-conscious 1980s, no record company could simply expect to release records of well-produced pop music and hope that the public would buy them purely because of their musical merits. However, ZTT went a little further than most other record companies of the time, realizing from the outset that, as a cultural phenomenon within the mass media, pop was now firmly established as a mixed art form relying on music, image, dance, poetry, etc. Unsurprisingly, many of the artists signed to ZTT are associated with strong, highly defined and complex images: The Art of Noise, Frankie Goes to Hollywood, Propaganda and Grace Jones typify the range. Time and again one finds vivid and memorable record sleeve artwork including intriguing or provocative pieces of prose, challenging video imagery, and a highly polished, clearly studio produced (and modern audio-technology dominated) sound, as well as unusual and fashion-defining T-shirt designs employing sophisticated advertising techniques.

This emphasis on the importance of image was an integral part of ZTT's 'corporate identity' and it placed the recordings in a contemporary (that is, mid-1980s), often thought-provoking and intentionally associative context: in other words, the listener would be unable to disassociate the sound of a particular recording from all those other, non-aural elements which accompanied it. A further aspect of this associative enhancement is provided by explicit reference to high art, and particularly the high art of the early twentieth century.[1] The name of the company, for example, is derived from a description in 'free words' by the poet Marinetti of the sound of warfare from the trenches of Adrianopolis, as quoted by Luigi Russolo in the Futurist Manifesto *The Art of Noises*.[2] To offer another example of 'high art' referencing, in an intentionally blatant piece of commercialism, a 1984 advertisement for Frankie Goes to Hollywood merchandise includes: 'The Kurt Weill sweat shirt', 'The sophisticated Virginia Woolf vest', 'The Jean Genet boxer shorts', 'The Edith Sitwell bag' and 'The André Gide socks' (quoted in Frith and Horne, 1987, p. 23). While hijacking the positive connotations of the high art forms of the twentieth century, it nevertheless is able to keep an ironic distance, and hence wins on both fronts. The linking of a commodity-based industry like the record industry (or the clothing and mass fashion industry) with the highly idealist, anti-Romantic search for originality which typifies the art of the early twentieth century was an original and unusual idea. These references had the effect of conferring an intriguing ambiguity on the product – a pop recording adorned with the language and imagery of 'high art' – and were an intrinsic part of ZTT's marketing strategy. While many might find this apparent lack of idealism cynical and quite contrary to the artistic beliefs of 'high art', Warhol has suggested that 'market success (money!) is the only authentic form of aesthetic validation' (quoted in Frith and Horne, 1987, p. 109). And, of course, Andy Warhol was one of the main representatives of Pop Art, which opened 'high art' to commercial imagery and artefacts.

Another band from Liverpool

> The Liverpool band was discovered by Malcolm Gerrie of the now sadly defunct Channel Four music show, *The Tube*. The Frankies were given a small budget by Gerrie with which to make a video for screening on the show. The song was 'Relax' and Horn saw its transmission while producing Yes's *90125* album at Battery Studios. (Cunningham, 1996, p. 274)

The success of Frankie Goes to Hollywood[3] was firmly built on the production and sale of singles. During 1984 the group released three singles ('Relax',[4] 'Two

Tribes'[5] and 'The Power of Love'[6]),[7] all of which sold extremely well: 'Relax' for example, 'became the biggest-selling single ever in Britain' (Hardy and Laing, 1990, p. 282). Yet no album was forthcoming. Frankie Goes to Hollywood's first album, *Welcome to the Pleasuredome*,[8] was finally released on 10 November 1984. In fact, the sale of singles in the UK had been steadily declining since 1979 (89.1 million). By 1983 sales were down to 74 million and this trend continued to 1992 (52.9 million). 1984 was one of the few years which saw the sale of singles increase over that of the previous year (see *BPI Statistical Handbook* – BPI, 1997). The production of singles was generally becoming less and less cost-effective, partly because of a shrinking market, partly because of the high-risk nature of the venture and partly because of a marketing system which revolved almost entirely around exposure on radio and television. Today many singles tend to be produced in order to promote albums. By releasing singles that sold in large quantities and not promoting an album, Frankie Goes to Hollywood took the unusual step of pursuing success through the singles chart. In fact, the band also sold an enormous number of 12-inch remixes and at the same time exploited and developed merchandising to the full: 'Frankie merchandising, in particular "Frankie Say" T-shirts, was shipping nearly as fast as the records' (Gambaccini, Rice and Rice, 1994b, pp. 298–9).

Another remarkable feature of Frankie Goes to Hollywood is that they did not promote their three successful singles with much live performance. Tours and guest appearances on radio and television that involve some elements of live performance tend to be associated with rock and the more old-fashioned, 'traditional' popular musicians. While in videos and personal appearances on television programmes Frankie Goes to Hollywood may have appeared to be playing their instruments and singing, it was in fact extremely rare. Perhaps more surprisingly, there were questions raised as to their actual contribution to the recordings.[9] Audio and video recording technology makes this separation between music and image possible but disrupts creative and legal preconceptions. In extreme cases the separation is complete with the video artist(s) apparently responsible for the audio recording having played no part in its actual conception or realization.

Finally, Frankie Goes to Hollywood were firmly linked to their record company not just financially but also aesthetically. As already noted, ZTT was a small company formed by a music journalist and a record producer, and, as such, was keen to promote an image of creativity and artistic involvement. This was partly to differentiate it from the larger, and more anonymous major record companies, and partly because the ZTT executives were so personally involved in making aesthetic decisions. As Johnny Rogan suggests, 'the Frankie phenomenon had less to do with management in its traditional sense than the efforts of a journalist turned record company executive and a hot-shot producer' (Rogan, 1989, p. 395). In other words, the record company took over the role traditionally played by the manager. Although this proved to be a highly effective arrangement initially, it eventually led to acrimony and litigation: Holly Johnson, the lead singer of Frankie Goes to Hollywood, contested the contract he had with ZTT in a court case that began on 18 January 1988.

The image

'The group's peculiar image of Liverpool laddishness coupled with the unashamed homosexuality of vocalists Johnson and Rutherford merely added to their curiosity value and sensationalism, while also providing them with a distinctive identity that their detractors seriously underestimated' (Larkin, 1993, p. 475).

Unlike a number of pop ensembles, Frankie Goes to Hollywood had formed as a band well before signing with ZTT and had already received a certain amount of national media exposure: as well as appearing on *The Tube*, they had done a session on the John Peel radio show and had featured in an article in the *New Musical Express* (*NME*). Considering the unusual and remarkably complex image of the band, it is perhaps hardly surprising that their genesis was the result of a series of chance encounters rather than the work of a manipulative manager attempting to realize a cliché. They were all young working-class men from Liverpool and their spectacular success in 1984 prompted comparisons with The Beatles, which were encouraged both by the record company and the media generally. Like any convincing pop ensemble, Frankie Goes to Hollywood had a number of identifiable 'characters' within the band. This meant that any performance, mimed performance or promotional video would display a disparate group of individuals, each presenting a different set of physical mannerisms and visual characteristics. Indeed, one of the main reasons why the group finally disbanded was the result of friction between 'two separate factions' (Johnson, 1995, p. 188) within the band. A third characteristic of the band's image was the numerous overtly homosexual references, in terms of clothing and movement, of Holly Johnson and the dancer/vocalist Paul Rutherford: 'These two group members had superbly complementary appearances and personalities, and both exuded an essentially gay sexual aura: Johnson's that of the camp, more flamboyant theatrical queen; Rutherford's of the macho, leather-clad, moustachioed clone' (Beadle, 1993, p. 66). A typical Frankie Goes to Hollywood performance would involve this rather unlikely pair centre stage vying for attention. The rest of the band, continually referred to as 'The Lads' by Johnson in his autobiography, adopted a more youthful and clearly heterosexual image.

Jeremy J. Beadle links the band's image with the overtly individualistic political message associated with the premiership of Margaret Thatcher and the radical Conservative doctrine. He writes:

> The consciously aggressive stances of Frankie fitted well with the sense of conflict generated at home by the miners' strike, presenting increasingly unpleasant

spectacles of violence on TV screens and in newspapers every day, and in foreign affairs by the belligerent noises of Ronald Reagan, at odds with the equally gerontocratic rulers of the USSR. This latter image was well exploited in Godley and Creme's otherwise indifferent promo video for Frankie's second single, 'Two Tribes'. Essentially Frankie gave a face to the early, don't-give-a-fuck consumer days of the booming 1980s. (Beadle, 1993, p. 67)

Simon Frith, however, questions the group's political impact when he writes:

It's the smoothness of Frankie's success which unnerves me – it's hard to find anyone (other than ZTT) who thinks that Frankie, or their records, are changing the way people understand their lives. They're a best-selling group without real fans, more like The Archies than The Sex Pistols. And this reflects the way they've made it – through marketing rather than performance. (Frith, 1988, p. 195)

Certainly the marketing of popular music is often viewed, especially by those writers who specialize in cultural studies, as one of the least acceptable aspects of mass culture since it explicitly links a work of art with the machinery of consumer capitalism. However, Frith's view that 'Frankie's records make best sense in a cheap British disco where the elemental chorus chants, the beat machines' seedy grandeur, and the stodgy vocals offer distinct echoes of Gary Glitter' (ibid., p. 194) smacks of either naivety or prejudice: as we shall see 'Relax' is a finely produced and musically sophisticated product.

Too much, too young?

We were in awe of Trevor and whatever he said we went along with. (Johnson, 1995, p. 162)

Holly Johnson's autobiography, *A Bone in my Flute*, provides some fascinating insights into the relationship between a young and newly signed pop group and their record producer. Financially and aesthetically, the producer wields a great deal of power. Johnson implies this by the above quotation and also when he writes: 'On one occasion Trevor said to me that he had considered sacking the musicians from the band, leaving just Paul and me to front the act' (ibid., p. 164).

Such an arrangement is by no means uncommon, especially since many young pop musicians lack the experience and technique to perform adequately in a professional recording studio. A myth still persists that modern recorded pop music accurately reflects the musical skills of young, untrained musicians. Listening carefully, from a performance perspective, to any of the records in the Top 10 will confirm that, on the contrary, these records tend to be extremely sophisticated, highly balanced and strongly musical performances. The producer must decide whether it is worth taking up expensive studio time to work with the musicians in the group or hire in session musicians who can be relied upon to play to the required standard immediately.

Since the musicians in Frankie Goes to Hollywood 'were between sixteen and eighteen years old, and inexperienced as studio musicians' (ibid., p. 161) at the time 'Relax' was being recorded, it is hardly surprising that they encountered problems. This highlights a central paradox in a good deal of popular music: while it is created explicitly for a young audience, often has lyrics which deal with the experiences of youth and employs the vocabulary of youth, as a musical artefact it is often the result of highly talented and, more importantly, highly experienced musicians. And that experience usually is acquired slowly. Furthermore, the celebrity status conferred on young pop stars places them under enormous pressures, which few are able to survive completely unscathed. Certainly in the case of Frankie Goes to Hollywood's final tour the 'behaviour of the band seemed to get worse and worse as the tour progressed – hotel carpets were ruined and rooms trashed. It was all such a cliché' (ibid., p. 246).

The making of 'Relax'

As well as providing excellent background information on 'the Frankie phenomenon' (Rogan, 1989, p. 395), *A Bone in my Flute* details the creative role played by Trevor Horn and his working practices.[10] The genesis of the recording of 'Relax' appears to have been a long and surprisingly complex process involving four separate versions. Initially, Horn attempted to record the song with the musicians in Frankie Goes to Hollywood, however he 'soon got tired of their playing and started to construct a rhythm track on his Fairlight' (Johnson, 1995, p. 161). The second version of the song was played by Ian Dury's Blockheads, a highly rated and extremely professional session band. The third 'hybrid' version was created using elements from the earlier recordings plus contributions from Andy Richards (keyboards and programming) and Steve Lipson (guitar). This too was finally scrapped. Eventually a fourth version was recorded which adopted 'a new, machine-like electronic version of the backing track' (ibid., p. 161). This was made with 'the help of J.J. Jeczalic, Andy Richards on keyboards and Steve Lipson on guitar' (ibid., p. 162). Johnson perceptively describes this final version as 'a hybrid of the kind of disco records I had heard in the gay clubs, but with a significant rock edge to it' (ibid., p. 162).

It should be evident from the account above that as a record producer Trevor Horn is extremely hard-working, highly determined and rather obsessive in the pursuit of his aesthetic goals. Also evident is the tenacity with which such a record producer investigates the potential of musical material. The recording studio not only offers the facilities to realize a recording, it also enables producer, engineer and musicians to go over the material again and again, until the ideal timbre, performance and context is found for each element. Inevitably a thorough understanding of the material develops and, as it develops, so the confidence of the creators in their artefact grows. It is a process that is both highly creative and fulfilling. In the case of Trevor Horn and Frankie Goes to Hollywood, the production process was also highly expensive. It was the cost of producing the two albums which was to prove an important factor in the subsequent legal proceedings: the final recording costs for the first album totalled £394 000, while the second claimed a further £760 000, and these expenditures had a marked impact on the royalties the band subsequently received.

Johnson's account of the recording of the follow up to 'Relax' confirms this aspect of Trevor Horn's production techniques:

> After 'Relax' had been such a huge hit, Trevor became very nervous, afraid that he would not be able to produce 'Two Tribes' to a sufficient standard to make it a hit. He was also scared that we might become just a one-hit wonder ... Later Trevor cobbled together an electronically sequenced version of 'Two Tribes' that to my mind sounded fantastic. It wasn't up to his standards however, and was scrapped. Another three-month process began in which Trevor and his team worked on 'Two Tribes' over and over again. (Johnson, 1995, pp. 178–9)

This passage also reveals a certain degree of doubt and insecurity, which is clearly an integral and necessary part of Horn's creative process.

The presence and importance of technology in the recording studio as a fundamental part of the creative process, and the far-reaching changes that were taking place in equipment during this period, are evident in another passage from Johnson's autobiography:

> 'Two Tribes' and all subsequent Frankie tracks were recorded digitally, in contrast to 'Relax' which was recorded on one twenty-four-track analogue tape. I believe that on the 'Two Tribes' sessions, Steve Lipson learnt to use Trevor's new toy, the Synclavier (an extremely expensive instrument that was to replace the Fairlight as the premier sampling tool). (Ibid., pp. 178–9)

'Remix, Re Use It'

Having invested so much effort and money into the recording of 'Relax' and also generated much material that did not appear on the final 7-inch single version,[11] ZTT released several remixes. Johnson writes:

> Dave Robinson had the idea of multiple twelve-inch record releases to prolong the life of the record. This started off another round of controversy. We were accused of trying to rip fans off by releasing multiple mixes of the same track, when in reality the fans adored it. This eventually led to a 'Spitting Image' skit of the band ... I was asked to actually sing the lines for the sketch: '*Remix, re use it*', to the tune of 'Relax'. It was an offer I foolishly declined. (Johnson, 1995, pp. 174–5)

The view that remixes are purely produced to exploit gullible fans is widespread but open to question. First, it presumes a level of innocence on the part of fans that is hardly credible. Second, it refuses to acknowledge the possibility that 12-inch remixes are purchased *because they are wanted* by fans, because they are perceived as separate and distinct from the original, and worthy of consideration in their own right. Finally, as well as there being clearly a healthy market for remixes, it is possible to posit a series of artistic/creative reasons for remixing. Asked about the 'Relax' remixes, Trevor Horn said: 'I wasn't being clever. It wasn't some great scheme that I dreamed up to make three 12-inches: I was just desperately trying to get the record right' (quoted in Buskin, 1994, p. 38).

This statement highlights some of the dilemmas that a record producer can face. Unlike live performance, which offers numerous unpredictable elements for each performance, recordings are fixed forever. As a consequence, the record producer will want to get the best results possible – anything less would be frustrating, disappointing and regarded as a missed opportunity. Furthermore, the absolutely fixed quality in recording – the sense of 'this and no other' – can be alleviated to a certain extent by making several different versions. Finally, there could well be a functional reason why several different versions of the same song are produced: they may be intended for different kinds of audio media or environment. Given that the buying public will first hear recordings on the radio and television, many record producers mix specifically for these media in order to make the best possible impression. As for records clearly intended to induce dancing, they must sound impressive when played over the very particular sound systems that are used in dance clubs, discotheques and similar venues. Horn has stated: 'Although I myself had already had a couple of big 12-inch hits, I'd never heard them being played on a big sound system, and so I then went back and mixed "Relax" again and that was the version which sold a couple of million over here' (quoted in Buskin, 1994, p. 38). Hence, while the production of 12-inch remixes may simply be dismissed as a cynical ploy to sell more records, there are actually a series of artistic and aesthetic factors which may go some way to justify their production and consumption.

Banned

There is a long tradition of censorship of the arts, both popular and otherwise, in Britain. The British Board of Film Censors, established in 1912, is legally empowered to demand that scenes which it finds unacceptable are edited. Furthermore, films and videos that cannot easily be edited or are considered blasphemous are 'refused a certificate', effectively making it illegal to show them to the general public. The case of censorship in popular music is complicated by the dominant role played by the BBC. The lyrics of pop records, like any other art form, may be regarded as a violation of the obscenity laws, in which case the manufacture of the recording then becomes an illegal act. Such instances are rare. A more regular occurrence for controversial records is the denial of airplay by the BBC. This is a well-established convention,[12] which can either ruin a record's chance of success or, as was the case with 'God Save the Queen' by The Sex Pistols, promote it very effectively. A rather unusual situation ensued in the case of 'Relax'. Following its release it received airplay on BBC Radio One and was even performed on *Top of the Pops*. However, at some point, the lyrics were discovered to be too sexually explicit – allegedly by the BBC DJ Mike Read – and the record was subsequently denied all exposure by the BBC.[13] Most commentators agree that 'Relax' had the ideal circumstances – some exposure followed by the media furore that erupted when the belated ban was announced – to be successful. The BBC looked naive and out of touch, particularly since the lyrics of other records, most notably Lou Reed's 'Walk on the Wild Side', released in 1973, had made reference to similar sexual practices yet was regularly played on Radio One. It is doubly ironic that having been partially responsible for the huge success of 'Relax' through the imposition of the ban, the BBC subsequently had to relent and play the record because its very success conferred a kind of 'classic' status to it.

The sound of 'Relax'

'Relax', the band's first single with ZTT, was the song that they had earlier performed on Channel Four's *The Tube*. However, it had been greatly changed through the lengthy process of production and, apart from vocals and tempo, bore only scant resemblance to the original. The rather old-fashioned pseudo-rock 'n' roll riffs on electric guitar were replaced with a wide variety of synthesizer-generated sounds, producing timbral diversity and fulfilling a range of musical functions. Synthesizers provide bass lines, brass section stabs, swirling sonic backdrops and sounds clearly designed to enhance the meaning of certain lyrics (timbral word painting). In spite of this diversity, the record is actually dominated by a simple, repetitive, yet highly effective backbeat, like so many productions associated with Trevor Horn. The simplicity of the backbeat belies its originality: surprisingly few records before or since have used a similar technique. The backbeat of 'Relax' is made up of the typical 'four to the floor' disco-style bass drum plus a pitched bass sound in crotchets. Bass drum and bass pitch share the same short envelope shape. 'It was just a Linn 2 bass drum, but it had a sampled E note on the bass guitar going with it' (Horn quoted in Buskin, 1994, p. 40). The result is an absolutely relentless, utterly undeviating beat reminiscent of a metronome, and a bass pitch which appears to function rather like a traditional pedal note. Paradoxically, one effect of such a simple and rigidly enforced backbeat is musical liberation. Pop music, and particularly pop music intended for dancing, is often criticized for its heavily repetitive nature.

Few are willing to support the notion that this actually enables rhythmic diversity in many of the other parts: fundamental to the effect of syncopation is knowing where the beat is in the first place. This is implicit in James Brown's concept of 'The One' (that is, the first beat of the 4/4 bar) which instead of destroying the 'funky beat', actually enables it to work properly. Similarly, the pedal note in pop music often functions in a different way from the pedal in classical music. Rather than providing tension through a dominant pedal or establishing, or re-establishing, stasis through a tonic pedal, the pedal in pop music provides a kind of base pitch (no pun intended) from which all the other pitched instruments can deviate, often wildly, without threatening the almost hypnotic effect of an unchanging, omnipresent tonic. In this sense, the pedal in pop music is more like the drone pitch found in much World Music.

A novel approach to musical form

Generally the way tonality functions in pop music is quite different from the classical model. Through repetition, non-developmental harmonic sequences, highly sectionalized structures, scales which tend to avoid sharpened leading notes (and often have ambiguously pitched thirds) and a rejection of any musical movement which might threaten to imply modulation, pop music tends to establish a fundamental pitch[14] which either permeates the whole song or is replaced by a different pitch in different sections (typically the chorus). 'Relax', with its virtually omnipresent bass note/bass drum, allows for no change in fundamental pitch throughout the song. While, as already noted, the backbeat tends to act as a liberating influence on pitch and rhythm in the song, it may also demand a rather more unpredictable and original approach to structure in order to provide the necessary diversity to excite and give pleasure. This is perhaps the reason why so many pieces of pop music intended for dancing, and dominated by similar, highly repetitive and utterly undeviating backbeats, adopt a similarly unpredictable approach to structure. One could, for instance, cite the work of George Clinton in the 1970s: often there are no recognizable structures in these pieces and instead there is a semi-improvised quality as short ideas seem to come and go, apparently at random. While it is possible to assign standard labels to the constituent parts of 'Relax' (verse, bridge, chorus, etc.), the backbeat provides a through-going continuity and undermines any possibility of truly contrasting sections. Indeed, it is mainly through repeated vocal phrases that different sections become established. Trevor Horn has described 'Relax' as 'a kind of non-song … it was an advertising jingle, and a brilliant one' (quoted in Buskin, 1994, p. 38). However, the production of this recording not only transformed much of the original material but also brought about a highly inventive and novel approach to musical form.

A startling variety of musical ideas – bass lines, brass-like rhythmic stabs, keyboard pads, idiomatic guitar gestures, vocal interjections, woodwind-like melodies, swirling or evocative keyboard gestures – appear in 'Relax', partly to offset the unchanging and relentless backbeat, but also because the piece is made up of a number of short sections that require differentiation through timbral and melodic diversity. While certain sections reappear quite regularly, most notably the section dominated by the word 'relax' and the section that alternates synthesized brass and synthesized bass figures, a number of other sections appear only once in the song. Since most of these sections are of quite regular phrase lengths of eight bars (with a few notable exceptions, as we shall see later) and inevitably all have some kind of motivic continuity simply by virtue of the omnipresent backbeat, one finds that the non-repeated sections tend to function rather like bridges or middle eights: material that acts purely to separate more musically dominant ideas.

However, the two repeated sections are not really intended to fulfil the traditional verse and chorus roles. First, the A section (see Table 6.1) has some

Table 6.1   The structure of 'Relax'

Intro.	Swirling synths., 'honking' saxophone, lead vox (reverb.)
A	(8 bars: 6 + 9 + 9 + 8 beats) – minimal orchestration, mainly sounds from the introduction, simply carrying chord changes
A	(8 bars) – voice and backing voices (delay-like), 'plucky banjo' sound, brass section sound
B	(4 bars) – brass figure followed by bass line (this appears with several different timbres – bass, guitar and [sampled?] voices)
A	(8 bars) – full sound with vocals always double tracked
B	(7 bars) – bass line followed by brass
C	(8 bars) – 'Shootin' in the right direction' – chords: I-flatVII-flatVI-IV major
B	(8 bars) – bass and brass together, countered by 'banjo'
D	(8 bars + 2 bars) – A and C combined harmonically, kick drum in semiquavers on last two bars
B	(8 bars) – bass and brass together in first bar, guitar line/'banjo' in second
A	(8 bars) – elements of B present here (e.g. bass line)
E	(6 bars + 2 bars) – 'When you wanna come' + synth. 'come' as word painting. This is a new idea timbrally and harmonically
B	(8 bars) – brass and bass often in same bar; guitar and 'explosive' synth. sounds in the other bar. This is rather like a M8 in feel
A&B	(8 bars) – contains elements from both sections and, although the lyrics change, the full backing is largely made up of previous material
F	(4 bars + 'Come') – kick on semiquavers

of the characteristics of a chorus: the lyrics are usually the same and they emphasize the title of the song. Yet musically this section is often rather muted in character and hardly has the rousing, anthem-like qualities that would be appropriate with a song like this. Furthermore, this section tends to be used rather like the A part of a rondo form: it is simply repeated between contrasting sections rather than successfully and dramatically reached after a bridge section. Second, the B section has no discernible lyrics at all and instead has a rather transitional character, although the bass line and brass stabs are quite distinctive. The reasons why both these sections lack truly memorable musical material will soon become apparent.

What's the hook?

The unusual structure and the absence of sections with strong verse or chorus characteristics make 'Relax' an unusual pop song. The listener's expectation is somewhat disrupted, partly through this structure and partly because the piece apparently has no strongly discernible 'hook'. Burns defines the 'hook' as 'a musical or lyrical phrase that stands out and is easily remembered' ('A typology of "hooks" in popular records', *Popular Music*, vol. 6, pp. 1–20; quoted in Moore, 1993, p. 14), however, also implicit in the 'hook' is the notion of capturing and keeping the listener's attention. Generally speaking the strongest musical and lyrical material is reserved for the chorus, which most pop song structures then exploit through underrepresentation: fading out before the listener has a chance to really immerse themselves in it. Hence, it is usually the chorus that is the hook, capturing the listeners' imagination and leaving them wanting more.[15] However, in 'Relax' the two sections (A and B) do not function in quite this way and instead there is a remarkably unpredictable but satisfying unfolding of the song (see Table 6.1).

On closer inspection it becomes evident that this highly repetitive piece of pop dance music has a number of unusual and unpredictable qualities, many of which disrupt one's expectations in subtle ways. For example, following the 'swirling' pulseless introduction, the entry of the relentless backbeat is presented within some unusual phrase lengths, as defined by the chord changes.[16] The first phrase is six beats long, the second nine, the third nine, and it is only the fourth phrase that settles down to the more typical eight beats. The sum of the four phrases is 32 beats and hence could simply have appeared as eight bars of 4/4. Instead, an extremely unusual phrase arrangement is adopted. A further unusual feature of the song is the often repeated B section characterized by its alternation of bass and brass figures. Its first appearance begins with the one-bar brass figure followed by the one-bar bass line. However, subsequently the order of these bars is reversed with the bass followed by the brass. Later on in the song, both bass and brass figures occur together in one bar, answered by a solo guitar in the second bar. Both these examples may well be not consciously perceived by most listeners, nevertheless, there can be little doubt that they are intentional modifications which run contrary to expectation and instead subtly disrupt conventions.

Overall, the most surprising characteristic of 'Relax' is that, far from being a rather rambling structure, it is a highly organized song: the two distinct and most repeated sections, A and B, go through a series of modifications as the song develops and finally appear together as a single section (see Table 6.1). In other words, the structure is made up of a dynamic process of convergence between two initially distinct musical sections.

As the song progresses, each section grows and diversifies in terms of arrangement but, in so doing, starts to lose its distinctive characteristics. The result is an unusual musical form that has few parallels in classical music. Since the fundamental nature of this structure is the reconciliation of distinct musical ideas, it is also highly satisfying musically.

Yet although the structure of 'Relax' is unusual, it is not unique in pop music. Indeed, such structures have become increasingly common in the past 20 years and may be seen, at least partly, as a result of musicians working with sequencers. The development of MIDI, and particularly MIDI sequencing programmes, during the 1980s enabled the manipulation of musical material in new ways: ideas can be developed by working directly with sound and then copied, 'pasted' and, if necessary, modified wherever might seem appropriate. Hence, rather than beginning with a specific structure in mind, musicians can allow structures to evolve through an investigation of the potential for combining the various ideas. The results of such working practices are especially evident in the various styles of dance music which have been so popular in the last 20 years. And these have, in turn, been highly influential on singles chart pop music during the period.

Repetition in 'Relax'

'Relax' relies heavily on the repetition of musical material: many elements – synthesized brass gestures, bass lines, lyrics – appear on several occasions and whole sections are repeated. Furthermore, the backbeat which permeates the entire song (sequenced disco-style bass drum and pedal bass note) is a model of repetition since it is clearly derived from a single sample and simply repeated at the same level over and over. Repetition is a feature of the song and is also evident in other elements. In the A section, for example, one finds that words are often repeated in a kind of call and response manner: 'Relax (Relax), don't do it (do it)', etc. Like the bass drum sample, these repetitions further serve to emphasize the pulse with the stressed syllables of both original and repetition falling firmly on the beat. Furthermore, the liberal use of delay is noticeable in several parts of the song. Delay is one of the earliest audio effects used in popular music and was originally generated using a tape recorder to record and then replay the new recording after a short delay. Delay provides a mechanical and exact repetition. A crucial element in the use of delay is the time interval between the original sound and its repetition. Very short delays (less than 50 ms) result in it being difficult for the listener to differentiate between the two sounds (original and repetition). Longer delays produce more recognizable echo effects. Generally, the delay times in 'Relax' have been set to ensure that the repetition coincides with the following beat and hence once more serve to emphasize the dominance of the beat. A list of examples of the use of delay and repetition appears below (see Table 6.2). Once again, there is a strong sense that 'Relax is underpinned by highly defined and purposefully presented elements which provide both aesthetic cohesion and functionality.

> Within a year Frankie split having crammed a decade of sales, creativity and controversy into less than 24 months. (Rogan, 1989, p. 395)

The remarkable success that the group experienced in 1984 was not repeated. Instead, conflicts within the group developed and escalated, and had a direct effect on their growing number of live performances. Furthermore, ZTT rather than arbitrate in these disputes seemed to exacerbate the conflicts, culminating in the court case between Holly Johnson and the record company. One consequence of this meteoric rise and fall was that the group were perceived as having a fixed image that did not have the time to develop or change. That year, 1984, became the year of Frankie Goes to Hollywood: the group were iconically linked to that particular year in the same way that 1967 is linked to the 'Summer of Love'.

Frankie Goes to Hollywood remain, however, a fascinating topic for study. Their image captured the imagination of a particular time and subsequently has come to represent that time. Their youth, while being an essential part of that image, was also the reason why they played a relatively minor role in the production of their first single. The descriptions of the making of this record reveal a level of commitment and artistic striving on the part of the record producer that is hard to reconcile with the cynical 'exploitation of youth' view that is so often directed at record companies. This sense of commercial exploitation is especially associated with the release of three 12-inch remixes, yet, as should now be clear, the production of these records may have also been driven by artistic, rather than purely financial, considerations.

Commentators tend to agree that the BBC's belated ban on 'Relax' paradoxically aided its chart success. It would seem that censorship, so long associated with popular culture in the UK, simply encourages demand rather than stifles it. The record itself exhibits some interesting musical features. Its sound is dominated by a fiercely simple yet surprisingly original backbeat with synthesizers providing a wide range of timbres and also playing a variety of musical roles. The structure

Table 6.2   Repetition in 'Relax'

Part	Delay	Immediate repetition	Medium-scale
Intro.	Lead vocal	'My-hi-hiya'	
A(8)	Lead vocal Synths.	'Whoa-ho-ho-ho'	Chord pattern
A(8)	Lead vocal	'Relax (Relax), don't do it (do it)'	'Relax, don't do it' Banjo-like synth. motif Chord pattern
B(4)	Lead vocal		Synth. brass motif Synth. bass motif 'When you wanna come'
A(8)	Lead vocal	'Relax (Relax), don't do it (do it)'	'Relax, don't do it' Banjo-like synth. motif Synth. brass motif Chord pattern
B(7)	Lead vocal	'Ha-ha-ha'	Synth. bass motif Synth. brass motif
C(8)	Lead vocal	'Oh yeah', 'Hit me'	
B(8)	Lead vocal	'Ow-ow-ow' 'Ha-ha-ha'	Synth. bass motif Synth. brass motif 'Laser Beams'
D(8+2)	Lead vocal Synth. melody		'Relax'
B(8)	Lead vocal	'Ah-ah' 'I'm comin'' 'Ha-ha-ha'	Synth. brass motif Synth. bass motif
A(8) E(6+2)	Lead vocal 'Come' Final synth.		'Relax, don't do it' 'When you wanna come' Descending synth. motif
B(8)	L. voc./splashes	'Ow-ow-ow'	Synth. brass motif Synth. bass motif
A&B(8)	Lead vocal	'Relax (Relax), don't do it (do it)'	'Relax, don't do it' Banjo-like synth. motif Chord pattern Synth. brass motif Synth. bass motif
F(4+)	Synths/'Come'		

is not the rambling, motivically dominated 'jam session' it might first appear, but instead is a highly organized and highly original approach to musical form in pop, in part the result of Horn's obsessive pursuit of high standards while working on the Page R sequencer of the Fairlight CMI.

Notes

1. This is clearly not exclusively a characteristic of ZTT records since a number of groups in the early 1980s made some reference to high art: for example, Bauhaus, Cabaret Voltaire and Père Ubu.
2. Russolo (1986, p. 26). Surprisingly, the words actually used in Russolo's manifesto – 'ZANG-TUMB-TUUUMB' – are misquoted.
3. 'Two stories have been given as the origin of the band's name. It either came from a caption to a photograph of the young Frank Sinatra or from a headline in a Liverpool paper about Frankie Vaughan' (Hardy and Laing, 1990, p. 282).
4. ZTT ZTAS 1.
5. ZTT ZTAS 3.
6. ZTT ZTAS 5.
7. 'Relax' was actually released on 26 November 1983 but only reached the number one position in the UK singles chart on 28 January 1984.
8. ZTT ZTTIQ 1.
9. 'The press made much of ZTT's statement that on our first two number one hit records "Relax" and "Two Tribes" there was no actual playing done by any member of the band but me [Holly Johnson]. Parallels were drawn with The Bay City Rollers, The Monkees, etc., and the words "manufactured pop group" were bandied about a lot' (Johnson, 1995, p. 266). Johnson goes on to write: 'At least Trevor (Horn) had the decency to testify, "I could never have done these records in isolation. There was no actual playing by the band on either record but all the music was by the band and the whole feeling came from the band".'
10. See particularly Johnson (1995, pp. 161–2).
11. Significantly, both Johnson and Horn concur that the main musical contribution of the group (vocals excepted) was 'a bunch of samples of the group jumping in the swimming pool' (Buskin, 1994, p. 35).
12. 'Tell Laura I Love Her' (Columbia DB 4493), a number one hit for Ricky Valance in 1960, for example, was not played on BBC radio because its lyrics mentioned death. It became a hit because it was played on Radio Luxembourg.
13. There are discrepancies between the sources as to exactly when the record was banned by the BBC. *The Guinness Book of Number One Hits* states that 'Relax' 'pottered around the lower regions of the Top 75 until one morning Radio One's breakfast DJ, Mike Read, realized just what the lyrics were saying. He unilaterally declared his disgust and his refusal to play the disc led to an all-out BBC ban. This was just what the record needed'. While *The Faber Companion to Twentieth Century Popular Music* states that '"Relax" reached the Top 10 before the BBC imposed a belated radio ban on the grounds of obscenity'.
14. Naming this pitch the 'tonic' is rather misleading since it does not really function in the same way as the tonic in classical music.
15. Of course, it could be argued that lyrically 'Relax' has no verses at all and is made up purely of a chorus (the A idea) interspersed with contrasting musical sections.
16. This is a characteristic of a number of Trevor Horn productions: a mysterious, beatless introduction, often tonally ambiguous in character, is cut through by the first statement of the backbeat which is both loud, pulse-defining and imposes a strong sense of tonality through the pitches of the bass line. The effect is reminiscent of the notion of 'order out of chaos' and draws attention to the strength and immediacy of the backbeat. This effect is also found at the beginning of Horn's production of 'Crazy' by Seal, for example.

Chapter 7

Who's Afraid of The Art of Noise?

ZTT's disjointed image was typified by the quirky Fairlight workouts of The Art of Noise, a project ... which gathered together Anne Dudley, J. J. Jeczalik and Gary Langan to create the most unlikely, though ultimately successful, chart music. (Cunningham, 1996, p. 278)

The Art of Noise was formed while Trevor Horn was working on *90125*, adopting a name derived from the Italian Futurists. It was the first group to be signed to Horn's ZTT label. The four other members of the band were already closely associated with Horn. Gary Langan 'remained Horn's engineer throughout his early eighties productions' (ibid., p. 272) and worked extensively on the recording of *90125*. J.J. Jeczalik was the assistant engineer and Fairlight programmer during the Yes recording sessions. Anne Dudley had already worked with Horn on several occasions as a keyboard player and arranger, and Paul Morley was ZTT's publicist.

During their ZTT period,[1] The Art of Noise were characterized by the absence of a lead vocalist and extensive use of modern electronic technology.[2] Since the vocal part tends to be a fundamental aspect of pop music, successful instrumental groups are rare. Moreover, The Art of Noise used very few traditional musical instruments associated with pop music (that is, electric guitar, electric bass guitar or drum kit) on their recordings. The influence of Trevor Horn seems apparent here: Gary Langan has described him as 'the first person I knew who had a great command of machines and he had this obsession about everything needing to be strictly in time' (ibid., p. 272). On The Art of Noise recordings sounds are created with synthesizers, samplers and recording studio technology: equipment which even today has some associations in the popular imagination with either toys or magic. Toys because often, like musical boxes and other mechanical musical devices, no dextrous playing technique is required, and magical because, at the touch of a switch, acoustic sound is broadcast from apparently motionless 'black boxes'.[3]

However, The Art of Noise were not alone in adopting this kind of technology-based approach to the creation of popular music. The German group Kraftwerk, who exclusively used synthesizers, had opened the way in the 1970s, and a number of British pop groups adopted a similar approach in the early 1980s: Depeche Mode, Scritti Politti and The Human League, for example. This was at least partially because synthesizer technology during the period was beginning to make use of digital processing and, as a result, was becoming more reliable, resourceful, and accessible. Moreover, in 1983 MIDI first started to appear on synthesizers. The success of such pop groups was also partly due to an acceptance on the part of the buying public that the exclusive or at least extensive use of such technology represented an appropriate way of making pop music, and particularly pop dance music characterized by a fiercely accurate and mechanical beat.[4] As mentioned, disco had already celebrated the notion of dancing to synthesizer-driven, studio produced records. This trend has continued to the present day and remains firmly associated with British and European singles chart music.

Although a few vocal parts did appear at times on The Art of Noise recordings, there was no lead vocal as such. On rare occasions a named vocalist was invited to make a 'guest' appearance: in later years the band collaborated with a number of other musicians including Duane Eddy and Tom Jones. The absence of a lead vocalist in The Art of Noise has wide-ranging implications, going beyond the aural dimension: the lead vocalist often largely defines the image of the group both in terms of performance and public relations; and they inevitably carry the poetic message (the lyrics) normally present in the pop product. By not having a lead vocalist, The Art of Noise had no focal point with which to present their image and they also denied themselves the traditional vehicle with which to deliver the verbal element. In pop terms, this sense of absence is compounded by their avoidance of live performances and personal appearances as a band or as individuals. They had decided to never appear in their own videos and even their record sleeves gave no indication of the physical appearance of the members of the band. Unlike masked performers such as The Residents or Frank Sidebottom who surround their identity with secrecy, The Art of Noise were without bodily image and instead tended to define themselves aurally through their recordings. Like the record producer, they were at the heart of the pop product yet remained visually anonymous and unrecognizable. It is perhaps significant that this non-image goes hand in hand with modern audio technology.[5] Hence, this notion of the 'ghost in the machine', discussed with regard to 'Video Killed the Radio Star' emerges once again.

What's in a name?

Although The Art of Noise had no image constructed around their physical presence, they presented images in conjunction with their work through a series of vivid record sleeves, promotional videos and advertising material. Verbal imagery was presented through titles, as well as the words and phrases that appeared on the sleeves or could be heard, usually as samples, on their recordings. In effect, the absence of physical personality draws greater attention to, and as a result placed greater emphasis on, these very elements. The name of the group, derived from Russolo's Futurist manifesto entitled *The Art of Noises*,[6] is an oxymoronic formula: art, at least in the popular imagination, is associated with beauty and culture, while noise is perceived as being ugly and random. By making noise singular rather than plural, the group strengthened the oxymoron coined by Russolo. Furthermore, the phrase could be interpreted as a definition of a particularly harsh and challenging type of music and, as such, suggested a group making an explicitly aesthetic and self-referential statement.

A similar approach is evident in some of the album titles. *Into Battle with The Art of Noise* (1984), their second album, implied both the use of sound as a militant weapon and the artistic confrontations of the avant-garde, a term which itself originated with the military. Other titles tend to adopt word play and puns to amuse and perplex, and are reminiscent of the clues to crossword puzzles: *In No Sense? Nonsense* (1987); *In Visible Silence* (1987); and *Below the Waste* (1989). Such titles are both amusing and ambiguous.

Who's afraid of The Art of Noise?

The image promoted by ZTT, particularly as regards to modern art, was viewed by many commentators as rather pretentious: 'there's something about the karma of ZTT which annoys me. This incredibly pretentious veil they tend to wrap themselves in' (*Melody Maker*, single review, 27 October 1984). These objections resulted not only from an uneasiness about the references to high art within pop music but also from the impression of facile ambiguity as a result of the deliberate play on connotation (that is, implied meaning[s]) as opposed to denotation (that is, explicit statements or images).

The title of The Art of Noise's first album, *Who's Afraid of The Art of Noise?* (1984),[7] is a particularly striking and apposite example of their reliance on wide-ranging cultural references. First, there is an obvious similarity between the title of the album and that of the song used in Walt Disney's cartoon *Three Little Pigs* (1933), 'Who's Afraid of the Big Bad Wolf?', which is derived from the Little Red Riding Hood tale; the reference here is to American popular culture, parodies of nursery rhymes and more psychologically disturbing elements present in the original European folk tales. Second, the phrase also works as a reference to the play *Who's Afraid of Virginia Woolf?* (1962) by Edward Albee, itself a clear reference to the cartoon song; the popular success of the film version of this play, starring Elizabeth Taylor and Richard Burton, prevents it from being an obscure cultural reference.

In its formulation the title offers further ambiguity since it can be read as referring to either fear of the musical content or of the group itself. The use of contrasting colours for the title on the front cover ('Who's Afraid Of' in red and 'The Art of Noise?' in yellow) encourages both interpretations. Hence, the album title, which is one of the first elements to reach and possibly attract the consumer, asks a direct question that had more than one possible answer.

Cover imagery

The cover of this album is also worthy of some consideration. The absence of human figures enabled the group to retain their anonymity. In addition to the title in red and yellow, the front cover bears two silver masks, one sad and one happy – a recognized symbol of the dramatic arts – against a blue/black backdrop which looks like velvet but on closer inspection has the grain typical of an enlarged photograph; and six lines of text on the right:

> this record includes moments in love, a time for fear and close (to the edit) … the music was compiled by the art of noise between February 28th 1983 and April 1st 1984 … on April 2nd 1985 the art of noise had this to say: 'our contemporaries irritate us, we detest the neighbour to our right, we detest the neighbour to our left, above all, we detest the one on the floor above us, just as much, anyway, as the one on the ground floor. (good heavens! we live on the ground floor ourselves !!!)' … the buzzy buzzing flies are of some use after all … sleeve design: xlztt for the enjoyment of zang tuum tumb. zang tuum tumb's musical director is trevor horn.

Most noticeable here is the repeated use of suspension points that denote words or phrases that have been omitted: once again a sense of uncertainty is created. The use of different colours for the title facilitates a further interpretation: perhaps the title of the album is simply 'Who's Afraid of', with the name of the group appearing afterwards? Such an interpretation is slightly undermined by the inclusion of the question mark after the name of the group, but the ambiguity remains.

The masks clearly encourage a theatrical interpretation of the title. This is supported by the back cover which has three photographs each containing stylized paper masks which are either sad or happy. These masks – particularly one which has only one hole cut out for the eye – have a more sinister quality: robbers wear masks; people with disfigured faces (like *The Phantom of the Opera*) wear masks; and actors wear metaphorical masks. A figure dressed in a cowl on a deserted seaweed-strewn beach appears on another photograph, but the figure has the insubstantiality of a scarecrow ('who's afraid?'). Identification is denied, adding a further level of ambiguity and supporting the recurring motif of fear.

The grainy and indistinct backdrop of the cover provides a suitably neutral background to draw attention to the silver masks, however, even this is capable of several interpretations. First, the poor resolution partially evokes a landscape or cloudscape. Second, the masks are strangely small in relation to the overall dimensions of the cover, making the backdrop more significant and more insistent. Finally, one can see a relationship, either contrived or fortuitous, between the grainy quality of the backdrop and the lack of resolution in the samples on the recording. The word 'grainy' is often used to describe the kind of eight-bit samples which dominate this record.

To summarize, many of the elements on the sleeve of this record are open to several possible interpretations. The specific references to art and artifice further encourage these multiple interpretations. The ambiguity and subsequent unease evoked by the cover reflect a fundamental aspect of audio recording: the acousmatic. Originally a method of instruction during the time of Pythagoras which involved the teacher presenting information from behind a screen, the acousmatic has come to refer to the absence of visual aids to the comprehension of pre-recorded sound. The sensation of hearing creates an expectation of a visible and physical source. However, recorded sound always emerges from the apparently motionless cones of loudspeakers. Moreover, many recorded sounds are immediately identifiable – speech for example – and, as a result, create a specific visual expectation in the listener which is not fulfilled. The dichotomy between these two conflicting pieces of sensory data (sound and sight) inevitably induces some slight unease. The use of digital sampling as a means of creating new recordings, a fundamental musical attribute of The Art of Noise, further compounds this disturbing phenomenon.

Sampling

With a few notable exceptions, it was only with the advent of the tape recorder that new music derived from recorded sound really began to develop. The collage techniques that had already been so important in other art forms, only appeared to any significant degree in music in 1948 with Pierre Schaeffer's inauguration of *musique concrète*.

The use of pre-recorded material (as the basis of the work of art) began to permeate a far greater range of musical genres with the invention and development of the digital sampler in the late 1970s. The sampler enables the composer to work directly with sound – even the physical reality of tape, and the physical expertise necessary to manipulate it, has been eradicated. The routines, strategies, processes and working practices that the sampler imposes on the act of composition are profoundly influential: samplers make 'sampler music', which is often a collage made from other recordings. Of course, this sense of collage is also present in the recording process itself: most classical recordings are created by splicing different takes together, while most pop recordings are a mix of different, and separately recorded, individual tracks.

Any sound source that can be recorded can be sampled. This has resulted in many unusual samples being used as the basis of musical composition. Often the characteristics of these samples tend to be musically disruptive, drawing attention to non-musical parameters. First, a single sample may contain a range of pitch, rhythmic and/or timbral information. Although this sample appears on a keyboard as a single note it can be a remarkably complex musical idea. Second, the sample may contain sounds which inevitably evoke a 'real' situation. The sample is made up of sounds that suggest a particular physical environment. Third, the sample may contain sounds which relate to a particular time and place – a sample of a Second World War air raid siren, for example. Finally, the sample may contain sounds which are specific to and derived from the process of audio recording and reproduction. Using samples with any of these characteristics in a piece of music gives rise to a conflict between musical and extra-musical elements.

Moreover, sampling offers a musician a way to explore systematically those parts of their musical imagination which developed *as a result* of listening to records. Sampling may begin with a fascination for a particular recorded sound. The process of sampling, and particularly sample editing, refines and focuses that fascination.

Unlike the tape recorders of the 1950s, digital samplers tend to be controlled by a MIDI keyboard. However, with the keyboard-controlled sampler, pitch control, the primary function of the keyboard, will often be utterly disrupted: timbre replaces pitch as the main control parameter. As a result, one often finds that the most imaginative manipulators of keyboard-controlled samplers are neither highly proficient nor formally trained keyboard players: people who have as little expectation as possible of the traditional pitch implications of the keyboard. The manipulative skills necessary to use a sampler are minimal, the expert sampler operator is both composer, instrument maker and performer. They need not be a physical virtuoso, only a virtuoso of the imagination with an expertise in the manipulation and organization of sound. This extreme distinction between the infinite variety of sounds and sound combinations, and the few relatively simple, fixed manipulations is one of the characteristics which makes the sampler both so attractive yet also so defining as a musical instrument. Like all machines, the sampler performs a few tasks very well and the most successful pieces of music that are generated by this machine are made by people who work efficiently within these constraints: the music is conceived as a result of the sampling process, not abstracted from it.

Recording records

The fact that the sampler can deal with any recorded material would seem to be a major liberating factor rather than a constraint. However, anything that is recorded is, by definition, anything that is not live. Playing a sampler is, in this sense, closer to playing a record player than playing a musical instrument. This highlights a fundamental difference between musical and mechanical repetition: every time a musician repeats a musical phrase it is performed anew, while the sampler simply replays exactly the same recording. The potentially infinite repetition of an acoustically unique event has no natural parallel.

The generation of much sampler music is the result of listening to, and then sampling, audio recordings. Hence, the person listening to a piece of sampler music hears something that is itself derived from a process of listening. This might tend to create a particular bond between the listener and the composer, which is rarely present in other kinds of music. Furthermore, sampling would seem a particularly appropriate technique for the pop musician whose musical imagination is likely to have developed largely through listening to recordings.

Audio recording could be seen as a mere example of the desire to preserve and to, literally, *record*: 'Since at least the beginning of this century, our culture has been oriented towards historicism and conservation' (Boulez, 1986, p. 6). The sampler represents a creative response to the notion of preservation: manipulating and organizing bits of the old to make something new. Evan Eisenberg writes of 'the freedom, once the cathedral of culture had been wrecked, to take home the bits that you liked and arrange them as you pleased' (Eisenberg, 1988, p. 24).

Listening to samples

Turning to the listener and the artwork, Nattiez's notion of an *esthesic* dimension, where listeners 'construct meaning in the course of an active perceptual process' (Nattiez, 1990, p. 12), is particularly useful when dealing with sampler music, since the importance of the 'lived experience of the "receiver"' (ibid., p. 10) can have immediate consequences in the process of reception. When a listener identifies the source of a sample, the extra-musical connotations (be they physical, cultural or phonographical) inform the purely musical response. These non-musical associations become part of the interpretative process: the listener's understanding of the piece is dependent on whether identification takes place, and a culturally informed response is quite different from a musically informed response. Physical, cultural or phonographical signs replace or override musical signs and, as a consequence, a different kind of communication takes place.

Sampling, like all the important techniques in twentieth-century art, is subversive. It challenges and undermines traditional musical notions, replacing them with radical and disturbing alternatives. Fundamental to this challenge is the creative use of recorded sound: the sampler records recordings, which are then assembled to make new recordings. This self-referential quality clearly links the sampler to parallel practices in other art forms of the twentieth century. Subversion takes place at several levels. First, by imposing a rigidly defined operating system, sampling channels and constrains the composer's methods. Second, the traditional pitch parameters associated with the keyboard are undermined: with the sampler, the keyboard is used simply to select and trigger specific samples. Third, the use of commercial recordings as source material raises important questions regarding intellectual property and copyright. Fourth, sample identification disrupts the listening process that is associated with more traditional music. Finally, sampling subverts the division between composer, player and listener, showing that active, imaginative listening and the relatively simple skills required to operate a sampler can form the basis of musical composition.

Sampling and The Art of Noise

While sampling is a feature of 'Buffalo Gals', 'Owner of a Lonely Heart' and 'Relax', it is a fundamental element in recordings by The Art of Noise. Indeed, in their early work they are often explicitly associated with one particular sampler: the Fairlight CMI Series II. A great deal of what one hears when listening to *Who's Afraid of The Art of Noise?* is derived from this instrument and, as a result, has a defining influence on the sound of the recordings. The Fairlight CMI Series II was an eight-bit sampler with a maximum sampling rate of 35 000 samples per second, individual samples were monophonic and the maximum sample length was 16 kilobytes. In contrast, more modern samplers offer at least 16-bit resolution, sample rates comparable or superior to the compact disc (44 100 samples per second), stereo sampling capabilities and the possibility of recording very long samples if required. Because of these limitations, sounds produced by the Fairlight Series II tend to lack dynamic range and timbral definition. Moreover, it is particularly prone to aliasing: a high-pitched noise that occurs when the low-pass output filter on the digital to analogue converter is set too high. When the converter is set low the samples tend to have a veiled, indistinct quality. As a consequence, sounds produced by the Fairlight Series II are often described as 'grainy': a quality which at the time was regarded as a deficiency but which nevertheless has a particular charm and character. Such samples are often rich in the phonographic connotations mentioned earlier. This is especially noticeable when these samples are mixed with sounds of a higher resolution and sound quality. The Art of Noise often contrast the grainy samples of the Fairlight Series II with bright, clear sounds produced by synthesizers. This differentiation is not only timbrally marked: the more traditional musical parameters – melody and harmony – tend to appear as synthesized sounds, while the special effects, noises and rhythmic elements are produced through samples. Perhaps as significant as its sampling capabilities, the Fairlight Series II also had the ability to arrange samples into musical sequences. Although the sequencing system was created pre-MIDI, the sequencing software (known as 'Page R')[8] has a number of similarities with early MIDI sequencers: a layout that follows the multitrack formula; notation (rhythms only) to indicate the presence of data on a particular track; on-screen editing (with a 'light pen'); and a limited number of tracks (eight). The sequencer enables and encourages highly rhythmic arrangements of samples, and is ideal for the generation of pop music intended for dancing rather than the normally somewhat less pulse dominated rhythmic characteristics of much electroacoustic music.

The first track on *Who's Afraid of The Art of Noise?*, 'A Time to Fear (Who's Afraid)' begins, after a few introductory sounds, with what appears to be a recording of a political speech in praise of the people of revolutionary Cuba: a recording (in fact a recording within a recording) with explicit cultural references. Thus, although there are very few words on the album, and none that are definitely spoken or sung by any of the members of the band, it begins with a stream of words.[9] This speech is far too long to be a digital sample, particularly a Fairlight Series II sample, and has been made using the analogue magnetic tape editing techniques associated with *musique concrète*. It is interrupted by extremely short drum samples sequenced into a simple 4/4 dance pattern – a typical product of the Fairlight CMI. The stark contrast between these two essentially similar ideas – they are, after all, both derived from pre-recorded material – highlights the difference in practice between *musique concrète*, which is firmly associated with the musical avant-garde, and the kind of sequenced samples found in pop music: the sequencer/sampler arrangement enables and encourages the specifically rhythmic use of pre-recorded music. Hence, an album which begins with techniques associated with *musique concrète* subsequently establishes the strongly stressed dance rhythms of pop music. As if to reinforce this point, later in this piece the short phrase 'military forces', clearly derived from the original speech, appears this time as a sample, and is treated in a far more rhythmic manner.

Another characteristic of the use of speech on *Who's Afraid of The Art of Noise?* is 'the half-heard voice': here speech contributes to the musical fabric of a piece and is also perceived as spoken words. It tends to occur with speech which is usually quite low in the mix and combined with other sounds which tend to obscure the articulation and make the exact meaning unclear. A particularly noticeable example is the repeated phrase 'moments in love' in the track of the same name. The listener's attention is drawn specifically to this phrase because it is so difficult to actually hear – at the end of the track one is still not entirely sure of the exact words and has to make the assumption that it must be 'moments in love'. Another example of this technique is the phrase 'bright noise', once again on the track of the same name on the album *Into Battle*. In a world of insistent and demanding advertising using a variety of media to stress a particular message, the creation of interest through understatement is an intelligent and subtle way of involving the listener – in these examples, once curiosity is aroused, concentration is required in order to decipher the words.

The sampler allows exact repetition time and again, in the same way as the replaying of any other kind of audio recording. This unchanging, repeated quality can often be used to create a kind of aural 'constant' and this in turn can enable other sounds to be presented with a greater rhythmic flexibility. In this sense it is similar in function to the 'four to the floor' disco beat of the late 1970s which also tended to allow greater rhythmic freedom for the other parts, as mentioned in the previous chapter. Perhaps the most notorious example of one of these 'constants' is the vocal sample which permeates 'O Superman' by Laurie Anderson.[10] A similarly high level of repetition of a sample is noticeable on 'Moments in Love', the sixth track of *Who's Afraid of The Art of Noise?* Like 'O Superman', it is a simple, single vocal sample following the four beats of the bar, the only difference is that it changes pitch, following the basic harmonic structure of the piece. A rather more unusual use of sample repetition on the album occurs when the same sample appears in several different pieces. For example, the female vocal sample 'Heh!' which crops up on both 'Close (to the Edit)' and 'Who's Afraid (of The Art of Noise)', provides continuity and cohesion between the various pieces rather like a particular instrumentalist's timbre or a singer's voice would. Finally a further rhythmic effect is achieved in sampling by repeating the start of a short spoken phrase, almost in the manner of a stutter. As previously mentioned, this technique is particularly evident on 'Nineteen'[11] ('N-N-N-Nineteen') by Paul Hardcastle, and can also be heard on 'A Time for Fear (Who's Afraid)' with the phrase 'Can I – Can I – Can I say something?'. The spoken phrase takes on a mechanical, and distinctly non-human quality when subjected to this treatment. It is no accident that a computer-generated 'celebrity', Max Headroom, who is subject to these bouts of phrase repetition, would appear on a later recording by The Art of Noise.[12]

Many of the samples used on *Who's Afraid of The Art of Noise?* contain physical associations and hence are unlikely to be appreciated as 'pure music'. By evoking non-musical responses on the part of the listener, the use of such samples undermines the normal parameters which define musical aesthetics. It is most noticeable on the track 'Momento' which is made up almost entirely of samples of sound effects: thunder, footsteps, a tolling bell, a peel of bells and the singing of birds. The physical associations that these samples evoke are immediate and undeniable, and since they are derived from clichéd sound effects are immediately recognizable. However, these samples do not evoke a linear narrative interpretation. They are neither pure music nor pure effect, but sounds that activate cultural memory, functioning in a similar way to the numerous non-original musical ideas so often found in pop.

Finally, another musically disruptive use of sampling is evident with the single samples of chords which are then combined sequentially to provide the basic harmonic movement of a piece. Disruption here is the result of unusual harmonic sequences which run counter to conventional harmonic language. At one point in 'Moments in Love', for example, a sample of a single minor chord is used to underpin the melody: one minor chord (the tonic) is followed by another minor chord, a tone below. Obviously, by traditional Western harmonic standards, this sounds unusual, yet the sampler, with its keyboard-based control, not only allows but also positively encourages such ideas.[13] It is likely that this kind of harmonic movement will become established, in much the same way as parallel chords on the electric guitar.

Studio made

The genesis of 'Close (to the Edit)' illustrates the extremely close relationship between sampling and recording. It is no accident that the title makes reference to Yes's album *Close to the Edge*[14] and the substitution of 'edit' for 'edge' can be interpreted as referring to the specific techniques adopted. Significantly, the tape edit was an important technique in the production of earlier Yes albums. Mark Cunningham writes: 'it might seem that the computer-assisted mixdown technology prevalent today was born for mixing the long and highly complex tracks for which Yes became famous. Yet all they and Offord (Yes's engineer and co-producer) could rely on was the editing block and a razor blade' (Cunningham, 1996, p. 159). The relationship between 'Close (to the Edit)' and the work of the progressive rock group is extremely close. Cunningham later notes:

> The idea originated during the nine months it took Horn to produce Yes's *90125* album ... Langan says: 'After about seven months of working virtually every day of every week at a variety of studios ... we had been up at AIR in Oxford Circus to cut a track but it was scrapped. I kept the multitrack though because the drum track was just phenomenal. A month later, when the band had gone home one night, myself and J.J. (Horn's assistant and Fairlight programmer) had the idea for putting the drums from this multitrack into the Fairlight as a complete sample. The idea wasn't to have separate samples of the bass drum, snare and hi-hat, like everyone else was beginning to do with AMS's, but have it as a composite sample of the whole kit ... we just looped the drum sample and added a few other things on top. (Ibid., p. 278)

Unlike the recordings so far reviewed in this study, those by The Art of Noise are not credited as being produced by Trevor Horn on the album cover.[15] On *Who's Afraid of The Art of Noise?* he is described as 'zang tuum tumb's musical director' and is credited with contributing to the composition of six of the nine tracks. This important distinction once again highlights the problem of assigning specific creative roles to particular individuals. While Horn's influence is apparent in several aspects of this recording – most noticeably in the use of timbre, space and structure – he is to be considered simply as one member of the team involved in production. This may be regarded as somewhat similar to some of the working practices adopted in several fine art studios during the Italian Renaissance. In spite of Horn's somewhat ambiguous personal role, the use of timbre and space on this album is worthy of closer scrutiny.

Timbre

Once recorded sounds with specific physical connotations are subjected to the manipulative facilities of the sampler and sequencer, musical and cultural messages may be combined in unusual ways. 'Close (to the Edit)', for example, begins with a sample of a car motor starting, which is then used to play a short melody: the noise of the car engine is manipulated *as though it were* musical. The melody appears several times in the piece, often with more traditional musical timbres. When sampled and manipulated melodically, those resonant frequencies which directly relate to the physical size of the sound source (formants) also change pitch, suggesting similar changes in the actual size of the resonating body. Hence the physical connotations are somewhat undermined but not eradicated, while the musical potential is explored and emphasized. The listener is encouraged to have a musical response to the timbre – the 'noise' becomes 'art'. A somewhat similar situation has long been apparent in the artistic use of sound effects in radio, television and film: sounds are used for dramatic effect rather than acoustic accuracy: 'The art of creating and using sound effects has become so sophisticated that sounds rarely appear in film or television as they are found at the source' (Mott, 1990, p. 53), and 'since the advent of sound in film, it has become increasingly popular to tamper with the reality of natural production sounds' (ibid., p. 76).[16] Many of the sampled timbres on *Who's Afraid of The Art of Noise?* rely on the listener's appreciation of the physical qualities of the sound sources which are then disturbed and disrupted by the musical processes that the samples are subjected to.

As noted, the synthesized timbres on the album contrast strongly with the samples in a number of ways: resolution, noise level, frequency range, etc. Musically, their function differs, too: they tend to carry the more traditional melodic and harmonic ideas. For example, 'A Time for Fear (Who's Afraid)', the first track on the album, begins with a political speech and is followed by drum-like samples that are sequenced in a harsh mechanistic rhythm which builds up with several other samples (orchestral sounds, the repeated phrase 'military forces', etc.). This sample-generated and rhythm-dominated texture is replaced at 1 minute and 55 seconds by a far more gentle, melodic section played by synthesized timbres. The violent, insistent rhythms of the noise-like drums are contrasted with clearly pitched sounds suspended within a sustained and pitch-dominated texture. Moreover, the synthesizer timbres on the album are not generally imitative of acoustic instruments, while the sampled sounds are all clearly directly derived from acoustic sounds, producing a further paradox.

Space

Just as timbre is an important and featured parameter on *Who's Afraid of The Art of Noise?*, so is the manipulation of space. The potential for artistic investigation of space using the typical stereo speaker arrangement would appear somewhat limited, yet this is deceptive. In fact, the two axes (left/right and depth) as well as various psychoacoustic emulations offer an enormous range of positional possibilities which are further enhanced by the artificial and technological nature of the recorded medium: sounds can not only move within one field but can also occupy different fields *within the same recording*. With the multitrack tape recorder, several recording spaces within a studio, and a variety of digital signal processors, the possibilities for evoking different kinds of space and movement are virtually endless. For example, a guitar played in what sounds like a huge, bright space could be accompanied by close, highly defined drums, with exact stereo positions for each part of the kit, and also a booming bass guitar, whose sound suggests a relatively small, dark space. Even this extremely simple example illustrates the 'unnatural' and artificial nature of the medium: the two guitars (solo and bass), while playing together (in tune, in time, following identical harmonic and structural patterns) apparently occupy entirely different spaces.

Furthermore, recordings not only place the instrumental or vocal timbre in a particular spatial position, they also define the position of the listener in relation to that sound: the spatial elements in the recording present the listener with a specific point of view. Claudia Gorbman, writing specifically on the relationship between sound and image in films, places great emphasis on the spatial qualities present in soundtracks:

> Cinema also had the psychological effect … of flattening the real onto a two-dimensional plane. Thus, first, music came to replace, or at least compensate for the lack of, speech. Second, all sound exists in three dimensions; music as sound gave back, or at least compensated for the lack of, the spatial dimension of the reality so uncannily depicted in the new medium. (Gorbman, 1987, p. 37)

While film soundtracks, and particularly diegetic sound effects, are likely to follow and simply support the visual elements of film, no such constraint is imposed upon sound recordings. Unlike much film, in recorded music there is no need for any kind of 'natural' diegesis. With recordings, the implied environment of a specific timbre is accepted by listeners as part of a musical statement about that instrument or voice.

Popular music has, since the crooners of the 1930s, used audio technology to create unnatural or at least unlikely spatial effects, intended to impress the listener rather than depict reality. During the 1960s and 1970s a great many new signal processors were introduced and refined explicitly to expand the highly artificial nature of the recorded medium. With the introduction of digital reverberation around 1980, sound manipulation within entirely unnatural and 'impossible' spaces became a possibility. During this period, Trevor Horn and the work of ZTT consistently embraced the latest digital technology and explored the artistic potential it offered, challenging and subverting the expectations of the listener.

The manipulation of space as a significant musical parameter is a characteristic of much of Horn's work (see Chapter 9). However, to depict exactly how space is implied and used in these recordings is problematic since it involves several parameters simultaneously: different sounds in different spatial positions over time. A possible solution would be the use of computer animation running in synchronization with the specific recording: a kind of moving score. Cartoons based on the use of abstract images which evolve with music are far from new. See, for example, the opening sequence in Disney's *Fantasia* or some of the abstract work of the Canadian animator Norman McLaren.

The Art of Noise is an unusual and unlikely pop group with no vocalist, no visual personification of the band, and a general sense of the equivocal. Their album covers, publicity photographs and the use of texts support the 'high art' image associated with ZTT, and are rich in ambiguity. Although Trevor Horn is not personally credited with the production of *Who's Afraid of The Art of Noise?*, some of the sonic characteristics of the record strongly suggest his influence. The band's image makes reference to the use of modern studio technology and a central feature of the band's sound is their use of the Fairlight Series II sampler. The band's use of the sampler is innovative – unusual samples are arranged rhythmically and the physical associations of some samples are manipulated in interesting and surprising ways. Contrast is created between the sounds of synthesizers and those of the sampler. Hence, the manipulation of timbre (with the use of the sampler) and space (with the use of digital reverberation) are fundamental to the musical aesthetic of *Who's Afraid of The Art of Noise?* With the benefit of hindsight, The Art of Noise would seem to encapsulate many of the characteristics of the early 1980s through their exploitation of specific current audio technologies in much the same way as slapback echo is an intrinsic aspect of the sound of rock 'n' roll during the 1950s.[17]

Notes

1. Trevor Horn and Paul Morley left The Art of Noise after their first album and the rest of the band signed a new contract with China Records.
2. 'At their first group meeting, on February 2nd 1983, they decided that they would never appear in their videos, they would not have a lead singer, they would never officially finish off a track, they would use technology to liberate the imagination' (http://www.hiponline.com/artist/music/a/art_of_noise/).
3. It is perhaps significant that the second track on The Art of Noise's first album is called 'Beat Box'.
4. It is rather ironic that 'Beat Box' 'became something of a blueprint for new styles in the rhythms of hip hop and electro and won ... [them the] Best Black Dance Act in many dance polls' (http://imusic.artistdirect.com/showcase/club/artofnoise.html).
5. In contrast, Kraftwerk stressed a half man/half machine image – their sixth album was actually called *The Man Machine* (1978). For further details on Kraftwerk see Bussy (1993) and Barr (1998).
6. Russolo (1986).
7. ZTT 4509-94746-2. Entered the UK albums chart on 3 November 1984.

8. The Fairlight Series II's monitor was a green and black screen and each of the editable areas was known as a 'page': a particular screen shot. 'Page R' was the 'Rhythm Composer' and significantly emphasized the rhythmic capabilities of the system.

9. The use of political speeches became widespread in later music using samplers and is especially associated with black rap groups with a strong political message like Public Enemy. An early example is the extremely successful single 'Nineteen' by Paul Hardcastle (Chrysalis CHS 2860), although The Art of Noise pre-dates this.

10. Warner Bros. K 17870, 17 October 1981.

11. Chrysalis CHS 2860, released 4 May 1985.

12. Max Headroom is featured on 'Paranoimia' (China WOK 9), 21 July 1986.

13. The orchestral stab became such a regular sample to appear on dance records during the 1980s, including the enormously successful 'You Were Always on my Mind' by Pet Shop Boys, that it not only quickly acquired cliché status, but also appeared on virtually every MIDI keyboard and tone generator of this period as a preset sound.

14. Atlantic K 50012 entered the UK charts on 23 September 1972.

15. Although Sarm Productions attribute the production to Trevor Horn. See Appendix 2.

16. This can give rise to conflicts between 'real' reality and imagined reality: 'A veteran of World War II gave this rather startling account of his first day in combat at Anzio. "Believe it or not, the first thing I thought about was [how] it didn't sound like a war. Having grown up watching Hollywood war movies, I expected a lot more sounds and much bigger sounds, it wasn't until I [was] hit that I realized what I was in was real"' (Mott, 1990, p. 77).

17. That The Art of Noise are, after James Brown and Kraftwerk, the group most often sampled by other musicians, is an ironic indication of the importance and influence of their recordings.

Chapter 8

'Jewel', 'Duel' and 'Jewelled' by Propaganda

In addition to his work with ZTT, Trevor Horn was still acting as an independent producer. Between the release of *Who's Afraid of The Art of Noise?* and the first Propaganda album, he produced the 12-inch version of 'Do They Know It's Christmas?'[1] by Band Aid and the single 'Cry'[2] by Godley and Creme. However, the dynamic relationship between creativity and technology, the central focus of this study, is best exemplified by his ZTT work with Propaganda.

Recordings revisited

In spite of differences engendered through the various contingencies of playback environment and medium, the audio recording, once released as a record, tends to remain a forever fixed and unchanging artefact. Although it is naive to consider it literally a 'record' of a particular acoustic moment or moments, nevertheless the sound of a recording can often come to represent something of a 'record of its time'. Many popular music recordings often manipulate and artificially reconstruct this sense of 'historical' presence for aesthetic or nostalgic purposes (see Chapter 3).

It is the composition, performance and technology involved in the production of a recording that enable the listener both to place it historically and to recognize it as a unique and 'un-recreatable' sound artefact.[3] However, a number of types of recording provide exceptions to this general rule: remastered recordings, cover versions, re-recordings and remixes. Although this chapter will focus on remixing, it may be worthwhile to first review the other forms of re-recording mentioned above, given the crucial role technology plays in each case.

Remastering involves the enhancing of existing master tapes (or, for earlier recordings, master discs), often using modern digital technology, which can remove a great deal of the noise generated by the original recording system, and a variety of devices which are intended to improve the audio characteristics of the recording. Many of the original analogue multitrack recordings by Yes have been 'digitally remastered by Joe Gastwirt at Ocean View Digital'[4] for the CD format, for example. Remastering covers a range of transformations from simply one of medium (78 rpm disc to compact disc, for example) to far more radical changes to the sound elements of the original artefact. Perhaps paradoxically, remastering often raises questions of authenticity, only here it is applied to the 'authentic recording experience' of the listener, rather than the more usual context of authentic performance practice.

Recorded cover versions – new recordings by different musicians of popular songs that have already been recorded – can also display a diverse range of characteristics. Some cover versions attempt to re-create the original as closely as possible: the rendition of 'Axel-F', for example, on *Greatest Synthesizer Hits*[5] by Star Inc. In other cases, popular material is rearranged and played by particular instrumental ensembles: *The Hollyridge Strings Play Instrumental Versions of Hits Made Famous by Elvis Presley*[6] or *Frank Pourcel Plays Abba*.[7] There is another kind of cover version, however, which is characterized by the intention of subtly undermining or conflicting with the aesthetic of the original. Hence, Devo's quirky and humorous cover version of The Rolling Stones' 'Satisfaction' on the album *Q: Are we not men? A: We are Devo!*[8] bears little resemblance to the original; and similarly 'It's my Party' by Dave Stewart with Barbara Gaskin[9] is an intensely dramatic, almost Gothic, version of the original 1963 Lesley Gore hit.[10] These radical reworkings tend to play on the differences and similarities between the new version and the original, while many of the highly imitative cover version recordings come about because record companies specializing in budget priced compilation albums of popular songs are unwilling to pay for the copyright of the original.[11] Similarly, highly imitative recordings of backing tracks of successful recordings are produced for karaoke. However, in all cases these recordings reinforce the notion that every record will have a particular collection of unique attributes which are impossible to re-create exactly: with even a relatively superficial acquaintance with the original, most listeners can easily identify the ways in which the new version differs. Hence, every record has a unique set of sound qualities and, as Steve Jones writes, 'the primary impact of recording technology has been to make the sound of a recording its identifying characteristic' (Jones, 1992, p. 12).

The third exception is the re-recording. Here a solo artist or group already responsible for a pre-existing, and often successful, record go on to make a completely new recording, based on the original composition, usually to produce a more modern-sounding artefact which benefits from contemporary audio technology, yet also retains some aspects of its original historical dimension. Examples include *Switched-On Bach 2000*[12] by Wendy Carlos with 'Authentic Bach Tunings, Dolby Surround' and '4-D Digital Sound', and *Tubular Bells II*[13] by Mike Oldfield.[14] In fact, this process of re-recording may be regarded as an inherent aspect of pop music production since most pieces are first realized as demonstration recordings, often on domestic equipment, and only later go on to be re-recorded in a professional studio. Clearly technology again plays an important role in this process.

The final exception, the remix, is a relatively recent phenomenon and indeed only became possible in its present form with the advent of multitrack recording.

Remixing involves the production of a new master recording from a pre-existing multitrack recording and first became popular with disco DJs during the late 1970s. While some disco was successful in the singles chart, its main purpose was to induce dancing in discotheques, and here the demand was for recordings which lasted longer than the 7-inch vinyl single. It is possible to produce 7-inch singles that contain more than five minutes' playing time on each side; however, the grooves have to be less deep as they must be closer together and, as a result, have less dynamic range, providing less output to the amplifier. Record companies, realizing the demand, developed the '12-inch single' – a 12-inch vinyl disc that played at 45 rpm and could be used with existing record players. Although these records were primarily intended for disc jockeys in discotheques, they quickly attained a cult status and sold in quantity. This was especially profitable to the record companies since the price of 12-inch singles was often three times that of 7-inch singles. The 12-inch extended remix was usually derived from the 24-track tape of the original single. The same sections were mixed in a variety of ways down to a two-track tape recorder and these were then assembled using traditional tape-editing techniques. However, during the 1980s, remixes were often created that introduced new material not present on the 7-inch single or even the 24 track tape. As noted with Frankie Goes to Hollywood, the remix may be regarded as either a marketing ploy to sell more records or an artistic striving to explore more fully the potential of the recorded material.

The remix has established itself as an important part of pop music production and continues to enjoy a great deal of popularity, especially among dance music aficionados. Twelve-inch remixes are often sold in quantity purely on the basis of the name of the producer – one of the few areas where the record producer is appreciated by an audience. The remixes of William Orbit are a case in point and his remix of Trevor Horn's production of 'Crazy' by Seal on the compilation album *Zance – A Decade of Dance from ZTT*[15] is particularly impressive and markedly different from the original.[16] The remix also provides the analyst of pop music with a particularly useful artefact since it enables comparison with the original and highlights the stylistic and aesthetic characteristics of specific record producers. The significance of remixing is certainly evident in the work of ZTT's Propaganda.

Propaganda

Propaganda was a German group made up of Michael Mertens, Suzanne Freytag, Claudia Brücken and Ralf Dorper. Unlike many European pop musicians, Propaganda made their nationality something of a feature both within their music and as part of their image. Their first single 'Dr Mabuse'[17] refers directly to a character from early German cinema and, although their songs have lyrics in English, they are delivered and recorded with marked German accents. While this sense of 'German-ness' is never over-stressed and avoids caricature, it ensures that the band had very few of the characteristics that link pop music with the USA – blues inflections, glamorous American image, words or phrases of American slang, and any imagery or subject matter within the lyrics that might specifically refer to American culture. The group also managed to avoid the trap of appearing simply as another rather superficial 'Europop' group. In an affectionate article, Bob Stanley describes Europop as an 'irresistible blend of techno, hi-energy, house, hip hop and melancholy-yet-uplifting melodies' (Stanley, 1995).

The work of Europop groups or solo artists, often associated with the Eurovision Song Contest, has been, at times, perhaps rather unfairly perceived as having 'linguistically baffling' (ibid.) lyrics. Their visual presentation may often have appeared either slightly bewildering or even non-existent. Of Italian House, for example, Stanley writes 'no one had a clue what the artists looked like' (ibid.). In contrast, Propaganda's image was carefully considered – serious, dark, enigmatic rather than bewildering, and distinctly 'arty' in line with ZTT's general profile. Through photographs of the band, for example, in which they appear dressed in severe black clothes with 'sensible' hairstyles, rarely smiling, often with synthesizers and other complex machinery, Propaganda managed quickly to establish their somewhat purist and relatively original image.[18]

Propaganda also positively emphasized the role that technology played in their music: for example, 'P Machinery', one of the songs on their first album, is virtually an anthem to the machine. The following can be found on the sleeve notes of this album, 'For those who heed the call of the machine, we salute you ... ', which is hardly the language of the technophile keen to extol the virtues and benefits of equipment, but rather that of the obsessive – enthusiasm without reasoned justification, fascination almost suggesting idolization, the machine as ideology. This is reminiscent of an aesthetic that emerged earlier in the century, visible in Fritz Lang's silent film *Metropolis*, Chaplin's *Modern Times*, Aldous Huxley's book *Brave New World* and Orwell's *1984*. In these works the tending of machinery requires human beings to accept their loss of freedom and individuality for the sake of security and relative material comfort. In effect, people become machine-like – capable of endlessly repetitive movements, cold, emotionless – in order to reap material benefits. The rise of mass-production techniques pioneered by Henry Ford at the turn of the century presented both a threat and a challenge to Western society: the effects of working in such an environment were unknown but felt to be potentially destructive.

While these concerns were of primary importance during the first half of the twentieth century, during the 1980s, especially in Britain, manufacturing industry had either fallen into decline or become fully automated, requiring virtually no work force in the production process. A paradox emerges: at the very time when British manufacturing industry was quite evidently declining, a pop group makes great play of the aesthetic of the machine as part saviour and part demon; this could well have been a direct result of the Orwellian connotations inevitably attached to the previous year – 1984. Propaganda's use of this kind of imagery, which incidentally is by no means entirely original,[19] produces a kind of dislocated and purely aesthetic reference: an earlier age's predictions for the future had proved to be rather inaccurate yet nevertheless retained a certain fascination. This sense of style without commitment, a characteristic often associated with postmodernism, lies at the heart of Propaganda's image. It is evident in the name of the group: Propaganda is the organized dissemination of information and is associated both with repressive and highly organized states tied to a specific ideology. In a perceptive review of the group's first album, Helen Fitzgerald wrote: 'Like magpies they steal quotations from Edgar Allen Poe, Roland Barthes and a host of other literary figures ... They enjoy *scattering* ideas more than trying to make something of them' (Fitzgerald, 1985). She goes on to describe this technique as 'amusingly highbrow' and in so doing evokes the 'high' versus 'popular' art debate.

Some of the responsibility for Propaganda's image can be attributed to Paul Morley, 'former arbiter of public taste for *NME*' (Beadle, 1993, p. 67) and ZTT's publicist, who was incidentally married to Claudia Brücken. Anne Winder, in a review of Propaganda in concert at Salford University, described the band as 'a designer label off the Morley shelf', while also sustaining the machine imagery by describing the band as having 'a mechanical sound and clockwork performance' (Winder, 1985).

Like The Art of Noise and Frankie Goes to Hollywood, the image of the group is an important aspect of their art and was encouraged and fostered by the record company. Record companies, particularly smaller, newer ones, often try to ensure that there is a strong commonality of aesthetic between their various signings. Although the artists signed to ZTT were of necessity appropriately distinctive and individualistic, they nevertheless tended to possess common elements: a modern sound based on the use of the latest technology; reference to 'high art' movements of the earlier twentieth century; a British/European rather than American image and sound; and a clear commitment to pop music (singles chart, dance music, vivid immediacy, etc.) rather than rock.

A Secret Wish: pretentious packaging

Propaganda's first album for ZTT, *A Secret Wish*, which followed on from the success of their singles 'Dr Mabuse'[20] and 'Duel',[21] has been described as 'one of the highest pop achievements of the mid-1980s' (Beadle, 1993, p. 66). Yet the artwork on the cover and inner sleeve is rather muted: there are few vivid, eye-catching colours here; instead, blues and greys tend to be dominant. Furthermore, the imagery is rarely simple and direct: small black and white photographs are imposed upon larger colour images, which are then littered with text.

The central image on the cover of *A Secret Wish* is the wire torso of a dressmaker's dummy photographed in profile. This distinctive object is worn as a garment by an otherwise apparently naked Claudia Brücken on two more photographs included in the inner sleeve. Finally, it appears on the back cover as a small line drawing with the logos/trademarks of ZTT and Island Records, who were responsible for the distribution of the recording. This image also features on the cover of *Wishful Thinking*, a set of remixes of the original tracks (more of which later), presented mostly as almost abstract patterns generated from the repeating curves and twists of the wire from which the dummy is made. Like the masks used on the cover of *Who's Afraid of The Art of Noise?*, this image is rich in connotation. Although the dressmaker's dummy evokes the female body and the world of fashion, it is an abstracted, amputated and thus dehumanized form. Being made entirely from twisted wire gives it a cage-like quality. While the patterns of the wire are rather like those of thread in fabric, supporting its relationship to the dressmaker, they are also cold and unyielding. Hence, the inner photographs, where it is presented no longer as a model used to shape garments but as a garment itself, are slightly disturbing: a metal, cage-like object fitted to a naked woman's body has sado-masochistic overtones: an individual's body forced into an abstracted form. This aspect is reinforced by other elements on the album cover and inner sleeve: several of the photographs show the two female members of the group with red, scar-like smears on their faces and necks, for example.

The numerous lines of text which appear with quotation marks on the cover and sleeve notes seem to be unreferenced quotations. The central pages of the sleeve notes list the song titles in the order they appear on the record, giving a picture and a quotation for each one. The texts are as follows:

'Dream Within a Dream' – 'the most merciful thing in the world, I think, is the inability of the human mind to correlate all its contents'

'The Murder of Love' – ' ... the idea of crime is able always to ignite the senses and lead us the lubricity [*sic*]'

'Jewel' and 'Duel' – 'the imagination is like an engine that can work on many different fuels: but it must be powered, and sex, properly used, is a fuel of high potency'

'Frozen Faces' – 'the contemplation of the world independently of the principle of reason'

'P Machinery' – 'the dark religions are departed and sweet Science reigns'

'Sorry For Laughing' – ' ... always two strangers uniting in the interests of torment'

'The Chase' – 'reliance on powers of reason does not come easily: it is opposed to our basic animal instinct'

'Dr Mabuse' – 'the greater an individual's power over others, the greater the evil that might possibly originate with him'.

Although it is hard not to dismiss all this as simply pretentious packaging, the fact remains that these statements – couched in the language of academics, poets and philosophers – encourage an intellectual and distinctly 'highbrow' response.

The back cover has a further list of the songs with start times, end times and song lengths in minutes, seconds and frames, preceded, as mentioned before, by the phrase 'for those who heed the call of the machine, we salute you … '. This is followed by 'Recording Data: Sony 1610, 44Kh, no pre-emphasis, continuous SMPTE 30F/s audio CH2, PQ subcode (SONY DA Q1000), audio CH1' and 'Noise Information: Clicks at 13'05, 13'06, 14'05 – vocal; track five slight vocal & synth clicks evident throughout; track six vocal "pop" at 31 57 21 and clicks at 32 57 29 and 33 51 26, +20 db peak at 53 05 27. There is no cause for concern!'. Apart from the errors in measured unit abbreviations ('Kh' and 'db' as opposed to 'kHz' and 'dB') and the reassuring final phrase, this would appear to be genuine information concerning the two-track master recording. Its inclusion is a novel way of listing the playing order of the songs and emphasizes the technological nature of the realization of the recording. This aspect is strengthened by the extremely accurate measurements of time. Hence time, a universal aspect of the art of music, is quantified by the very technology which has been used to produce the recording.

From engineer to producer

The artistic relationship between producer and balance engineer is clearly an important link in the recording process. If producer and engineer share similar goals on a project and, at the same time, share similar tastes on a more general level, then the collaboration is far more likely to be fruitful. While engineers often affect a business-like and detached manner, and appear concerned simply with carrying out the producer's wishes, at the practical level their influence is both inevitable and, at times, far from negligible. Balance engineers are responsible for the practicalities of making a recording – they choose which microphones are used, decide the most suitable placements, define how the signals are routed through the mixing desk, decide on appropriate signal levels to send to the tape recorder, define the type and extent of signal processing used, etc. – for each track of the multitrack. Every one of these manoeuvres offers a number of possibilities and the specific choices made by the engineer inevitably will have some bearing on the final result. Experience, amount of time available, convention and advice can all play a part in the engineer's decision-making processes.

The evidence suggests that the relationship between Trevor Horn and Steven Lipson in the mid-1980s was particularly important and significant. Lipson is credited as engineer or assistant producer on *Welcome to the Pleasuredome* and *Slave to the Rhythm*, and described as producer on *A Secret Wish* and some of the Simple Minds singles.[22] That Lipson can evidently alternate between the two roles of engineer and producer with apparent ease is impressive. But taking into account the quality and stature of some of the above recordings, his achievements are quite considerable. There are important similarities between those records produced by Horn and those produced by Lipson. When asked about his working relationship with Lipson, Horn replied:

> Well, that changed as the years rolled by. Steve originally just showed up as the engineer … In the end, when we did *Slave to the Rhythm* … I was acting almost like the artist and he was almost like the producer. I was having all the mad ideas and he was executing them. (Buskin, 1994, p. 34)

The important and demanding role played by technology in this relationship is evident in an interview with Lipson. Of the Synclavier, for example, Lipson states:

> We both got quite excited by its possibilities and ended up investing loads of money in it. Every time an upgrade came out, we got it – but this would mean we'd do another version of a track just because there'd been an upgrade … Hi-hats would take a week – because it could be done. (Ward, 1995, p. 72)

The recordings of Horn and Lipson have much in common: they tend to be highly organized, timbrally diverse pieces, carefully paced, with a clear sense of direction and growth. These similarities are due to three distinct yet interrelated elements: technology, technique and taste. First, these recordings were created in the same studios with the same equipment. Each recording space has its own particular acoustic characteristics which resourceful engineers learn to exploit. The use of the same microphones, mixing desks, tape recorders and signal processing are all likely to contribute to the similarity of sound, and the use of the same sound-producing equipment – synthesizers, samplers and drum machines – is bound to result in further marked similarities. Hence, particular equipment will impart particular sound qualities to recordings. Second, recording studio operators often tend to use audio technology in idiosyncratic ways: the same operators working on different projects are likely to produce recordings with certain sonic similarities, which are often described as their 'trademark sound'. Finally, it is clear that this particular set of recordings have aesthetic similarities: they tend to strive to be effective through the emphasis and manipulation of similar parameters – structure and timbre, for example. Many of the above characteristics are evident in Lipson's work with Propaganda.

The music of *A Secret Wish*

We make records rather than music.[23]

S.J. Lipson is credited with the production of *A Secret Wish*, while the album was 'mixed and matched by Lipson and Horn'.[24] The assistant engineer was Bobby

Kraushaar. Paradoxically, Propaganda's first album was produced by Trevor Horn's balance engineer and their second album was produced by 'Bob Kraushaar'. This illustrates both the flexibility of roles within the recording studio and also the level of creative sympathy that can become established between balance engineers and record producers. The credits go on to 'acknowledge the participation, with some voice and instruments, of: Andrew Richards, Steve Howe, David Sylvian, Glenn Gregory, Trevor Horn, Ian Mosely, Jonathan Sorrell, A. Thein, Stuart Coppland [*sic*] and Allen L. Kirkendale, S. J. Lipson.' This is an impressive list of names: Steve Howe had been one of the guitarists in Yes and also was part of the group Asia established by Geoff Downes (the other half of The Buggles); David Sylvian had been the lead vocalist with Japan and went on to pursue a successful solo career during the 1980s; Ian Mosely was the drummer with Marillion and 'a veteran of many progressive rock bands, including Curved Air and the Gordon Giltrap Band' (Larkin, 1993, p. 748), and Stuart Coppland may actually have been Stewart Copeland, ex-drummer of The Police.

The music on *A Secret Wish* is quite diverse in character. The album begins with 'Dream within a Dream', a long (9 minutes and 8 seconds) and complex song dominated by a spoken rather than sung vocal track, a trumpet melody (perhaps synthesized and played on a MIDI wind controller) which acts rather like a ritornello, and a strong backbeat dominated by a pedal note on the bass guitar, reminiscent of the pedal note in 'Relax' by Frankie Goes to Hollywood, which continues throughout the song. The complexity is provided by the chord structure, which is repeated with variations throughout, and the unusual overall structure of the song. The chords above the unchanging bass pedal, played mostly by shimmering synthesized strings, are rich in added notes, unpredictable in terms of harmonic movement, and avoid any strong, cadential resolution. The structure of the song comprises four sections (A, A1, A2, A3), each one longer than the last (15, 21, 51 and 70 bars respectively), and each based on reiterations of the same chord pattern but with added internal repetitions. The powerful backbeat provides immediate presence and involvement – through its persistent emphasis of the unchanging pulse and the pedal note pitch – while the structure and underlying chord sequence remove any strong sense of harmonic direction. The hook – that musical element designed to excite the listener most – could be regarded as the omnipresent backbeat with pedal note upon which other musical elements are cumulatively added, only to return to its purest presentation at the end of each section. The characteristics of the music (hypnotic single pitch repetition provided by the pedal note, and the omnipresent pulse of the backbeat; flexible, complex chord sequence which always avoids resolution; and structure of gradually expanded sections which nevertheless all contain the same basic material) both support and enhance the dreamlike yet obsessive lyrics of the song.

The second track on the album, 'The Murder of Love', is dominated by a heavily four-square drum pattern, a wide range of bright synthesized stabs and interjections, and a very straightforward structure (ABABCB where A is the verse, B the chorus and C is the middle eight). 'Jewel' and 'Duel', the third and fourth tracks on *A Secret Wish*, will be looked at in closer detail later. 'Frozen Faces', the fifth track on the album, begins with the sound of voices whispering in German. The music which follows is in two distinct parts: the first is dominated by a synthesizer and sequencer generated backbeat emphasizing the semiquaver division of the beat, strongly reminiscent of Kraftwerk (particularly 'Abzug'[25]), and almost spoken vocals; the second has the 'four to the floor' bass drum characteristic of dance music, a rhythmically syncopated and 'featured' bass guitar part, harmonies provided by synthesizer generated sounds sequenced in repetitive semiquavers, and sung vocals. The song which follows, 'P-Machinery', not only reinforces the man/machine imagery of the cover through its lyrics, but is also an impressively 'produced' piece, rich in delicate synthesizer flourishes and timbral variety. Again the influence of Kraftwerk is evident: first, in the 'bubbling' synthesizer sound at the beginning which is so similar to the beginning of Kraftwerk's 'The Robots'[26] or the central section of 'Pocket Calculator';[27] and, second, the very mechanical setting of the words 'Power, Force, Motion, Drive' which is reminiscent of Kraftwerk's 'Radioactivity'.[28] The seventh track, 'Sorry for Laughing', is the only cover version on the album (credited to Paul Haig and Malcolm Ross) and, in spite of some interesting and highly processed timbres, tends to lack the sense of growth and presence found on the other tracks. 'The Chase', which follows, is full of delicate synthesizer gestures but has a rambling and rather aimless structure, almost as though it is illustrating some unknown narrative. The final song on *A Secret Wish* is an extended version of Propaganda's first British hit single 'Dr Mabuse'. As already mentioned, this character appears in early German cinema, however, the reiteration of the phrase 'selling your soul', in the chorus of this song, links it to another important character in German culture: Faust. This is a bright and rather 'flashy' production, full of careful timbral balance and copious use of digital reverberation, and in these respects is typical of the predominant sound of pop singles of this period. However, as this extended album version progresses it deviates more and more from the rather predictable formula associated with singles. Five minutes into the song, for example, a long section (over two minutes) based entirely on drums, string orchestra and later backwards female voice begins. The string writing is extraordinarily 'modern' for pop music, using glissandi, pizzicato, multiple trills, *sul ponticello* and a variety of other unusual techniques, and is beautifully recorded in stereo, to produce a sound highly reminiscent of Bernard Herrmann's score to Hitchcock's film, *Psycho*. This is followed by a return to the synthesized sounds of the original song, but towards the end the strings appear again, this time without drums, accompanied by the sounds of heavy rain and thunder.[29] This highly dramatic and evocative section is both unusual and surprising. The string writing and sound effects such as thunder give the impression of a film sound track rather than a pop record. It provides a fittingly impressive end to a recording that tends to pose questions rather than offer answers.

'Jewel'/'Duel'/'Jewelled'

The third and fourth tracks on *A Secret Wish* deserve greater attention for the purposes of this study as they highlight a number of important characteristics of pop music production, offer analytical opportunities for direct comparison, and are two of the strongest pieces on the album. 'Duel' was the second single taken from the album and attained a higher position in the UK singles chart than any other Propaganda record. In fact, 'Jewel' and 'Duel' are two startlingly different versions of the same song. Furthermore, Propaganda's second and last album with ZTT, *Wishful Thinking*,[30] which comprises eight remixes by Bob Kraushaar and Paul Morley of the tracks on *A Secret Wish*, includes 'Jewelled', which uses material from both 'Jewel' and 'Duel'.[31]

The lyrics, underlying chords and phrase structure hardly change between these three versions, while the structure is subjected to some important changes. The tempi for these three recordings are slightly different: 'Jewel' runs at 154.5 bpm, 'Duel' at 145.6 bpm and 'Jewelled' at 152.3 bpm. The greatest divergences between the tracks, however, are in the arrangement, production and 'sound'.

'Jewel'/'Duel'/'Jewelled' – the structure

Although the two recordings on the first album sound very different (the third recording is simply constructed from the other two) they are derived from the same basic musical material (harmonic and melodic patterns) and have the same lyrics. Tables 8.1, 8.2 and 8.3 show how this material has been divided up within each of the pieces. 'Jewel', while having verses, bridges and choruses of lengths typically associated with pop music (that is, 8 and 16 bars), has a long and unusual introduction (52 bars) and an extended 'middle eight' (30.5 bars). The bars of two beats at different points within the structure ensure the relentless momentum of the piece, they precipitate change at aesthetically appropriate places and subtly disrupt expectation. In contrast, 'Duel' is a model of regularity by adopting standard section lengths throughout. This gives it a rather formal and constrained quality in comparison to the more 'organic' nature of 'Jewel'. Finally, 'Jewelled' tends to reveal the structural characteristics of the extended remix: the result of splicing together mixes of various sections; and choruses, in particular, tend to be subject to a far greater level of repetition.

A much simplified version of the structure analyses presented in Tables 8.1, 8.2 and 8.3, in which 'A' represents verse material, 'B' bridge material, and 'C'

Table 8.1   The structure of 'Jewel'

Section	Bars	Characteristics
Noise		Bright metallic crash in claustrophobic reverberation
Count in	1	Shouted and not in time
Intro.	4	Basic drum pattern
	4	Brighter snare added + fills
	12	Bass and sustained notes added
	4	Chord IV introduced
	6	Return to chord I
	7 (+ 2 beats)	Bass follows line from verse
	6	Cascading pipe organ figure
	6	Altered repeat of pipe organ figure
	2 (+ 2 beats)	
Verse 1	16	Single vocal; chords on distorted guitar-like sound; bass acting almost like a pedal
Bridge	8	Guitar out; more bass pitch movement
Chorus	16	Brighter, more synth.-like and syncopated bass line
	4	Gestural non-pitched synth. sound
Verse 2	16	As verse 1
Bridge	8	As previous bridge
Chorus	16	As previous chorus
Middle Eight	8	Guitar-like sounds as stabs which fall in pitch
	22 (+ 2 beats)	Bass out; many unusual synth. noises presented rhythmically and extreme panning
Chorus × 2	32	Doubled vocal (original plus inarticulate roar); bass in
Outro.	2 (+ 2 beats)	Bass out; scream
	16	Impressive bright synthesizer chords
	16	Added noise samples from Middle Eight
	4	Fade-out on single synth. suspended chord

chorus material, reveals that the three different pieces are in fact structurally very similar:

'Duel'	Intro.	A B C A B C D C
'Jewel'	Intro.	A B C A B C D C
'Jewelled'	(CAB)	A B C A B C D A C

Table 8.2   The structure of 'Duel'

Section	Bars	Characteristics
Intro.	4	Piano/strings without pulse
	4	Slap bass; bright synth. sounds; clean sharp reverb.
	4	Snare
Verse 1	8	Sung vocal; warm pad
	8	Synth. response to bass figure; fuller pad
Bridge	8	More sustained pad; extra synth. figures added
Chorus	16	Orchestral figures at the end of each line
Verse 2	4	Similar to intro.
	16	As verse 1
Bridge	8	As previous bridge but with subtle double tracking on vocal
Chorus	16	As previous chorus
Middle Eight	8	Animal-like noises; disco bass drum (no snare)
	8	Addition of snare and synths.; sense of crescendo
	8	Sequenced piano; synth. added later
Chorus × 3	16	As previous chorus
	16	Orchestral stabs rather than figures at the end of each line
	16	Fade-out

This suggests that the initial instrumental chorus, verse and bridge in 'Jewelled' functions rather like an extended introduction. Indeed, if the crucial issue of section length is not taken into account, 'Jewel' and 'Duel', produced by Lipson, follow the same basic structural pattern.

'Jewel'/'Duel'/'Jewelled' – the sound

From the very first shouted count-in which is so reminiscent of punk, 'Jewel' presents a driving, aggressive sound dominated by the almost incessant quavers of the backbeat. The drum sounds are bright and highly unnatural in terms of timbre, with a strong sense of presence and a dark, claustrophobic reverberation. The quaver feel is emphasized by the throbbing, reiterated pitches of the supporting bass line which, particularly at the beginning and during the verses, functions as a pedal note. While there are a variety of other sounds on this track, they never really compete, and in fact often hardly distract from the omnipresent backbeat. These sounds include sung/shouted vocals, organ, pitched and non-

Table 8.3   The structure of 'Jewelled'

Section	Bars	Characteristics
Intro.	4	Sequenced synth. from Middle Eight of 'Duel'
Chorus × 3	12+16+16+1	No vocal; 'Jewel' bass; 'Duel' orchestra
Verse	12	'Jewel' bass; 'Duel' synths.
	8	'Duel' guitar
Bridge	4	'Duel' bass
Verse	16	Vocal; octave jumping bass – figure from 'Duel'; timbre from 'Jewel'
Bridge	8	'Duel' pad with triggered noise gate
Chorus	16	'Jewel' bass; 'Duel' orchestra
Verse × 1.8	12+8	No vocal; 'Jewel' bass; 'Duel' synths.
	16	Vocal with verse 2
Bridge	8	Vocal and spoken vocal together
Chorus	16	Warm 'Duel' pad
Middle Eight	8	No bass; guitar-like sounds from 'Jewel'; animal-like noises from 'Duel'
	8	Synths. from 'Duel'
Verse	8	No vocal; sustained sounds
Chorus × 6	16	No vocal
	16	Vocal plus extra sounds
	16	Doubled vocal (one from 'Jewel' and one from 'Duel')
	16	Single vocal from 'Duel' with 'roaring' vocal from 'Jewel'
	16	Mixture of vocals
	8	No vocal or bass; drums and stabs only
	4	Drums as loop only

pitched synthesizer sounds, distorted electric guitar and bright percussive samples in the middle eight. There are three factors which ensure that these sounds retain a secondary role within the piece. First, unlike the backbeat, they are all intermittent rather than continuous: there are none of the harmonious pads found in 'Duel'. The single exception is the sustained chords of the synthesizer at the end of the song which produces a remarkable sense of release: strong, diatonic harmony finally appears. Second, they are often mixed with a highly artificial reverberation producing a tunnel-like sound which places them at a perceived distance from the listener. Finally, certain melodic lines are 'confused' by having similar sounds playing different melodic material simultaneously. This is particularly noticeable on the two organ phrases near the beginning and on the lead vocal towards the end, where the main vocal is accompanied by the same voice moaning, roaring and singing the words roughly, out of tune and like someone suffering from a severe speech impediment. The piece contradicts its title by being made up of predominantly rough and mostly non-pitched, noise-like timbres.

'Duel' presents a stark contrast to 'Jewel' with its extensive use of bright, 'clean' and often sustained synthesized timbres. The backbeat is more rhythmically varied but less dominant, the vocal lines are more sweetly sung, and the arrangement is full of purely pitched sounds. This is rather surprising since the violent nature of the lyrics is more clearly discernible in this version. The delicacy and attention to detail is impressive rather than thrilling.

'Jewelled' is perhaps the least satisfactory of the three versions timbrally, since it attempts to combine the violence of 'Jewel' with the sweetness[32] of 'Duel'. As a result, the sense of purity of intention and aesthetic homogeneity is lost. The pairing of the rough, driving 'Jewel' followed by the constrained and delicate 'Duel' on *A Secret Wish* is an extremely effective way of presenting the same basic musical material in two very different forms. This contrast highlights not only the remarkable range of timbral possibilities available in the pop recording studio but also shows two very different kinds of beauty: the wild, raucous and 'natural' against the ordered, balanced and artificial.

Technology and Propaganda

Increasingly, the technology used to create pop music defines aspects of the finished artefact. Using the same musical material in different recordings results in new artefacts – different interpretations with often radically altered aesthetic emphases. Modern audio technology might be seen not only to allow but actually encourage such practices, giving rise to several new forms: remastered recordings; cover versions; re-recordings; and remixes. The transition from analogue to digital technology during the mid-1980s clearly facilitated such practices.

As should be evident, the whole complex relationship between technology and creativity is a persistent feature of *A Secret Wish*. It not only appears in both the lyrics of the songs and the texts of the cover, but is also a central and significant feature of the sound of the record itself. The use of synthesized timbres for harmonic, melodic and rhythmic figures is extensive, and these are often further enhanced with fiercely 'metallic' sounding artificial reverberation, the result of digital signal processing. As well as the 'machine-like' precision of the parts performed in the studio by instrumentalists, the record is dominated by the use of digital sequencing which ensures an exacting level of rhythmic accuracy. In other words, most of the timbres and the performances one hears on these recordings have a distinctly un-human, and intentionally mechanical, quality entirely in keeping with the image the band wished to promote.

For this record Lipson experimented with the manipulation of the latest studio technology and discovered the technique which subsequently became known as 'the tapeless studio': essentially the use of a computer to sequence as many of the parts (synthesized and sampled sounds) as possible, rather than record them all on a multitrack tape recorder.[33] Fifteen years later this became the standard production procedure for pop records, but at the time it represented a highly novel approach.

By presenting the same song in two highly contrasted versions on *A Secret Wish*, Propaganda illustrate the creative potential offered by the audio technology of the mid-1980s. Their realization of some of this potential results in a novel and original pop artefact – a new form made up of two timbrally contrasting yet harmonically, melodically and structurally similar pieces. This creative exploitation of timbre and gesture through technology is an intrinsic aspect of the sound of modern pop music, giving rise to new musical forms and perhaps demanding a different kind of musical appreciation. Issues such as these need to be addressed if some of the important aesthetic characteristics of the genre are to be fully understood. As Steve Jones writes: 'it is at the level of composition and realization that one should begin to analyse the relationship of technology and popular music, for it is at that level that popular music is formed' (Jones, 1992, p. 7).

Notes

1. Mercury FEED 1. For several years the 7-inch version of this recording held the record as the highest selling UK single.
2. Polydor POSP 369.
3. This is another area in which the use of the sampler has tended to subvert expectation: recordings that bring together samples taken from records of different periods.
4. Text on the CD cover of *Drama* (Atlantic 7567-82685-2).
5. Star Inc. Records 4-5100.
6. Capitol Records (S)T2221.
7. EMI Records 10 CO64-016.550.
8. Virgin Records V2106 (1978).
9. BROKEN 2 (1981).
10. Mercury MF 829.
11. Attempts at exact imitation of pre-existing recordings are sometimes also produced for humorous purposes: creating an expectation that is then thwarted by new ideas (usually new lyrics). For example, 'N-N-Nineteen Not Out' (Oval 100) by the Commentators (in fact, the impressionist Rory Bremner) which imitated the hit single 'Nineteen' by Paul Hardcastle (Chrysalis CHS 2860).
12. Telarc CD-80323, 1992.
13. WEA 4509-90618-2, 1992.
14. Another rare example of re-recording is when a record company which owns a copyright refuses to allow the recording to be used as a sample in a new recording.

The original recording artist is then given a new record contract explicitly to re-record their song, and it is this which will then be sampled. Hence, when Jive Bunny were refused sampling rights over Wizzard's 'I Wish It Could Be Christmas Everyday' by Harvest Records (HAR 5079), they offered Roy Wood a recording contract to re-record the song.

15. ZTT 4509-96055-2.

16. Indeed, it was Orbit's skill in remixing which first established him as a record producer and working on remixes has now become a recognized route for young, aspiring producers.

17. ZTT ZTAS 2.

18. Propaganda's image is not dissimilar to that of another group from Dusseldorf: Kraftwerk. Indeed, the influence of Kraftwerk is evident in the work of many UK pop groups during this period. For a fuller exploration of this see Bracewell (1998, pp. 204–6).

19. 'Metal Postcard' by Siouxsie and the Banshees, on their album *The Scream* (POLD 5009 (2442 1571), for example, was released in 1978 and has similar imagery. It is dedicated to John Heartfield.

20. ZTT ZTAS 2.

21. ZTT ZTAS 8. 'Duel' entered the UK singles chart on 4 May 1985 and reached number 21. *A Secret Wish* entered the albums chart on 13 July 1985 and reached number 16.

22. Specifically 'See the Lights' (Virgin VS 1343) and 'Let There Be Love' (Virgin VS 1332). Lipson also co-produced 'Belfast Child' and 'Mandela Day' on the *Ballad of the Streets EP* (Virgin SMX 3) with Trevor Horn.

23. 1985 interview with Ralf Dorper (http://micksinclair.com/zigzag/propazz.html).

24. Although on Sarm Production's discography Trevor Horn is credited with the production of *A Secret Wish*. See Appendix 2.

25. From the Kraftwerk album *The Mix* (EMI EM 1408) released in 1991.

26. From the Kraftwerk album *The Man Machine* (Capitol EST 11728) released in 1978.

27. From the Kraftwerk album *Computer World* (EMI EMC 3370) released in 1981.

28. From the Kraftwerk album *Radioactivity* (Capitol EST 11457) released in 1976.

29. The thunder is highly reminiscent of 'Momento' on *Who's Afraid of The Art of Noise?*. Moreover, an almost identical effect of thunder, rain and string orchestra appears before the final verse of 'The Days of Pearly Spencer' on Marc Almond's 1991 album *Tenement Symphony*, which was produced by Trevor Horn (Some Bizzare YZ638).

30. *Wishful Thinking* (ZTT ZTTIQ 20) entered the albums chart on 23 November 1985 and reached number 82.

31. A further extended remix of 'Duel' appears on the album *Zance* credited to Lipson. None of the sounds from 'Jewel' are used. This track provides an excellent example of the delicate and complex orchestration of the original since the material is presented with a number of sections which have been 'cut-down' through the use of channel muting on the mixer. In this sense it is a more typical and traditional remix. With the exception of a guitar solo at the very end, no new material appears.

32. This sense of sweetness was clearly evident to Lipson who named the later *Zance* remix 'bitter-sweet'.

33. For 'Dr Mabuse' Lipson used 'a Linn, a Fairlight, a DMX, a DSX and a Roland M5, interconnected them and programmed the whole song in each machine. A special device called "conductor" was used to help synchronize the instruments with each other' (http://www.trevor-horn.de/).

Chapter 9

Slave to the Rhythm
by Grace Jones

He [Trevor Horn] asked us to record a song called 'Slave to the Rhythm' written by Bruce Woolley and Simon Darlow. No one in the band was keen about the idea but it was hard for us to say 'no' to Trevor. A version was recorded, but to no one's satisfaction. (Johnson, 1995, p. 178)

The enormous success of Frankie Goes to Hollywood as a complete popular musical package – music, image, 'attitude' – the year before, brought ZTT credibility from a public keen for something which had the reputation of being a little more demanding than the typical chart singles of the time. It also must have encouraged and given confidence to a company that had consistently signed and supported acts which ran contrary to the more dated but nevertheless highly prevalent teen-directed glamour image and retrospective musical style, as exemplified by such artists as Shakin' Stevens. Similarly, while Propaganda failed to establish themselves as a consistently successful chart band, for a time they received a high level of critical acclaim.

In 1985 Trevor Horn and the ZTT publicity/marketing machine began working on a recording project with the Jamaican/American disco singer, Grace Jones. Unlike previous ZTT bands and artists, Grace Jones was already well established as a pop singer with a highly distinctive image. Having previously worked successfully as a fashion model appearing on the covers of *Vogue* and *Elle*, then as a disco singer, in 1985 she was given a leading part in the James Bond film, *A View to a Kill*, and it appeared that her future career would be in films.[1] Yet unlike so many other black disco singers, Grace Jones would hardly be described as a highly accomplished soul singer.

Slave to the fashion

What makes pop videos 'postmodern' is not their 'exploding signifiers' but their equation of art and commerce. Their aesthetic effect can't be separated from their market effect; the desires they address can't be realized except vainly in exchange. The fashion industry, as Pat Aufderheide notes, was quick to realize the video point: 'Since 1977, when Pierre Cardin began making video recordings of his fashion shows, designers have been incorporating video into their presentations'. (Frith, 1988, p. 206)

As mentioned in Chapter 1, there are clear parallels between the worlds of fashion and pop music. Both are luxury commodities, which undergo stylistic change on a similarly short timescale in order to renew themselves: pop music and fashion do not wear out they 'go out'. Both rely on a high profile in the mass media, either explicitly within dedicated programmes or as ways of defining topicality. Both involve potential buyers by exciting and fascinating them. People want, rather than need, particular creations of fashion and pop music around them.

In spite of these similarities, pop music and fashion tend to remain separate and distinct. Of course pop stars dress fashionably and fashion shows (and fashion shops) often use pop music as a suitable backdrop to their displays. Indeed, some fashion models have made pop records – the late 1960s fashion model Twiggy, for example, released the single 'Here I Go Again'[2] and went on to become something of a 'popular family entertainer' – and a few pop stars are seen modelling fashion clothes on occasion. However, these are definitely the exception rather than the rule. Like any other highly competitive area of human endeavour, the extreme specialization necessary to succeed in fashion or pop music tends to preclude access to the other. Grace Jones is one of the few people who have achieved some success in both areas.

Slave to the image

Grace Jones's background as a fashion model was both an enabling and a restricting influence on her subsequent career in pop music. The beneficial elements are clearly evident in the quite stunning range of photographs of her that have appeared on record covers and promotional material. The quality and diversity of these images are far superior to similar material by many of her often more successful contemporaries. The limitations of Grace Jones's background are plainly audible in her singing which tends to lack both technique and character.

There can be little doubt that Grace Jones presents a forceful and attractively androgynous image to her audience. Androgyny has long been associated with pop music and is evident in the images of artists as diverse as Little Richard and David Bowie. This characteristic is often explicit in the work of Grace Jones with lyrics like '"feeling like a woman" and "looking like a man"' (Hughes, 1994, p. 153) and is captured by Jean Paul Goude in a description of an early performance, read out by Ian McShane on the track 'The Frog and the Princess':

> She was singing a hit song 'I Need a Man' to a roomful of shrieking, gay bobby-sockers. The ambiguity of her act was that she herself looked like a man: a man singing 'I Need a Man' to a bunch of men. I could see how the average guy could get a little scared by her physical appearance – it was so powerful.

However, as an image it relies almost entirely on the visual media: there is little audible character to reinforce and support her visual image. Her most successful albums prior to *Slave to the Rhythm*[3] – *Warm Leatherette*,[4] *Nightclubbing*[5] and *Living My Life*[6] – were dominated not by her voice, nor by displaying her compositional skills, but by the dance-based backbeats provided by the electric bass guitar and drum kit playing of two extremely successful Jamaican session musicians: Sly Dunbar and Robbie Shakespeare. These recordings, produced by Chris Blackwell, who was the founder of Island Records, present a variety of musical styles – disco, reggae, tango, punk[7] – but the emphasis is always firmly on rhythms derived from dance. Grace Jones's vocal contribution is quite limited and at times seems almost superfluous to the simple but powerful music created by the other musicians. She sings tunes, she half sings, and she speaks through these songs. Her delivery is generally in time with the pulse and in tune but has very little character to command attention or any of the subtle phrasing associated with accomplished pop or soul singers. This is not really a question of physical technique, although Grace Jones is clearly not an accomplished singer, but much more a question of evoking a sense of presence to the listener. If anything, her vocal role in *Slave to the Rhythm* is even less pronounced. On some of the tracks she hardly seems present at all while others clearly use samples of her voice derived from her vocal contribution to other songs rather than original performances. For example, on 'The Frog and the Princess' she only shouts a single word, 'Slave', which is clearly a sample, while 'Operattack' is constructed entirely from vocal samples. As a consequence *Slave to the Rhythm* may well be better viewed as an album *about* Grace Jones rather than *by* her. In fact, the album is subtitled 'a biography'. Steve Sutherland writes, 'Grace Jones doesn't exist, she's a creation and this is an album *about* her' (Sutherland, 1985). Furthermore, while the title of the album manages to draw attention to Grace Jones's ancestry[8] and a racial cliché (Black people are supposed to have an 'innate sense of rhythm'), it also suggests and encourages a more personal interpretation: that Grace Jones is allowed to express little will of her own, and instead is subjugated to the rhythms of the music she is associated with yet does not play, compose or produce. Once again, Steve Sutherland captures this quality when he asks: 'Is she so devoid of scruples that she'll allow Horn and his cronies to concoct this kaleidoscopic soundtrack around the absence of her talent in praise of her *presence*?' (Sutherland, 1985). The image of the flashy female mannequin, the vacuous mind and the beautiful body, manipulated by mysterious yet powerful men, svengali-like, would seem to be positively encouraged in this album. Trevor Horn has said: 'Grace is pretty off the wall anyway and how she presented herself suggested to me that she should be handled rather like an art object' (Cunningham, 1996, p. 277). In this sense, Grace Jones may be regarded as the antithesis of ZTT's earlier group, The Art of Noise. She is presented as an overwhelming physical/visual presence whose audible contribution is vocal, while The Art of Noise are defined by their physical absence and their non-vocal sound.

However, another possible interpretation of the title is, appropriately enough, concerned explicitly with music technology and recording. By 1985 it was possible to synchronize the running of a multitrack tape recorder with a MIDI sequencer through the use of timecode.[9] The timecode is recorded onto one track of the tape recorder (the master) and this signal is then sent via a conversion box to the MIDI sequencer (the slave) set up to synchronize with the signal. In this sense the MIDI sequencer is a 'slave to the rhythm' (or more accurately the tempo) of the tape recorder. This technology was originally developed for video production and it is significant that 'the boundaries between audio and video operations are less clear these days' (Rumsey and McCormick, 1994, p. 286). This is hardly surprising since the synchronization of image and sound is a fundamental requirement in television which is a natural medium for a mixed art form such as pop music.

Finally, pop music production itself is often the result of the slavish pursuit of new musical fashions. Steve Lipson says:

> Chris Blackwell told Trevor [Horn] that he wanted to do a Grace Jones *Best of...* , and Bruce Woolley had presented this song called 'Slave to the Rhythm'. Chris loved the title, and we did it very up-tempo and Germanic. Blackwell thought it was too straight, and suggested we did it with a go-go rhythm. None of us knew what go-go was, but Bruce did a demo and off we went to New York where Blackwell had assembled this combination of authentic musicians. Up went the faders, and we heard this rhythm which was completely different from what Bruce had written ... We found this 2-minute sequence which ... I copied and edited ... to create a 5-minute song complete with drum fills. (Ward, 1985, p. 70)

Slave to the cliché

Clearly linked to the slave motif is all the imagery associated with the fantasy role-playing games of sado-masochism. The poetic introduction, attributed to I. Penman's 'The Annihilation of Rhythm' with which *Slave to the Rhythm* begins, includes further hints with lines like 'lacerations echo in the mouth's open erotic sky'.[10] Walter Hughes, in his article 'In the Empire of the Beat – Discipline and Disco' (Ross and Rose, 1994, pp. 147–54), suggests a strong link between the gay disco culture of this period and sado-masochistic imagery when he writes: '"Love", in disco lyrics, tends to be described in hyperbolic terms as enslavement, insanity or addiction, a disease or a police state, as anything that rivals the despotism of the beat itself' (Hughes, 1994, p. 150). Perhaps inevitably, Hughes regards *Slave to the Rhythm* as an obvious example of this phenomenon:

> Nowhere is this exchange of identity more forcefully articulated than in Grace Jones's use of the imagery of forced labor to describe the discipline of the disco in 'Slave to the Rhythm'. According to the song's lyric, the rhythm regulates every aspect of bodily existence, breathing, dancing, labor and sex, and so becomes a

universalized disciplinary apparatus: 'you learn to the rhythm and you live to the rhythm.' (Ibid., p. 151)

An interesting extension to this idea is posited by Hughes:

> By allowing the synthesized disco beat to move you, you surrender yourself to becoming an extension of the machine that generates the beat, and consequently what is variously called a 'man-machine', a 'dancing machine' or a 'love machine'. The fearful paradox of the technological age, that machines created as artificial slaves will somehow enslave and even mechanize human beings, is ritually enacted at the discotheque. (Ibid., p. 151)

It would seem that Grace Jones and, particularly, the album *Slave to the Rhythm* provide a clear focus for this social phenomenon.

Of course, imagery often associated with sado-masochism permeated certain kinds of popular music well before this album. The leather-clad 'bikers' of American rock may be loosely regarded as part of this tradition. This is perhaps most explicitly evident in the rock parody 'Don't Touch Me There' by The Tubes. The work of Trevor Horn also reveals some precedents: the collaboration with Malcolm McLaren, who introduced bondage clothing to The Sex Pistols, and some of the imagery associated with Frankie Goes to Hollywood and particularly the 'Relax' videos.

Slave to the Rhythm

> We made all these records, and one day I said: 'Enough!' We made all these records that were like flashbulbs – they sounded very bright and new suddenly, and then it seemed to me that they quickly sounded old-fashioned. I thought why don't we make a record more like a standard lamp – one that's going to last without burning out the bulb just like that. Something deeper, that wouldn't necessarily go in at Number One and then disappear as quickly. I said this as we were working on *Slave to the Rhythm* with Grace Jones. He looked puzzled for a moment, then Horn looked up and said: 'Yeah – what a great gimmick: we make a record with no gimmicks'. (Stephen Lipson, quoted in Ward, 1995, p. 70)

Slave to the Rhythm is certainly an unusual pop album, many of whose characteristics are directly related to the influence of technology. A closer inspection of the orchestrations/arrangements and structures present in the album tend to reveal modern audio technology and the working practices it engenders as determinant factors at the heart of the creative process. Yet, as with all the other recordings studied, it is not purely the qualities and characteristics of the technology which define many of the aspects of the album, but more the way in which producer and engineer interact with them.

'Re-written by machine'

Unlike most pop albums, *Slave to the Rhythm* is a collection of separate songs/ instrumental pieces which nevertheless share recorded material between tracks. Pop albums often rely on common timbres, and harmonic and melodic similarities between songs to ensure cohesion. The use of common material within the separate songs of an album, however, is very rare. Although Propaganda's 'Jewel' and 'Duel' on *A Secret Wish* use similar musical material, *Slave to the Rhythm* uses the same recordings across several tracks. Table 9.1 shows some of the repeated recorded material which appears in different pieces, while Table 9.2 lists the phrases from the lyrics which appear in several tracks.

Table 9.1   Musical repetition in *Slave to the Rhythm*

Repeated material	Appears in tracks
Chord pattern (IV-IV-I-I)	2, 4, 8
Go-go backbeat	2, 4, 7, 8
Melodic line	5 (bass) and 6
Whole accompaniments	4(B section), 7
	2(A section), 4(A section)
	2(C section), 8
Tempo 84 bpm	5, 6
Tempo 98 bpm	2, 4, 7, 8

There are several possible reasons for the use of common material over several songs. One such is that the processes of digital multitrack recording and sampling have encouraged a different approach to musical structure.[11] Multitrack recording, and particularly digital multitrack recording which enables virtually infinite copying with no loss in audio quality, separates timbres and material both in time (the recording of each part is a serial rather than parallel process) and space (each separate track is assigned to a separate channel on the mixer, with its own set of controls), and in doing so draws attention both to the individuality of each musical gesture and to its potential as an isolated element. These individual elements, which can be completely isolated from their original musical context, may then be sampled so that they become available at the press of a key on a keyboard. The ability to isolate, copy and recall, in turn is likely to encourage reuse of material between songs. While it is unusual to see such reuse in an album, it has become an accepted technique in the production of dance music recordings: during the late 1980s/early 1990s

Table 9.2   Verbal repetition in *Slave to the Rhythm*

Phrase	Appears in tracks
'Slave__'	1, 2, 3, 4, 5, 8
'Slave to the rhythm'	1, 2, 3, 4, 8
'Dance to the rhythm'	1, 3, 8
'Axe to wood in ancient time'	1, 8
'Man machine, production line'	1, 8
'Fire burns, with heartbeat strong'	1, 4, 8
'Sing out loud the chaingang song'	1, 4, 8
'Keep it up'	1, 2, 4, 8
'Never stop'	1, 4, 8
'Work to the rhythm'	1, 2, 3, 4, 8
'Live to the rhythm'	1, 4, 8
'Baby'	2, 8
'Don't cry'	2, 8
'You slave'	2, 8
'Work all day …'	2, 4, 8
'… to keep the flow'	2, 4, 8
'Build on up don't break the chain'	2, 4, 8
'Sparks will fly when the whistle blows'	4, 8
'… the action'	4, 6, 8

the breakbeat from James Brown's 'Funky Drummer'[12] appeared on many dance records, for example.

Concerto for Synclavier

Just as the recordings of The Art of Noise are firmly associated with the use of the Fairlight CMI Series II, so *Slave to the Rhythm* is strongly associated with another particular electronic musical instrument: the New England Digital Synclavier II. From the late 1970s, two companies – the Australian-based Fairlight and New England Digital of the USA – had dominated the 'luxury end' of the music technology market. There are a number of clear similarities between the two: both employ a computer at the heart of the system and enable the user to synthesize, sample (eight-bit) and sequence. The difference between the two tends to be one of sound rather than system.[13] The Fairlight produced a distinctively veiled, 'grainy' and highly evocative sound which permeated all the samples, regardless of their particular content. It had a strong sense of character and individuality, particularly evident in some of the more successful sounds of the sample library with which it was supplied: the breathy vocal sound (as heavily featured in 'Moments in Love' by The Art of Noise) or the ubiquitous orchestral stab, for example. The Synclavier was rather different in character. Unlike the Fairlight, it was able to produce (or reproduce) bright, clean samples and synthesized sounds, rich in overtones, which created a powerful sense of presence and resolution. However, unlike the later (and cheaper) FM-based Yamaha DX7 – the most successful synthesizer to date – many of the sounds produced by the Synclavier had a much stronger sense of analogue-like warmth. The lack of system noise and on-board signal processing, which can enhance poorly defined sounds, often at the price of real presence, enabled the Synclavier to produce a rich range of highly defined sounds from its single audio output.

An extreme example of the Synclavier used purely as a sampler is the track 'Operattack', which is entirely constructed from a few sampled phrases taken from other tracks (see Table 9.3).

Table 9.3　Sampled phrases in 'Operattack'

Section	Sampled phrase
A	'Work to the rhythm'
	'Slave to the rhythm'
	'Dance to the rhythm'
	'Annihilating the rhythm'
B	'Huh' (panned with and without reverb, getting faster)
A	'Dance to the rhythm'
	'Slave_'
	'Work to the rhythm'
	'Annihilating the rhythm' (descending in pitch)
	'Slave to the rhythm'
	'Slave_'
B	'Huh' getting faster
A	'Dance to the rhythm'
	'Dance to the'
	'Work to the'
	'Annihilating the rhythm' (low pitch)
B	'Huh' panned with and without reverb, with distinct pitches
A	'Slave_'
	'Dance to the rhythm'
	'Work to the rhythm'
	'Slave to the rhythm'
	'Annihilating the rhythm' (very low pitch with repetition)

There are numerous examples of the Synclavier used as a synthesizer in *Slave to the Rhythm*, but it is particularly prominent through the bass and many of the accompanying sounds on 'The Frog and the Princess'.

Slave to the sampler

Although the presence of the Synclavier is felt, in different guises, throughout *Slave to the Rhythm*, a range of other timbres appear on a number of tracks: most notably electric guitars, orchestral timbres, and vocal and choral sounds. The effect of these, and especially the orchestral and choral colours, is to broaden the scope of the music, offering not only a remarkably rich palette of sounds but also opportunities to manipulate musical significance. While these sounds are often used to add timbral contrast and diversity, they are also used as icons of musical style. What is fascinating here is the apparent influence of sampling on the orchestration of *Slave to the Rhythm*. In the same way that sampling encourages the creation of collages in which each element has both its own significance and provides further significance due to its context, so many of the acoustic sounds in *Slave to the Rhythm* have both a musical and a referential role. This referential role is then compounded through the context in which the particular gesture appears. Naturally, for such a system to function successfully one must take into account not simply the tone colours of the instruments/voices and their combinations, but also the rhythmic, melodic, harmonic and gestural elements which will tend to support the reference points. Like a sampler which relies on capturing a sound bite which is rich in style, that style will be – must be – defined through a variety of musical means and not just through timbre. The strings and wordless choir which form the introduction to 'Slave to the Rhythm', for example, suggest a sense of wonder, peace and tranquillity, at least in part through their evocation of musical characteristics associated with religious music.

At times the diversity of timbre in *Slave to the Rhythm* is extremely wide, although clarity is never impaired, as exemplified by the first track on the album, 'Jones the Rhythm'. At other times the range of sounds is extremely narrow and constrained: as previously noted, 'Operattack' is constructed entirely from a few vocal samples and signal processing. Thus, the record not only contains a wide range of sounds, and a range of ways in which those sounds are used (musically and referentially, for example), but it also exploits the contrasts that are possible between the use of many and few timbres. Similarly, space, in terms of near or far, and left and right, is also thoroughly explored on this record.

Finally, it is possible to even suggest similarities between the cover image of *Slave to the Rhythm* and audio sampling techniques. The photograph of Grace Jones has several horizontal cuts across her hair and mouth, and extra portions have been inserted, causing a lengthening of these two parts of her head. This produces the visual equivalent of the mechanical 'stuttering' effect found on many early sample-based pop records. Consequently, sampling would seem to permeate not only at the physical level of the recording (that is, the sound) but also the conceptual level, influencing orchestration and even visual imagery.

Space

Slave to the Rhythm makes a feature of the evocation of space or, more accurately, spaces. This sense of space is evoked in two ways: the physical position of individual sounds and the spatial characteristics suggested by the ambience. The listener is always able to distinguish each of the various timbres used – pop/ dance bass and drums, percussion, rock guitar, exotic synthesizer timbres, solo voices, choirs and orchestral instruments – partly because of the impressively delicate orchestration/arrangement, partly because of the excellent audio quality of the recording, and partly because of the careful spatial positioning of each timbre. The result is a wide variety of textures and colours that are never too thick or lacking in clarity. In effect, everything has its own space. This is largely created through the sensitive and judicious use of breadth (that is, left/right) and depth (that is, close/distant). The specific position on the left/right axis is set by the panoramic potentiometer (pan pot) on each channel of the mixer, while the depth axis is controlled by the type of artificial reverberation and its balance with the original signal: more reverberation tends to give the illusion of greater distance. These two parameters only become available for this degree of manipulation as a result of multichannel and multitrack recording. By sending the signal on a particular channel, via an auxiliary, to a artificial reverberation emulator and having the resulting (reverberated) signal brought back into a new channel (or more usually two channels as the signal will normally be returned in stereo), the balance engineer is able to 'mix' the two signals (original and reverberated). The greater the ratio of reverberated signal to the original, the greater the illusion of distance from the listener. However, reverberation does not simply define distance, it also defines the acoustic qualities of the real or imagined space. As Michel Chion has written, 'the more reverberant the sound, the more it tends to express the space that contains it' (Chion, 1994, p. 79). The development of high resolution, low noise digital reverberation emulators in the few years prior to this recording had a profound effect on virtually all the professional pop recordings of this period. Digital reverberation permeates 'the sound' of this time and ranges from subtle spatial placement to absurd and surreal evocations of space.

Spatial orchestration

The complexity and subtlety of the use of space in *Slave to the Rhythm* is extremely impressive throughout the album, defining each timbre's role and musical importance in *context*. Indeed, the parameter of timbral spatial placement is so important an element within the composition that the notion of 'spatial orchestration' would seem justified here. However, like the spatial placements within a traditional orchestral concert, there is generally very little movement within the spatial dimension or any sense of dynamic change to individual timbres. The sixth and seventh tracks on the album, 'The Crossing (ooh the action)' and 'Don't Cry – It's Only the Rhythm', are, in different ways, exceptional in this respect and exploit the spatial parameter in a dynamically changing manner.

After the introduction, based entirely on multiple repeats of a single sample, 'The Crossing (ooh the action)' comprises a rhythm track supported by some percussion instruments and two synthesized sound effects. It is the timbres of the percussion instruments and sound effects which are manipulated spatially. The cymbal, shaker, rim shot, cowbells and synthesized bongos begin completely dry and panned either hard left or right, while the claves sound is saturated in artificial reverberation to an unnatural degree. Like the percussion, the synthesized sound effects – 'nightingale' and 'insect' noise – begin completely dry and hard panned right and left respectively. However, towards the end of the track the dry signals tend to gain reverberation and, since this spreads the signal across the stereo spectrum, lose some of their purely left or right pan characteristics. The final sound on this track, the cowbell, has as much reverberation as the initial claves sound. What is unusual here is not only the change in mix between dry and reverberant sound through the track but also the extremely unnatural sound of the reverberation itself: this effect is set up in such a way as to negate any notion of emulation of 'real' reverberation. As such, it presents the listener with an entirely artificial, 'phonographic' effect, which nevertheless refers to a real acoustic phenomenon.

The following track, 'Don't Cry – It's Only the Rhythm' is even more extreme and explicit in its use of unnatural effect, drawing the listener's attention to the artificial nature of the recorded product. Here the left/right axis which features on 'Operattack' and 'The Crossing (ooh the action)' is once again used. However, this time the whole mix is fed through one of the two channels while the other is completely silent. Table 9.4 shows exactly how the music is organized between the two channels through the song.

The first noticeable aspect of 'Don't Cry – It's Only the Rhythm' is the use of the monophonic signal. While the music is restricted to one channel, and hence one loudspeaker, the resulting sound is inevitably monophonic. But when spread between two channels a stereophonic mix is not only possible but normally also desirable. Yet here the piece begins and ends in mono; in fact, in the whole piece

Table 9.4   Space in 'Don't Cry – It's Only the Rhythm'

Bars	Use of space
Intro.	Mono
1–4	Mono
5–10	All left except for single, close right sound
11–22	All right except for single, close left sound
23–38	Full stereo
39–44	Mono with central close sounds
45–47	Right only
48–49	Fast pan between left and right
50–65	Mono (flanged) to fade

only one section is in stereo.[14] Were there no stereo section here it would be possible to suggest that the piece merely reflects the single monophonic output of the Synclavier. The inclusion of the stereo section undermines this theory and suggests that the monophonic nature of the sound is not only intentional but part of some grander scheme: it serves as a foil for the stereophonic character of the rest of the record perhaps. A second aspect of this piece is the use of the close digital-sounding synthesized interjections which regularly occur when the rest is in mono. The second and third sections, for example, have the music entirely in the left then right channels respectively, while the close digital-sounding synthesized interjections appear in the opposite channels. This serves to reassure the listener that both loudspeakers are actually functioning: the effect is so unusual as to suggest technical malfunction. It also shows how close a completely untreated sound (that is, not mixed with any artificial reverberation) can be, especially when listened to with headphones, and highlights the way in which the parameter of depth is manipulated within the album. The extreme nature of this particular track, even within the context of an album which puts such emphasis on the musical manipulation of spatial placement, is startling. The absolute distinctions which are made between left and right channels here force the listener to notice and appreciate this particular aspect: in effect then, space is presented as the main musical parameter and a structural principle on which the entire piece is based.

Words

While the use of space is an important aspect of *Slave to the Rhythm*, the lyrics, which are often spoken rather than sung, also command the listener's attention and require some explanation. Words, whether spoken or sung, are invariably compelling. Michel Chion, in his book *Audio-Vision*, highlights this effect in film soundtracks when he writes: 'Sound in cinema is primarily vococentric, I mean that it almost always privileges the voice, highlighting and setting the latter off from other sounds' (Chion, 1994, p. 5). It is hardly surprising, then, that words are used very carefully in *Slave to the Rhythm*. First, many of the tracks on the album are not songs in the traditional sense since they lack the rhyming couplets which are such a feature of pop music. Instead a few phrases are repeated, apparently in random fashion. Second, the more musically complex tracks (like 'Jones the Rhythm', for example) tend to have less words, presumably so as not to divide the listener's attention. Finally, important phrases are sampled and reappear, often in a different musical context. The result of all this is an album in which the listener hears the repetition of a few key phrases.[15] Furthermore, there are obvious differences between the audio cassette and CD versions of the album in respect to the appearance of spoken words. The cassette version includes spoken interviews between Grace Jones and Paul Morley, or monologues from Jean-Paul Goude, Jones's manager and partner, between each track, which are entirely absent from the CD. These differences aside, the spoken (as opposed to sung) voice still features largely, even on the CD version of *Slave to the Rhythm*. The album (both cassette and CD versions) begins with an extract from 'The Annihilation of Rhythm' by I. Penman read by Ian McShane. Apart from the impressive and professional delivery of the text by the actor, one is immediately struck by the unusual audio effect which has been added to the voice: a sampled and delayed version appears in the left channel while the right channel has a similar but much shorter delay. The final phrase, 'Jones the Rhythm', is presented with no effect on either channel (that is, central and monophonic). The addition of this effect is clearly intended to distance the listener from the intimate sounding, persuasive voice (which also benefits from a close microphone placement): the doubling of the sound gives the impression of distance through the emulation of echo but also imparts a mechanical, and hence unnatural, quality.

Slave to the remix

Slave features only one song, that single in various versions – a gorgeous plasmatic dub of clockwork precision. (Sutherland, 1985)

Grace Jones's *Slave to the Rhythm* album was originally conceived as a single until Horn's dissatisfaction with the work in progress instigated a number of different versions of the song. This culminated in what he describes as 'the ultimate 12-inch mix', and one which was a reference point for all mainstream pop producers in the mid to late eighties. (Cunningham, 1996, p. 277)

Slave to the Rhythm is certainly an unusual pop artefact. The repetition of verbal phrases and variations on musical ideas within and between tracks produces a sense of cohesion that is quite unlike most pop albums. As these techniques of repetition are normally a feature of remixes, *Slave to the Rhythm* may be viewed as a bizarre kind of remix of itself: a pop music hybrid that evolves by using the principles of remixing to continue and develop itself. It is evident that remixing is an intrinsic aspect of Trevor Horn's work and different versions (mixes) of the same material abound. With *Slave to the Rhythm* this process has been taken a step further resulting in an album of material which evolves through the use of remixing techniques. There are several important points here. First, there is little sense of the 'original' from which the remix is usually derived in this album, particularly since the title song only appears as the fifth piece on the album – after many of the key ideas have already been sounded on previous tracks. Second, each song has less individual character since elements of other tracks are continually appearing. Finally, one may get the impression of a single, relatively large-scale work with contrasting sections linked by a series of almost leitmotif-like elements: a structure that perhaps represents an attempt to reconcile the classical and the popular notions of musical form. 'So *Slave* is essentially a record about making a record' (Sutherland, 1985).

Slave to the Rhythm clearly shares a number of similarities with other productions by Trevor Horn. First, its emphasis on presenting a complete art package which involves not only sound but also image and attitude is characteristic of many ZTT records. Second, it is a hugely varied musical product that clearly represents the work of a large team, rather than an individual. The list of contributors on the sleeve notes is extremely long and Horn acknowledges the considerable contribution of Steve Lipson: 'It was a team,' he says, 'but then most hugely successful projects are not due to a single person. On *Slave to the Rhythm*, Steve was producing me being a producer, which is a weird concept but that's how it worked' (quoted in Cunningham, 1996, p. 277). Third, the emphasis on technology not only defines much of the sound of the album but may also be seen to inform more traditional musical parameters like structure. Fourth, the detailed and sophisticated use of the spatial dimension at times dominates the musical proceedings. And finally, the influence of the remix which, as a separate and distinct pop artefact, brings about some of the unusual repetitions within the album.

Certainly many of these factors are more pronounced and further developed in *Slave to the Rhythm* than in previous work. The use of technology and phonographic space[16] are extremely important and not only dominate the sound of the album but also seem to have given rise to much of its structure. The use of recording technology not only plays a large part in bringing about the sound of the recording, but also has a great influence on the musical concepts which underpin it. In this sense, the quotation by Steve Sutherland is entirely appropriate.

Although *Slave to the Rhythm* is the last recording to be studied here, Trevor Horn has continued to produce successful and often innovative records right up to the present day. He still tends to embrace the latest technological developments and is quite explicit in recognizing the impact that these may have on his work. Commenting on the new Super Audio CD format, for example, he states: 'a new format always gives me an opportunity to look at my work in a different way'.[17]

Notes

1. In fact, she had already appeared as an actress in several films – *Gordon's War* (1973), *Armee Der Liebenden Oder Aufstand Der Perversen/Army of Lovers or Revolt of the Perverts* (1978), *Conan The Destroyer* (1984), *Mode In France* (1985) – and went on to appear in *Vamp* (1986), *Siesta* (1987), *Straight to Hell* (1987), *Superstar: The Life and Times of Andy Warhol* (1991) and *Boomerang* (1992). However, her career in films remains patchy rather than blooming.
2. Mercury 6007 100.
3. 'Slave to the Rhythm' (ZTT IS 206) entered the UK singles chart on 12 October 1985; *Slave to the Rhythm* (ZTT GRACE 1) entered the UK albums chart on 9 November 1985.
4. Island ILPS 9592, 1980.
5. Island ILPS 9624, 1981.
6. Island ILPS 9722, 1982.
7. For example, on the album *Nightclubbing*, 'Pull up to the Bumper' is a disco track, 'Walking in the Rain' is reggae, 'I've Seen That Face Before (Libertango)' speaks for itself, and 'Demolition Man' has strong punk overtones.
8. In one of the interviews on the cassette version of *Slave to the Rhythm*, Jones talks of her similarity to her grandfather whose grandfather was from the Ibo tribe of modern Nigeria.
9. It is also possible to synchronize two tape recorders. In recent years more pieces of equipment in the recording studio have the facility to be synchronized: all the controls on certain mixers (which can then be stored and 'recalled' at any time); the playback of a hard disk recording system (so that these recordings replay in time with other devices); digital and analogue tape recorders; and MIDI equipped signal processors. A range of different timecode standards exist (SMPTE, EBU etc.) all offering a resolution of between 24 and 30 divisions (frames) per second.
10. A fuller version of this extract is given on the sleeve notes and includes the phrase 'violence of the voice affirming a subjugated state', again reinforcing this theme.
11. Appendix I, an interview with Trevor Horn, confirms how important the use of two digital multitrack tape recorders were in the production of *Slave to the Rhythm*.
12. Polydor 531 165-2.
13. By 1984 the Synclavier II was 32 note polyphonic (although this was rarely achieved as many of the best sounds employed up to four voices at once), had a 16-track sequencer, a monophonic sampler with up to 50 seconds sampling time, additive synthesis, FM synthesis and a single output. Later additions included 'Timbre Frame Synthesis' – a system of re-synthesis where the machine would analyse samples and re-create them – SMPTE, MIDI and the ability to interface with the Macintosh II computer.
14. Stereophonic recordings give the impression of directionality through the use of a

combination of time and level differences between the two channels. The level differences act on our hearing like any other sound source: loudness defines position. The time differences of up to 50 ms between channels give rise to the Haas or precedence effect: the first signal defines position. 'Theoretical correctness is one thing, pragmatism is another, and the history of stereo could be characterized all along as being something of a compromise between the two' (Rumsey and McCormick, 1992, p. 297).

15. An obvious exception to this general rule is the track 'The Frog and the Princess'. Here a monologue by Ian McShane is intoned over a highly repetitive yet subtly varying backbeat.

16. The limitations of stereo and the extreme use of clearly artificial reverberation imply a phonographic space (that is, an audio illusion of an, at times, impossible space) rather than acoustic space.

17. http://www.sacd.philips.com/b2b/news/ztt_frankie.html

Conclusion

The seven analyses which form the second part of this book explore a number of issues relating to specific pop records produced by Trevor Horn during the period 1979–85. The breadth of information presented in the previous chapters should not, however, make us lose sight of the central theme of this study: the relationship between technology and creativity. Hence the need to start this conclusion with a brief recapitulation of the important ways in which the seven records analysed here relate to the central theme of the book.

The robotic rhythms, contrasting vocal timbres and ambiguous narrative of 'Video Killed the Radio Star' are imbued with the presence of technology; the record, produced entirely with analogue audio equipment, both revels in the disco aesthetic of the time and plays with a sense of nostalgia and loss. 'Buffalo Gals' combines several disparate musical elements in a sonic collage largely made possible through scratching and sampling (that is, analogue and digital) techniques; it introduced hip hop – an important and lasting influence on pop music – to the UK and celebrates the old and the new both musically, lyrically and technologically. 'Owner of a Lonely Heart' takes the timbral constraints of progressive rock and transforms them with the innovative techniques of a technologically adventurous pop production; the result, with its machine-like drums, incongruous samples and alienated guitars, is a four-minute single which reflects the repeatable nature of the pop artefact.

The lengthy period of gestation for 'Relax' illustrates both the challenges of new and complex technology, and a determination to work to high artistic standards; the influence of digital sequencing is evident not only in the virtually omnipresent, machine-driven backbeat but also in the almost organic musical structure. The Art of Noise recordings are dominated by a single device – the Fairlight CMI – and represent the first thorough exploration of the musical/sonic implications of digital sampling and sequencing in pop music.

The contrasts between Propaganda's 'Duel' and 'Jewel', which are essentially the same musical material subjected to radically different productions, exploit the creative potential offered by recording studio technology; they also illustrate a new approach to pop music production: the remix – a form which is technologically enabled but artistically motivated. Finally, *Slave to the Rhythm* might be regarded as a bringing together of all the creative possibilities offered by digital audio technology mentioned above; the bright, crisp, and carefully positioned sounds are the result of digital recording, synthesis and signal processing; the rhythmic gestures celebrate and flaunt mechanical manipulation; and as an artefact it is closer to an extensively remixed single than an album.

Collectively, these analyses reveal the complex relationship between creativity and technology which is at the heart of pop music production. The record producer, as mediator between artist and artefact, emerges as a key figure in this relationship. While Horn's contribution should not be overestimated – these records are always the result of team creativity – his almost obsessive pursuit of extremely high artistic standards should not be overlooked. If 'Genius ... is an infinite capacity for taking pains' (Boulez, 1990, p. 125), then Horn has consistently demonstrated such a capacity throughout his career.

The analyses also make it possible to identify a number of common characteristics which strongly suggest Horn's influence. Musically, the use of forceful and impressive, dance-derived backbeats, timbral diversity and subtle structural innovation are especially noticeable. Furthermore, the importance of technology is manifest: much of the sound on these recordings is either sequenced, sampled, synthesized or digitally modified; there is a strong emphasis on the technological manipulation of space through the use of digital reverberation and panning, as well as recurrent use of technology-related imagery in lyrics and on record sleeves. Moreover, re-recording and remixing, which are such a feature of Horn's work, are evidently enabled and driven by the technological nature of the medium: 'enabled' because multitrack, and particularly digital multitrack, recordings allow for virtually endless revision; 'driven' because a single mix may represent too fixed an artefact.

While harmonic and melodic ideas are often more likely to be the work of a range of composers, Horn's contribution would appear to be in the 'sound' (that is, the choice and combination of timbres and the way those timbres are manipulated through technological processes), the 'feel' (that is, the subtle rhythmic/dynamic/timbral nuances and pitch deviations of performance which give a strong sense of individual expression) and the structuring (that is, the order and content of the various sections of a piece in relation to the whole). The resourceful manipulation of these three factors is an important creative aspect of pop music and often largely achieved through technology. The rapid pace of technological change which characterized the period 1979–85 led to the evolution of new working practices within the pop recording studio. Trevor Horn, perhaps more than any other producer of the time, both embraced and explored the creative potential of this new technology, producing highly innovative and highly influential records. As Albin J. Zak confirms: 'British recordings of the early 1980s marked a turning point in terms of both sound and public awareness. With an abundance of sound processing, new electronic instruments, and resurgent experimental attitudes, the distance between the natural sound world and the sound of records increased markedly' (Zak, 2001, p. 181).

There can be little doubt that Horn's work has generally achieved great popularity (see Table C.1, which shows the highest position attained in the record charts by the recordings studied). Both singles and albums sold in quantity and, indeed, all managed to attain at least Top 30 status. A similar picture of success emerges

Table C.1   **Horn's recordings and the pop charts**

Recording	Singles chart position	Album chart position
The Buggles:		
'Video Killed the Radio Star'	1	
The Age of Plastic		27
Malcolm McLaren:		
'Buffalo Gals'	9	
Duck Rock		18
Yes:		
'Owner of a Lonely Heart'	28 (No. 1 in USA)	
90125		16
Frankie Goes to Hollywood:		
'Relax'	1	
Welcome to the Pleasuredome		1
The Art of Noise:		
'Close (to the Edit)'	8	
Who's Afraid of The Art of Noise?		27
Propaganda:		
'Duel'	21	
A Secret Wish		16
Grace Jones:		
'Slave to the Rhythm'	12	
Slave to the Rhythm		12

from Horn's numerous other recordings, serving to confirm his reputation as one of the most consistently successful record producers in Britain over the past 25 years (see Appendix 2).

In the UK television Channel 4 programme, *The 100 Greatest Number 1 Hits* (shown at 8.10 p.m., Saturday 1 December 2001), which was the result of a nation-wide poll, 'Video Killed the Radio Star' was placed at number 53 while 'Relax' was at 40. This programme tends to suggest that some pop records are able to transcend the ephemeral nature of the Top 20 and establish themselves as part of a 'pop canon'. Again, while it would be naive to assume that such success is any guarantee of artistic worth, it does reveal the lasting popularity and influence of at least a few of the recordings analysed here. Moreover, the success of these recordings also suggests a wide appeal, from superficial background music to a far more intense response and, as should now be evident, these recordings do lend themselves to close scrutiny. 'He must be doing something right, but nobody seems to care what it is' (Charlie Gillette writing of record producer Stephen Street, in Gillette and Frith, 1996, p. 119).

Horn's later work has included recording projects with more established artists like the Pet Shop Boys,[1] Godley and Creme,[2] Simple Minds,[3] Mark Almond,[4] Mike Oldfield[5] and Tina Turner,[6] among others, although he achieved significant success with the relatively unknown singer Seal.[7] These later recordings tend to be more diverse in character, possibly in order to present the specific musicality and personality of the artist. At times this can result in a conflict of interests between the sophisticated, technologically driven, studio production techniques associated with Trevor Horn and the presentation of the particular artist's 'sound', as Neil Spencer comments: 'At times on her first new album in six years Turner reminds us that she's still a super-charged soul singer. Mostly, though, her bluesy spirit seems locked inside Trevor Horn's airbrushed productions; a comfortable prison which allows neither commercial error or artistic licence' (Spencer, 1996).

Throughout his long and successful career, Trevor Horn has continued to not only champion the latest audio technology but also to explore its creative potential. This ongoing exploration is a fundamental characteristic of his work; as he said in 1994: 'You can hardly separate music from technology.'[8] His awareness of the vitally important role that technology plays in the process of record production is evident in the interview with him, included here as Appendix 1. When Michael Chanan writes, 'the greater part of the music engendered by mass production is composed almost as mechanically as it is reproduced' (Chanan, 1995, p. 16) he, perhaps inadvertently, draws attention to the technological nature of creativity, which is at the heart of the pop artefact – many of the sounds on these recordings are the result of machines. However, as these analyses have shown, the human creativity involved in the manipulation of this technology, is far from mechanical.

Notes

1. *Introspective* (Parlophone PCS 7325), 1988.
2. *The History Mix Volume 1* (Polydor 825 981-2), 1985.
3. *Glittering Prize* (Virgin SMTVD 1), 1992.
4. *Tenement Symphony* (Some Bizzare WX 442), 1991.
5. *Tubular Bells II* (WEA 4509906182), 1992.
6. *Wildest Dreams* (Parlophone 7243 8 37684 2 4), 1996.
7. *Seal* (ZTT 9031-74557-2), 1991.
8. http://www.trevor-horn.de/.

Appendix 1

Interview with Trevor Horn

The role of technology in pop music

T.W.   How much is the sound of a particular recording, Slave to the Rhythm *for example, defined by the technology used to make it?*
T.H.   That's a tricky question. *Slave to the Rhythm* is an interesting example. It's the first time we ever tried making a drum loop where we kept all of the drums separate (separate bass drum, snare drum, etc.) across eight tracks. We looped them using two Sonys. It took a long, long time. But it's still a straightforward, very nice drum sound.

Technology does affect things enormously and in different ways too. There's the sound of the equipment that you put the sounds through. There's also the nature of what you're recording and then what you do to it with the technology. *Slave to the Rhythm*'s not a bad example, I suppose, because you have a loop made up from a hard-core go-go band. Half the members of the band were EU – Experience Unlimited – and the others were a go-go band called Chuck Brown and the Soul Searchers. The best musicians from each of them couldn't play an arrangement to save their lives – they couldn't play anything that wasn't instinctive – and so we had to make up a drum track from something that they played while having fun as we set up.

The sound of that record was enormously influenced by the technology. We had the first polyphonic Synclavier with the 100 kHz sampling. The potential of that was something that Steve Lipson was just beginning to understand. The fact that I had the budget to do something like that was the amazing thing since it started out as just a single.

It's such a wide question because technology has affected the music since people built cathedrals. There's no doubt that *Slave to the Rhythm* bears very little relationship to live performance. It's completely fabricated – the whole thing – and that's what makes it so interesting.

T.W.   Which pieces of equipment have been responsible for changing your sound, and how?
T.H.   The first important piece of equipment that changed what I did was string synthesizers in the late 1970s because real records used to be records with real orchestras on them, and I could never afford them because I had no budget. So when the first string machine came along, that opened things up for us.

The next thing was the first polyphonic synthesizer – the Polymoog. That was a revelation because we'd been trying to get something by tracking up Minimoogs and the result was crap. It was wonderful when, for the first time, you could put your hands on a keyboard and play a full chord. I can't begin to tell you how excited we were. Now we all take it for granted.

Then the next thing was the first drum machine that you could actually programme. I'd tried to make my own drum machine by getting a drummer to play onto tape with each sound separate, and keying them in and out and speeding the tape up and down; but it was still a bit wonky. And then Roland brought out the CR78. It was a rhythm box, but you could programme fills into it. Suddenly there was a deluge of rhythm boxes in the early 1980s: the TR808 and the Linn I and II. The Linn was an amazing thing: not only could you programme the drums but you could synchronize them up to tape. I don't think anyone's got any idea of how difficult it was to grasp the concept of being able to run the drums along with the track back then. We just couldn't get our head around it. We thought it wouldn't work but it did, and that really began to change things.

And then the real killer – the Fairlight – came along, and nobody understood what it was and what it could do for a long time. For three or four years it was only the people who could afford £20 000 who could do their own sampling. It was a really good time, nobody knew what was going on. But then, of course, sampling became cheaper. I can remember the very first time we sync'ed up a Fairlight and a Linn drum machine together. This was where a record like 'Relax' came from – the rhythm track was wholly due to the fact that we had a piece of equipment that enabled us to sync the Linn and the Fairlight.

Then the next really big thing was the Synclavier with 100 kHz sampling. At first, it was only monophonic. It was such a big thing, it was difficult to assess what it was capable of in just one or two records. It was also very slow and time-consuming. I put on a stone in the first three or four months that we had it because of the length of time I had to hang about while people did things. The whole game of being a record producer began to shift away from being a sociable boss of a group of musicians having an exciting time making a record to being somebody who visits people programming.

Then the next important development was digital multitrack audio. We were used to analogue where you record something but then if you want to move it you lose quality; you move it again and you lose more quality. You can do stuff like that but the quality goes down like a Messerschmitt on a power dive. Somebody suggested we try one of the new Sony digital multitracks in 1984. We had one of the first eight or nine of them. We got it and it kept breaking down and the tape kept going wrong. So I really had a go at Sony: I had hysterics down the phone at them because it had shredded up a Frankie master. I insisted that they lend me a second machine – which, to their credit, they did for a few years. We found that with two machines copying one another you could copy any number of times. We once copied something 50 times just to see that it really did work. And it did, there was no loss of quality. That meant that we could do a kind of editing that we'd never dreamt of before. We used it to make 'Welcome to the Pleasuredome'. It started out as a three-minute thing and we made it 16 minutes long just by adding bits to it. It was Steve Lipson's idea, I have to be honest. He said: 'Look what happens if we do this. If we offset this machine eight bars from this.' And then somebody said: 'Why don't you try putting the chords over the verse, running the two things together?' We tried all kinds of stupid things and discovered a kind of multitrack editing that nobody had been able to do before. That's how we came to do *Slave to the Rhythm.*

The next thing, probably the final thing that's been any real influence, was direct-to-disk recording. At the beginning of the 1990s I bought a two-track direct-to-disk recorder that locked up to a sequencer, and freed myself from having to use engineers. I could start editing things myself. Now I've got four or five direct-to-disk systems and we use them all the time, every day, to edit and put together performances by people on whatever record we're working on. We use them for fixing up vocals, orchestras, everything.

T.W. Do you ever feel constrained by the recording studio as a creative environment?
T.H.   The times when I mostly feel that is when I'm on my own. If I have people to help me then I don't find it frightening. I can find the sheer tedium of setting things up to be too much, but only if I'm really tired. Besides, I've always liked technology and been involved in it, so I don't look at it that way. There's a song and I need to make a record of it. The studio is just something I use to make the record.

T.W. It's your factory?
T.H.   Yeah, and I think about it quite a bit before I make a record. In reality a producer has become, to some degree, an interface between the musicians and the technical process of recording. This week for example, I'm doing a record that's a combination of programming and playing. It started off as a completely computerized track, which I've stripped away and mostly replaced with real players. But next week I'll be working with a group and it's a live performance of a song, so it's completely different. Obviously with live performance I use the technology in a different way.

T.W. Is the technology a major consideration at the pre-production stage?
T.H.   Yes, because the first thing you ask yourself is what kind of a track are you making? Is it a dance track? Is it something that has to have a really rock-solid groove? If it does, then you're going to do it with the computer. When you've got the groove and the backing track together to some degree on the computer, how are you going to structure it? Where are you going to structure it?

Where is it going to be played? Is it going to be played in the studio, is it going to be played in the pre-production room? Somewhere along the way, you have to get the arrangement right. Although using pieces of equipment is a mechanical process, you have to think about it.

T.W.   What were the effects of the development of digital reverberation in the early 1980s?
T.H.   It didn't give us anything that we didn't have before. Digital reverb is all very nice but we had the old EMT plate, which was a beautiful sounding thing, and delay devices have been around since I started. Although it might take a while to get it, you could always get some kind of echo.

We had one of the first digital reverbs. You're right, you know, I forgot about that. It did change the sound because once I heard one, I more or less abandoned the EMT plate. At least back then, I'd probably use it again now. We used to call the early EMT rack-mount digital reverb the 'crash box' because you could get a great, short, hard reverb out of it. You could also get really long reverb times – four and a half, five seconds – you could freeze things and fade them out, or freeze things and slow the tape machine down, and do effects with it that you couldn't do very easily with a plate. So you're right, looking back on it, it did affect things.

T.W.   What technological advances would you like to see? Does any new area of technology excite you?
T.H.   We've had so much new technology in the past 10 years that we could spend ages just figuring out what can be done with it. The real innovations in technology, at the moment, seem to me to be at the low end of the market. Mackie mixers for example, and all those great new little op. amps that they've got so that they can machine-make high-quality mixers. So a great big thing like this [points to studio mixer] has become a little bit of a dinosaur. But if you can get the budget it's a fantastic environment to work in. I'm very dubious about digital mixing consoles – even the low end ones. They're all right provided you don't do anything. The minute you put some EQ on something or move a fader, it sounds terrible. They haven't made a decent digital EQ yet. There are a lot of problems inherent in digital mixing consoles.

What's really interesting these days for me is people's idea of sound. We've got a whole new generation of musicians – people who, for instance, programme a beat box without any experience of a real drummer. When we first got beat boxes, we tried to programme them to do what a drummer would do. Nowadays people haven't got a clue what a drummer would do, but they make the box go 'do do do da bo baf', and it's fantastic, it's great. I really find that exciting. Drum programming has become quite amazing. The way people get things to sound these days is really quite unbelievable.

Music

T.W. Typically, what is the nature of the musical material at the start of the production process? In Slave to the Rhythm, *for example, what was the original starting material?*

T.H. It was written for Frankie Goes to Hollywood. What you have to realize about 'Slave to the Rhythm' is that it was a 'bogus' song. It was written for a purpose and the fact that, in the end, it was done by somebody like Grace Jones lent it a weight that in reality it never had. It was written by a couple of professional songwriters and then forcibly rewritten.

T.W. What did you actually get from the songwriters?

T.H. I got a very Germanic demo version of it that was dead straight – you probably noticed I got a writing credit because I changed part of the song. I made a quick track with Grace but I didn't like it. I said: 'I love the title but I don't like the song. It's got to be something much broader, something that sounds more spiritual.' I suggested that we try rewriting it over a go-go rhythm. We went to New York and that's what we did. It was a bit of a risky thing to do but it actually turned out quite well.

You asked me what I got. I got an idea. I got a demo with this song on it and I liked the title 'Slave to the Rhythm'. I liked the idea of being trapped in the inevitable. The first version of it is the first track on the album. That was the first version, and the last version was the one that came out as a single. There's an enormous difference: the first one's very unsubtle and is in an utterly different tempo with a completely different tune. Whereas the last version's beautiful: it's one of the best records that I ever made. I just started out with an idea and that's what songs are: ideas about something. I've always liked badly written songs so I could fix them up rather than professionally written songs because I get bored with them and half the time they're bogus, they don't mean anything. The person who wrote them, wrote them because he heard two good words. Whereas, sometimes, you get somebody like Seal coming over with a song like 'Violet' which he doesn't know how to structure. It's all about an old girlfriend that he left, and it's like going into somebody else's world and you understand what they're talking about. You just want to try and organize it so other people can understand it. You see, what I get from the songwriters is the idea.

T.W. What attracts you to a piece of music in the first place? (I'm thinking of 'Relax', for example, where your production changed so much of the original material.)

T.H. I wasn't so attracted to the song on *The Tube*. I thought the band was pretty stupid, they had women chained up and I thought that was funny. The kid had a good voice and I liked the look of the drummer. I didn't get the song first time round because it seemed a bit weird, but when I heard it again on the radio without seeing them, I thought the hook was very attractive. I thought that the way Holly sang it was brilliant because it sounded manic. In actual fact it isn't much of a song if you analyse it to any degree. Everyone told me that it wasn't a very good song, more like a jingle for television – just singing the same thing over and over again. But what's great about that track is all the stuff that's done in between, all that 'ho, hey', etc. That's what's really interesting about it and all the imaginary mayhem on the record. It was actually done in here, funnily enough, but the studio wasn't quite the same.

What attracted me to it? It was a great idea, I don't know what he was talking about. In fact, it wasn't pornographic, that's the interesting thing. People got the idea that it was pornographic because a guy that was working at ZTT put 'When you want to suck it, do it' on the cover which is not what he sang. He sang 'When you want to sock it to it' – it was about being positive. But obviously it had incredible sexual overtones: the whole thing, the whole band did. Holly and the other guy were gay, the rest of the band were aggressively heterosexual and all they could talk about was shagging, all the time. The beat of the record went 'boom boom boom boom' like a bed going up against a wall. So how could you not be thinking about sex if you were anywhere near it?

By the time we came to do the record, the band had long since departed: they were completely worn out and disillusioned because I couldn't get to grips with them playing the song. By the time we did the song we had all kinds of pictures in mind, well I did anyway. At the start there's a funny little sax note that was meant to be Holly standing on the roof of some mosque and calling the faithful to sex. That was the idea. We'd completely re-done the track starting that afternoon. We'd dumped the last version by the band and had the machines running. Holly came in and loved it and couldn't wait to sing it. At four o'clock in the morning, while he was waiting for us to finish it, he took my saxophone and played it up on the roof next door. He gathered a crowd of dreadies on the street below. He came running in and he told me, so I said 'Come on, play it on the track' and he did.

T.W.   How clear an idea of what you're aiming for do you have before you start a production? Does this idea change as you're realizing the track in the studio?
T.H.   It's really simple. You have some kind of idea of where you're going but if, during the journey, you stumble upon something brilliant, then dump whatever the original plan was and do that. Music's a funny thing and quite often it won't do what you want it to do but does something else. If you're sensible you say: 'Well this isn't what I envisaged but it's terrific. We'll have this.'

T.W.   What musical elements define a good pop record? Structure, harmonic language, melodic language, arrangement, the manipulation of the hook, individual recorded performances, the final mix, feel, a sense of pace, development and change, the use of technology … ?

T.H.   I think it's whether the record communicates. Whether it gives off something. It might not even be the message the songwriter thought was in the lyrics. It's just if it gives off something, I can't explain it. It's a combination of all those elements. You do all of those things to try and make it communicate something and hopefully, somewhere along the way, it does it.

T.W.   Harmonically, melodically and structurally pop music is often dismissed as unoriginal. So what is musically original in each new pop music recording?
T.H.   In pop music there are no rules, as such, but there are implied rules. You can break them but only if you really know what you're doing. Where there are rigid things then the fun comes in trying to subvert them in some way – trying to get away with things that you wouldn't normally get away with. Somebody like Dr Dre – the rap guy – makes brilliant records because he really knows what he's doing. He has a way of dealing with structure that's fascinating.

I always look at all this as entertainment. You're making a record, you're making a thing that people are going to listen to. It's something that has to inspire people to go into a record shop and buy this piece of recording. So it had better be good, it had better have something going for it that's going to turn them on somewhere along the way.

T.W.   Do you feel that a traditional music education helps or hinders a pop musician?
T.H.   Well, I don't think that it ever harms to know what you're dealing with. I don't think it's very clever to make yourself ignorant or be ignorant. I think that while lots of good things, interesting things, can come from non-musicians, that's no excuse. Historically producers and arrangers have been bass players in groups. Lately it's been DJs. One of the reasons is because DJs play music to people, and a very important part of learning how to make a record, or any kind of musical performance, is watching people respond to what you do. It gives you a sense of what people are prepared to put up with and what people's attention span is like. But very few DJs have got any sense of harmony: the wacko things they do harmonically are sometimes good and sometimes just plain crap. It's fascinating to hear somebody sample the major triad onto a keyboard key and then move it around up and down tones. It's very like what Debussy used to do but they're doing it without even knowing what the hell they're doing. It's terrific, but the chances are that they'll probably give it up in about 10 years and do something else. In order to really get into something you have to know what you're dealing with. Very few DJs think: 'Wow, this is a 12–tone scale I'm using here and if I vary the root I can get this really pleasing effect.' They won't know that and the likelihood is that they'll give up music.

T.W.   What are the high standards that you work to driven by? The audience, the market, personal integrity, or a combination of all these?

T.H.   I guess my father always used to go on about doing things properly so I've always looked at things like that.

T.W.   How important are lyrics, the promo video, or other cultural (extra-musical) references to the success of a pop record?
T.H.   The lyrics are utterly important, far more important than anyone could realize, because the thing that differentiates us from animals is that we have the power of speech. We're the animal that can talk and what's said on the record is of absolute paramount importance. There's the potential for communicating something on a pop record. Every couple of months or so, I get pretty depressed because I hear one awful song after another, and I start to feel that I'm getting like my parents. Then somebody writes something that I really like and I have faith again, because it is possible to do beautiful things in the most simple way. I don't know if you've ever listened to Massive Attack, I love that opening song on their album – 'Protection'. I thought it was such a beautiful piece of writing.

Videos are a different department. I sometimes fantasize about directing a video but that's all. If you get a good video with a record, great – and generally if you make a good record they make a good video of it – but that's about where it ends.

T.W.   Does your background as a bass player have any influence on your production work?
T.H.   No, quite the opposite. I think I neglect the bass sometimes because I was a bass player. One of the reasons bass players often become producers is because the bass is only fun if everything else is right. So you get everything else right so that when you plonk your one note E, everything sounds great.

T.W.   In Good Vibrations, *Mark Cunningham quotes you as saying that you wanted a rhythm track to sound machine-like. Why do you want musicians to play their instruments 'like machines'? What's the attraction?*
T.H.   I spent the whole of the 1970s listening to people playing groovy things, and there was a certain kind of decadence about the 1970s. Towards the end of the 1970s, I heard an album by Kraftwerk called *The Man Machine* and I just loved it and I saw the logic in it. I realized that most of what musicians played at the time, the people around me, was rubbish. Only really great people can get away with making groovy feel kind of records and I didn't have that open to me. I wasn't a great musician, the people around me weren't great musicians, although they may have been good. So I had to try and find some kind of way of getting through all that. I didn't necessarily inherently have a great feel. I could play a reasonable bass guitar but people didn't fall over saying: 'Wow! You've got a great feel. What a great sense of rhythm you've got.' It didn't happen like that, I wasn't really that talented. So I had to find something that I could shape into what I needed. The machines made a noise that appealed to me because I could pin it down: 'That's in time, I know it's in time.' Nobody could question it.

T.W. *Do you miss being involved in 'live' performance?*

T.H. Yes, I do sometimes, but only a bit because the reality of it is that live performance is always such a shambles. It's a very powerful thing when it works. The time I was with Yes, and the few times when I actually felt that I made something work in front of 20-odd thousand people, was an incredible experience. But it leads to all kinds of ego problems and god-like aspirations that turn you into such a turd sometimes. I'm really quite happy to stay away from it.

Record production

T.W. *In layman's terms what does a record producer do? What is the main role of a record producer?*

T.H. Primarily the record company assigns an artist. The artist has a song and has to make a record of that song. A record producer can make all the difference between that record coming out a hit, or not, and that's where we earn our money. If we can influence the record enough to make it saleable then we have a value, and that's what we do.

T.W. *When you're producing a record, do you take the complete image of the band or artist into account? In other words, does it influence the production process?*

T.H. Yes, it does, absolutely, because it affects the way you look at the record that you're making. What you're doing is developing somebody else's idea. The way they look and the way they present themselves is all part of that idea, as is the choice of song. That's where you can have real problems because sometimes people's image, and what they see themselves as, is at odds with what they're actually doing. And of course you take the blame for it.

T.W. *Is there a typical production process?*

T.H. The typical production process is songwriters demo to producer, pre-production of demo, into studio, make record and then mix it.

T.W. *How responsible do you feel for a production?*

T.H. If I'm producing it, totally responsible, it's got my name on it. Everybody gets their own bit of credit. Though I might be reasonably well known, my kind of fame is nothing compared to that of an artist.

Earlier this year I won a Grammy award for a Seal track. We both got the Grammy and we both walked through the media circus surrounding the Grammy. On the stage in front of the press nobody had any questions for me, whereas they were asking Seal all kinds of things. It didn't bother me, it's what I expected. My credit, and what I get, comes from a certain group of people in the industry, and that's really all that interests me.

*T.W.   Are recordings always the result of some kind of creative collaboration?
Do engineers – Gary Langan and Steve Lipson, for example – have an influential
role in the recording process? And how influential are the people that you work
with (the musicians and employees of the record company)? In what ways do
they influence the process?*

T.H.   I always try to be reasonably strict in the control room but very open. If
the cleaning lady came in and said the middle eight's too long I'd check it out. If
I do that with the cleaning lady, I do it even more so with the people I'm
working with. They have an enormous input into what I do, and the choice of
who I work with has a huge effect on the quality of the records I turn out. The
better the people I work with, the better the records. So they do affect my work,
particularly the people in the control room. There are only certain people I can
put up with and only certain people can take the pace. It's a grinding pace
sometimes, you know, 14, 15, 16 hours a day, day after day after day, on maybe
one song. It can give some people nervous breakdowns. Other people love it.
You have to find the people and hang on to them. Even then they only last a
couple of years, then they leave and try to get a life somewhere else.

T.W.   How do artistic decisions come about in the studio?

T.H.   Try never to decide, try never to make a decision. Try and make the
decisions make themselves because if the decision doesn't make itself then
you're just taking an option. Should the rhythm track be like this or like that? If
you don't know, then you're just selecting an option. Whereas if the decision
makes itself, well, it's obvious it should be this one. Because this one's simple
and you can hear the reverb and we can put repeats on this, everything works.
Whereas that one's busy and doesn't quite fit. The decisions should make
themselves, as much as possible.

   The minute you start making decisions in a kind of dictatorial way – 'we're
going to have this because this is what I want' – then everybody starts to close
down and starts to do what you want. It stops being fun, you're no longer
working together. With music, people respond. Somebody plays something and
everybody goes 'great!' and starts jumping round. And that's what you're hoping
to communicate with the record.

*T.W.   What would you say are the essential characteristics of a recording
produced by Trevor Horn?*

T.H.   It has an interesting arrangement. It shifts perspective at some point so
that it draws you in and takes you on a little journey. That's the sort of idea: it
engages you while it lasts. But on the other hand you could still just ignore it and
do the housework, or drive if you were listening to it in the car. That's really it,
you know, the arrangement's interesting. And the chords are not necessarily the
most obvious chords. There's some nice musical stuff in there, I try and put
some nice music in.

T.W.   Which of your recordings are you most proud of? And what is it about them that you most like?

T.H.   I don't often listen to them after they're done. But then, sometimes I do have a kind of binge if I'm feeling miserable. If something I'm working on isn't working, I go back and listen to a few things that did work. In fact, I'm lucky to find so many that I like when I go back. Some of them are a bit odd. You mentioned *Slave to the Rhythm*, I always liked the track that came out as a single. I always thought it was particularly good. The first Seal album also had some great stuff on it, and lovely moments partly because of the way it came together. In places, in studios, out in Los Angeles for example, things happened. There's an acoustic track on the first Seal album called 'Whirlpool' which is just Seal and Wendy and Lisa and a couple of overdubs. Making that track was like living in a Robert Heinlein book when we did it, it was a great time. So I like that one a lot. Some of the ones I had terrible struggles with, I listen back to them and try to remember. 'Boy! I was really miserable with this and I had a tough time with it but it sounds OK. What were we all getting mad about?' All in all, I like a lot of them.

T.W.   What are the most important attributes to becoming and remaining a successful pop music record producer?

T.H.   You've got to be prepared to work like a dog. You've got to have lots of luck and you've got to keep looking over your shoulder. Keep looking in your wing mirrors to see who's coming up behind you and what they're doing. Make sure that you don't get stuck somewhere along the way, in any kind of little eddy, making one kind of record. I've only just recovered from that, really. It happened with the old superstars in America. I think staying in England is fairly important. In America you'll have so many people up your rear end, you won't know which way's up.

T.W.   Which producers do you admire?

T.H.   I always used to admire George Martin. Then in the 1970s I really liked Gus Dudgeon, I thought he was great. I loved 10cc. Funnily enough one of the guys is my big friend now: Lol Creme. I always loved their productions – 'I'm not in Love', for example. To be perfectly honest, I never much cared for Phil Spector, I always thought he overdid it. I mean, I know I have myself but … Then in the 1980s I had a lot of respect for Mutt Langer because I always thought that he got great results, even if he murdered the artist in the process. And right now it's the rap kids. They make amazing records, amazing sounding records. I hate the content but I like the records.

T.W.   In spite of their contribution to recordings, producers tend to remain relatively anonymous to the record-buying public. Would you like greater public acknowledgement for your work?

T.H.   For a producer, I've had a lot of public acknowledgement of my work. I've got no complaints. Inside the business that I operate in, I'm pretty well known. That's what's important to me because that's what gets me access to work and studio time, and the rest.

Views on pop music in general

T.W.   Is pop music a fundamentally technological art form?
T.H.   Yeah. That's a fascinating question. In a lot of respects, even though the classical – you know the straight music people – might fancy themselves, we've got them fucking licked, they've been licked for yonks really! They're nowhere, they peaked around the turn of the century and in the twenties, and since then they've been history, they've just been crap. Their stuff's just got more and more out there and it's just rubbish. John Cage and that stuff – I mean piss off! For an electronic record that had content and also had a kind of relevance, the Human League wiped the floor with them back in the 1980s. I'm sorry, that's a pretty sweeping statement!

This thing that we call pop music is an incredibly exciting thing. Obviously it's also a huge business. Somebody said to me the other day: 'There's no limits to consumption, but only a limit to creativity.' Other people argue that there's no limit to creativity, there's only limit to consumption.

Is it fundamentally a technological art form? You know, I've got an awful feeling that to some degree it is, because it's whatever technological invention is amusing people at a particular point in time. At the turn of the century, if somebody came over with a squeeze-box or a barrel-organ, the barrel-organ was a bit of a vibe for a few weeks and so was the squeeze box. Then everybody bought squeeze-boxes. If you worked on a farm five centuries ago and then you got to go to the cathedral on a Sunday and you heard the choir – wow! – that must have been like nothing in the whole world to you.

T.W.   Should pop music be viewed simply as an ephemeral art form? Should there be some attempt at preserving pop music?
T.H.   I imagine we're going to be doing a lot of those kind of things over the next couple of hundred years. There's going to be the most incredible archive of stuff available to people, and people are going to start diving back into it. Just the fact that you're doing this is such a surprise. How could I not give you an hour of time if you're going to spend this amount of time doing something like that. So I think certain things will be of interest to people. Pop music is like anything, loads of it is disposable, but some things you're going to keep. I don't imagine myself as Beethoven, but there might be one thing out of everything that I've done that somebody still listens to in 50 years' time. It would be nice if there was. That's about as much as I could hope for.

T.W. Is there such a thing as the beautiful in pop music?
T.H.   Beautiful is a song like 'Protection', a song that says loads of things without saying them directly. A song that gives you faith in life. That's what's beautiful in pop music.

T.W. Is there something particular about British pop music?
T.H.   Yes. It's because none of us are very good and so we have to work desperately hard to make something interesting, whereas Americans are really good a lot of the time. It's this concept that we've got the best bad musicians in the world and the Americans have the best good musicians.

Queries

T.W. In the early days of ZTT, how did it come about that bands or solo artists got signed? Was there any underlying philosophy?
T.H.   No, chaos. That was all.

T.W. Was playing in a band that specialized in disco (Tina Charles) an important influence?
T.H.   Tina was a very important influence. I never played on any of her recordings but I got to go on *Top of the Pops* and hang out and watch how it worked. It focused me. I got to meet her producer – one very rarely meets a producer – and know him a little. I heard some of his work in progress. It was a guy called Biddu, and I learned some very important lessons from listening to his backing tracks.

T.W. Did your work with Yes influence Adventures in Modern Recording *(The Buggles second album)?*
T.H.   *Adventures in Modern Recording* is a kind of blueprint for most of the records I made in the next eight to ten years. Terrible songs but a good record. I used tricks from it because it was just loads of tricks. Yes did influence it because I fancied myself as a bit of a singer on *Adventures in Modern Recording*.

T.W. Drama *and* 90125 *(by Yes) are very different albums – what brought these significant changes about?*
T.H.   In *Drama* I was a singer and with *90125* it was back to being real professionals. *Drama* was a joke, it was one of those mad experiences: to join Yes and go and do Madison Square Garden in front of 26 000 people, pretending to be Jon Anderson when I'd been a fan for 10 years. It's the kind of experience that really gave me so much juice in the early 1980s because when I came off that I was fearless. Nobody could intimidate me because I'd played Madison Square Garden.

T.W.   Was working with Malcolm McLaren influential?
T.H.   Enormously. We hardly sold any records in reality, but I came out at the end of it with so much. I got more from that one album with him than from working with any other artist.

T.W.   Slave to the Rhythm seems to be a kind of culmination of your work up to that point – do you see it like this?
T.H.   Yes, it was the end of an era, I calmed down after that. I had to get a bit more sensible. I was the most famous record producer in the world at that particular point. The fact that *Slave to the Rhythm* didn't get to number one everywhere was the beginning of a certain kind of decline. Which is a bit of a relief sometimes, you know.

(Interview conducted at Sarm West Studios on 8 November 1996)

Appendix 2

Trevor Horn Discography

Trevor Horn

Key   Quotation marks: 7-inch single (for example, 'Video Killed the Radio Star')

        Italic: album (for example, *The Age of Plastic*)

Trevor Horn has three times won BPI Producer of the Year in 1983, 1985 and 1991 (nominated 1982, 1984, 1986, 1987, 1988, 1992, 1994); Radio One Award for Contribution to Pop Music 1984; Ivor Novello Award for Best Recorded Record for 'Owner of a Lonely Heart' 1983, Best Contemporary Song for 'Relax' 1984, Most Performed Work for 'Two Tribes' 1984 and Best Contemporary Song and International Hit of the Year for 'Crazy' 1991; BMI Award for 'Owner of a Lonely Heart' 1984; Grammy Award for Best Instrumental for *90125* and Record of the Year for 'Kiss from a Rose' 1996; Q Magazine Award for Best Producer 1991; Music Week Award for Best Producer 1991. In addition, Trevor Horn has had simultaneous number one records on both sides of the Atlantic with different songs, namely 'Relax' (UK) and 'Owner of a Lonely Heart' (USA). His producer credits include:

The Buggles	'Video Killed the Radio Star' No. 1 single
	Age of Plastic
	Adventures in Modern Recording
Dollar	*The Dollar Album* Top 20 album and singles
ABC	*Lexicon of Love* No. 1 album and Top 10 singles including 'Look of Love' and 'Poison Arrow'
Malcolm McLaren	*Duck Rock* Top 20 album and Top 10 singles including 'Buffalo Gals' and 'Double Dutch'
Art of Noise, The	*(Who's Afraid of) The Art of Noise* Top 30 album and singles including 'Moments in Love' and 'Close (to the Edit)'
Yes	*90125* album and singles including US No. 1 'Owner of a Lonely Heart'
Propaganda	*A Secret Wish* Top 20 album and Top 30 singles including 'Duel' and 'Dr Mabuse'
Band Aid	'Do They Know It's Christmas' original 12-inch mix

Frankie Goes to Hollywood	*Welcome to the Pleasuredome* No. 1 album and three No. 1 singles 'Relax', 'Two Tribes' and 'The Power of Love'
Grace Jones	*Slave to the Rhythm* Top 15 album and single
Godley and Creme	'Cry' Top 20 single
Pet Shop Boys	'Left to my Own Devices' and 'It's Alright' Top 5 singles
Simple Minds	*Street Fighting Years* No. 1 album and 'Belfast Child' No. 1 single
Paul McCartney	*Flowers in the Dirt* No. 1 album (four tracks)
David Coverdale	'Last Note of Freedom' for original soundtrack of *Days of Thunder*
Marc Almond	'Jacky' Top 20 single and 'Days of Pearly Spencer' Top 5 single
	Tenement Symphony (five tracks)
Rod Stewart	'Downtown Train' and 'Tom Traubert's Blues' Top 10 singles and 'Rhythm of My Heart' Top 3 single
	A Spanner in the Works Top 10 album
Mike Oldfield	*Tubular Bells II* No. 1 album
Seal	*Seal* No. 1 album and the singles 'Crazy', 'Future Love Paradise' and 'The Beginning'
	Seal II No. 1 album and the singles 'Kiss From a Rose' (US No. 1) and 'Prayer For The Dying'
Toys	Original soundtrack album
Shane McGowan and Sinead O'Connor	'Haunted'
Shane McGowan and Maire Brennan	'You're the One' (theme from *Circle of Friends*)
Eddi Reader	'Nobody Lives without Love' from US No.1 *Batman* original soundtrack album
Tom Jones	'If I Only Knew' Top 10 single
Cher	*It's a Man's World* (three tracks)
Wendy and Lisa	'This Is the Life' from US No. 1 *Dangerous Minds* original soundtrack album
Tina Turner	*Wildest Dreams* Top 5 album (eight tracks) including the singles 'Whatever You Want' and 'On Silent Wings'
Sting and Pato Banton	'Spirits in the Material World' for *Ace Ventura II* original soundtrack album
Gabrielle	'Forget about the World' Top 20 single
The Frames DC	Tracks from the forthcoming album *Fitzcaraldo*
Public Demand	Track for first single release 'Invisible'
Brian Ferry	'Dance with Life' for soundtrack of film *Phenomenon*

Aka   Track for forthcoming album
Boyzone   'A Different Beat' – forthcoming single
Gary Barlow   Tracks for forthcoming album

(Discography supplied by Sarm Productions on 8 November 1996)

Discography

Key   Quotation marks: 7-inch single (for example, 'Video Killed the Radio Star')
         Italic: album (for example, *The Age of Plastic*)

ABC, 1981: 'Tears Are Not Enough' (Neutron NT101)
ABC, 1982: 'Poison Arrow' (Neutron NT102)
ABC, 1982: 'The Look of Love' (Neutron NT103)
ABC, 1982: *The Lexicon of Love* (Neutron NTRS 1)
ABC, 1982: 'All of My Heart' (Neutron NT104)
Act, 1988: *Laughter, Tears & Rage* (ZTT ZQCD 1)
Almond, Marc, 1991: 'Jacky' (Some Bizzare YZ610)
Almond, Marc, 1991: *Tenement Symphony* (Some Bizzare WX442)
Almond, Marc, 1992: 'My Hand over My Heart' (Some Bizzare YZ633)
Almond, Marc, 1992: 'The Days of Pearly Spencer' (Some Bizzare YZ638)
Art of Noise, The, 1984: 'Close (to the Edit)' (ZTT ZTPS 01)
Art of Noise, The, 1984: *Who's Afraid of ...* (ZTT 4509-94746-2)
Art of Noise, The, 1984: 'Daft' (ZTT 4509-94747-2)
Art of Noise, The, 1985: 'Moments in Love'/'Beat Box' (ZTT ZTPS 02)
Art of Noise, The, 1988: *The Best of The Art of Noise* (China WOLCD 1010)
Buggles, 1979: 'Video Killed the Radio Star' (Island WIP 6524)
Buggles, 1980: 'The Plastic Age' (Island WIP 6540)
Buggles, 1980: *The Age of Plastic* (Island ILPS 9585)
Buggles, 1980: 'Clean Clean' (Island WIP 6584)
Buggles, 1980: 'Elstree' (Island WIP 6624)
Buggles, (1981) 1993: *Adventures in Modern Recording* (JICK-89266)
Dollar, 1992: *Dollar – The Collection* (Castle CCSCD 320)
Frankie Goes to Hollywood, 1983: 'Relax' (ZTT ZTAS 1)
Frankie Goes to Hollywood, 1984: 'The Power of Love' (ZTT ZTAS 5)
Frankie Goes to Hollywood, 1984: 'Two Tribes' (ZTT ZTAS 3)
Frankie Goes to Hollywood, 1984: *Welcome to the Pleasuredome* (ZTT ZTTIQ 1)
Frankie Goes to Hollywood, 1985: 'Welcome to the Pleasuredome' (ZTT ZTAS 7)
Frankie Goes to Hollywood, 1986: *Liverpool* (ZTTIQ 8)
Frankie Goes to Hollywood, 1986: 'Rage Hard' (ZTT ZTAS 22)
Godley and Creme, 1985: *The History Mix Volume 1* (Polydor 825 981-2)
Jones, Grace, 1981: *Nightclubbing* (Island ILPS 9624)
Jones, Grace, 1985: 'Slave to the Rhythm' (ZTT IS 206)
Jones, Grace, 1985: *Slave to the Rhythm* (ZTT GRACE 1)
McLaren, Malcolm, 1982: 'Buffalo Gals' (Charisma MALC 1)
McLaren, Malcolm, 1983: 'Soweto' (Charisma MALC 2)
McLaren, Malcolm, 1983: *Duck Rock* (Charisma MMLP 1)
McLaren, Malcolm, 1983: 'Double Dutch' (Charisma MALC 3)
McLaren, Malcolm, 1983: 'Duck for the Oyster' (Charisma MALC 4)

McLaren, Malcolm, 1989: *Waltz Darling* (Epic 460736 1)

McLaren, Malcolm, 1990: *Malcolm McLaren Presents The World Famous Supreme Team Show – Round the Outside! Round the Outside!* (Virgin CDV 2646)

Oldfield, Mike, 1992: *Tubular Bells II* (WEA 4509906182)

Pet Shop Boys, 1988: *Introspective* (Parlophone PCS 7325)

Propaganda, 1984: 'Dr Mabuse' (ZTT ZTAS 2)

Propaganda, 1985: *A Secret Wish* (ZTT ZTTIQ 3)

Propaganda, 1985: 'Duel' (ZTT ZTAS 8)

Propaganda, 1985: *Wishful Thinking* (ZTT1Q 20)

Propaganda, 1985: 'P Machinery' (ZTT ZTAS 12)

Seal, 1990: 'Crazy' (ZTT ZANG 8)

Seal, 1991: *Seal* (ZTT 9031-74557-2)

Seal, 1991: 'Future Love EP' (ZTT ZANG 11)

Seal, 1991: 'The Beginning' (ZTT ZANG 21)

Seal, 1991: 'Killer' (EP)(ZTT ZANG 23)

Seal, 1992: 'Violet' (ZTT ZANG 27)

Seal, 1994: *Seal II* (ZTT 4509-96256-2)

Simple Minds, 1989: 'Belfast Child' (Virgin SMX3)

Simple Minds, 1991: 'Let There Be Love' (Virgin VS 1332)

Simple Minds, 1991: 'See the Lights' (Virgin VS 1343)

Simple Minds, 1992: *Glittering Prize '81–'92* (Virgin SMTVD 1)

Spandau Ballet, 1982: 'Instinction' (Chrysalis CHS 2602)

Spandau Ballet, 1991: *The Best of Spandau Ballet* (Chrysalis CDP 3218942)

Turner, Tina, 1996: *Wildest Dreams* (Parlophone 7243 8 37684 2 4)

Yes, 1972: *Close to the Edge* (Atlantic K 50736)

Yes, 1980: *Drama* (Atlantic K 50012)

Yes, 1983: 'Owner of a Lonely Heart' (Acto B 9817)

Yes, 1983: *90125* (Atco 790125)

Yes, 1984: 'Leave It' (Atco B 9787)

Yes, 1987: *Big Generator* (Atco 7567-90522-2)

Bibliography

Abbott, K. (2001), *The Beach Boys Pet Sounds*, London: Helter Skelter Publishing.

Adorno, T. (1990), 'On Popular Music', in S. Frith and A. Goodwin (eds), *On Record: Rock, Pop and the Written Word*, London: Routledge.

Agawu, V.K. (1991), *Playing with Signs – a Semiotic Interpretation of Classic Music*, Princeton: Princeton University Press.

Angilette, E. (1992), *Philosopher at the Keyboard: Glenn Gould*, London: The Scarecrow Press.

Apel, W. (1970), *Harvard Dictionary of Music*, London: Heinemann Educational Books.

Armbruster, G. (1984), *The Art of Electronic Music*, New York: GPI Publications.

Barber, L. (1984), 'Horn of plenty', *Melody Maker*, 3 November.

Barnard, S. (1989), *On the Radio: Music Radio in Britain*, Milton Keynes: Open University Press.

Barr, T. (1998), *Kraftwerk – from Dusseldorf to the Future (with Love)*, London: Ebury Press.

Barthes, R. (1982), *Camera Lucida*, trans. R. Howard, London: Jonathan Cape.

Beadle, J.R. (1993), *Will Pop Eat Itself?* London: Faber and Faber.

Bellos, A. (1995), 'Law or no law, youth keeps dancing as raves become big business', *Guardian*, 6 May.

Benjamin, W. (1970), 'The Work of Art in the Age of Mechanical Reproduction', trans. H. Zohn, *Illuminations*, London: Jonathan Cape. Originally published in *Zeitschrift für Sozialforschung*, **5** (1) in 1936.

Blake, A. (1992), *The Music Business*, London: B.T. Batsford, Batsford Cultural Studies Series.

Blaukopf, K. (1992), *Musical Life in a Changing Society*, trans. D. Marinelli, Portland, OR: Amadeus Press.

Borwick, J. (1990), *Microphones – Technology and Technique*, London: Focal Press.

Boulez, P. (1986), 'Technology and the Composer', in S. Emmerson (ed.), *The Language of Electroacoustic Music*, London: Macmillan.

Boulez, P. (1990), *Orientations*, trans. M. Cooper, London: Faber and Faber.

Bracewell, M. (1998), *England is Mine – Pop Life in Albion from Wilde to Goldie*, London: Flamingo.

British Phonographic Industry (BPI) (1997), *BPI Statistical Handbook*, London: BPI.

Buskin, R. (1994), 'From ABC to ZTT – the Amazing Career of Trevor Horn, *Sound On Sound*, **9** (10).

Bussy, P. (1993), *Kraftwerk – Man, Machine and Music*, Wembley: SAF Publishing.

Cage, J. (1968), *A Year from Monday*, London: Marion Boyars.

Capel, V. (1991), *Newnes Audio and Hi-fi Engineer's Pocket Book*, Oxford: Butterworth-Heinemann.

Chanan, M. (1994), *Musica Practica – The Social Practice of Western Music from Gregorian Chant to Postmodernism*, London: Verso.

Chanan, M. (1995), *Repeated Takes – a Short History of Recording and Its Effects on Music*, London: Verso.

Chion, M. (1994), *Audio-Vision – Sound on Screen*, ed. and trans. C. Gorbman, New York: Columbia University Press.

Cloonan, M. (1996), *Banned! Censorship of Popular Music in Britain: 1967–92*, Aldershot: Arena.

Copeland, P. (1991), *Sound Recordings*, London: The British Library.

Corach, J. and Boone, G.M. (eds) (1997), *Understanding Rock. Essays in Musical Analysis*, Oxford: Oxford University Press.

Culshaw, J. (1981), *Putting the Record Straight*, London: Secker and Warburg.

Cunningham, M. (1996), *Good Vibrations – a History of Record Production*, Chessington: Castle Communications.

Eisenberg, E. (1988), *The Recording Angel: Music, Records and Culture from Aristotle to Zappa*, London: Pan Books.

Eisler, H. and Adorno, T. (1947) *Composing For The Films*, Oxford: Oxford University Press.

Emmerson, S. (ed.) (1986), *The Language of Electroacoustic Music*, London: Macmillan.

Eno, B. (1996), *A Year With Swollen Appendices*, London: Faber and Faber.

Everest, E.A. (1994), *The Master Handbook of Acoustics*, New York: TAB Books.

Fitzgerald, H. (1985), 'The dream academy', *Melody Maker*, 6 July.

Frith, S. (1983), 'Popular Music 1950–1980' in G. Martin (ed.), *Making Music*, London: Pan Books.

Frith, S. (1987), 'Towards an Aesthetic of Popular Music', in R. Leppart and S. McClary, *Music and Society*, Cambridge: Cambridge University Press.

Frith, S. (1988), *Music for Pleasure*, Cambridge: Polity Press.

Frith, S. (1990), *Facing the Music*, London: Mandarin.

Frith, S. (1996), *Performing Rites*, Oxford: Oxford University Press.

Frith, S. and Goodwin, A. (eds) (1990), *On Record: Rock, Pop and the Written Word*, London: Routledge.

Frith, S. and Horne, H. (1987), *Art into Pop*, London: Routledge.

Frith, S., Straw, W. and Street, J. (eds) (2001), *The Cambridge Companion to Pop and Rock*, Cambridge: Cambridge University Press.

Gambaccini, P., Rice, J. and Rice, T. (1993), *British Hit Singles*, 9th edn, Enfield: Guinness Publishing.

Gambaccini, P., Rice, J. and Rice, T. (1994a), *British Hit Albums*, 6th edn, Enfield: Guinness Publishing.

Gambaccini, P., Rice, J. and Rice, T. (1994b), *The Guinness Book of Number One Hits*, 3rd edn, Enfield: Guinness Publishing.

Gates Jr., Henry Louis (1988), *The Signifying Monkey: A Theory of African-American Literary Criticism*, Oxford: Oxford University Press.

Gelatt, R. (1984), *The Fabulous Phonograph 1877–1977*, London: Cassell.

Gillett, C. (1980), 'The Producer as Artist', in H.W. Hitchcock (ed.), *The Phonograph and Our Musical Life – Proceedings of a Centennial Conference 7–10 December 1977*, New York: Institute for Studies in American Music, Department of Music, School of Performing Arts, Brooklyn College of Music, School of Performing Arts, Brooklyn College of the University of New York.

Gillett, C. and Frith, S. (eds) (1996), *The Beat Goes On – The Rock File Reader*, London: Pluto Press.

Glaister, D. (1995), 'Rap on the knuckles', *Guardian*, 10 June.

Goodwin, A. (1993), *Dancing in the Distraction Factory: Music Television and Popular Culture*, London: Routledge.

Gorbman, C. (1987), *Unheard Melodies: Narrative Film Music*, London: British Film Institute Press.

Gould, G. (1987), *The Glenn Gould Reader*, ed. T. Page, London: Faber and Faber.

Gracyk, T. (1996), *Rhythm and Noise – an Aesthetics of Rock*, London: Duke University Press.

Griffiths, P. (1979), *A Guide to Electronic Music*, London: Thames and Hudson.

Gronow, P. and Saunio, I. (1999), *An International History of the Recording Industry*, trans. C. Moseley, London: Cassell.

Hadsley, N. (1992), 'Rule of the technocrats', *Guardian*, 25 July.

Hamm, C. (1995), *Putting Popular Music in its Place*, Cambridge: Cambridge University Press.

Hanks, P. (ed.) (1986), *Collins English Dictionary*, 2nd edn, London: William Collins.

Hardy, P. and Laing, D. (eds) (1990), *The Faber Companion to 20th-Century Popular Music*, London: Faber and Faber.

Hayward, P. (ed.) (1990), *Culture, Technology and Creativity in the Late Twentieth Century*, London: John Libbey.

Hebdige, D. (1979), *Subculture: The Meaning of Style*, London: Routledge.

Hennion, A. (1990), 'The Creative Process', in S. Frith and A. Goodwin (eds), *On Record: Rock, Pop and the Written Word*, London: Routledge.

Heylin, C. (ed.) (1993), *The Penguin Book of Rock & Roll Writing*, London: Penguin Books.

Hitchcock, H.W. (ed.) (1980), *The Phonograph and Our Musical Life – Proceedings of a Centennial Conference 7–10 December 1977*, New York: Institute for Studies in American Music, Department of Music, School of Performing Arts, Brooklyn College of Music, School of Performing Arts, Brooklyn College of the City University of New York.

Hughes, W. (1994), 'In the Empire of the Beat', in A. Ross and T. Rose (eds), *Black Noise: Rap Music and Black Culture in Contemporary America*, Hanover, NH: Wesleyan University Press.

Johnson, H. (1995), *A Bone in my Flute*, London: Arrow Books.

Jones, S. (1992), *Rock Formation – Music, Technology, and Mass Communication*, London: Sage Publications.

Kempster, C. (ed.) (1996), *History of House*, London: Music Maker Publications.

Kramer, J.D. (1988), *The Time of Music*, New York: Schirmer Books.

Lanza, J. (1995), *Elevator Music*, London: Quartet Books.

Larkin, C. (ed.) (1993), *The Guinness Encyclopedia of Popular Music*, concise edn, London: Guinness Publishing.

Leppart, R. (1988), *Music and Image*, Cambridge: Cambridge University Press.

Leppart, R. and McClary, S. (1987), *Music and Society*, Cambridge: Cambridge University Press.

Levarie, S. and Levy, E. (1983), *Musical Morphology – a Discourse and a Dictionary*, Kent, OH: Kent State University Press.

Lipsitz, G. (1994), *Dangerous Crossroads*, London: Verso.

Longhurst, B. (1995), *Popular Music and Society*, Cambridge: Polity Press.

Mackay, A. (1981), *Electronic Music*, Oxford: Phaidon Press.

Manuel, P. (1991), 'The cassette industry and popular music in North India', *Popular Music*, **10** (2).

Martin, G. (ed.) (1983), *Making Music*, London: Pan Books.

Martin, G. (1995): *Summer of Love – the Making of Sgt Pepper*, London: Pan Books.

Massey, H. (2000): *Behind the Glass – Top Record Producers Tell How They Craft the Hits*, San Francisco: Backbeat Books.

McLuhan, M. (1964), *Understanding Media – the Extensions of Man*, London: Routledge and Kegan Paul.

Middleton, R. (1990), *Studying Popular Music*, Milton Keynes: Open University Press.

Middleton, R. (ed.) (2000), *Reading Pop – Approaches to Textual Analysis in Popular Music*, Oxford: Oxford University Press.

Moore, A.F. (1993), *Rock: The Primary Text*, Milton Keynes: Open University Press.

Morrison, J. (2002), 'Pop stars claw back their lives from music label moguls', *Independent on Sunday*, 13 January.

Morse, T. (1996), *Yes Stories – Yes In Their Own Words*, New York: St. Martin's Press.

Mott, R.L. (1990), *Sound Effects*, London: Focal Press.

Murray, C.S. (1991), *Shots from the Hip*, London: Penguin Books.

Nattiez, J.-J. (1990), *Music and Discourse – Toward a Semiology of Music*, trans. C. Abbate, Oxford: Princeton University Press.

Negus, K. (1992), *Producing Pop – Culture and Conflict in the Popular Music Industry*, London: Edward Arnold.

Oliver, P. (ed.) (1990), *Black Music in Britain*, Milton Keynes: Open University Press.

Olsen, E., Verna, P. and Wolff, C. (1999), *The Encyclopedia of Record Producers*, New York: Watson-Guptill Publications.

Paynter, J., Howell, T., Orton, R., Seymour, P. (eds) and 'Introduction' by Mellers, W. (1992), *A Companion to Contemporary Musical Thought*, London: Routledge.

Payzant, G. (1978), *Glenn Gould – Music and Mind*, Toronto: Van Nostrand Reinhold.

Potter, R.A. (1995), *Spectacular Vernaculars*, Albany, NY: State University of New York.

Read, O. and Welch, W. (1959), *From Tin Foil to Stereo*, Indianapolis, IN: Howard W. Sams.

Rogan, J. (1989), *Starmakers and Svengalis*, London: Futura Publications.

Rose, T. (1994), *Black Noise: Rap Music and Black Culture in Contemporary America*, Hanover, NH: Wesleyan University Press.

Ross, A. and Rose, T. (eds) (1994), *Microphone Fiends: Youth Music and Youth Culture*, New York: Routledge.

Rumsey, F. (1990), *MIDI Systems and Control*, Oxford: Focal Press.

Rumsey, F. and McCormick, T. (1994), *Sound and Recording – an Introduction*, Oxford: Focal Press.

Russolo, L. (1986), *The Art of Noises*, New York: Pendragon Press.

Said, E.W. (1991), *Musical Elaborations*, London: Vintage Press.

Savage, J. (1996), *Time Travel – Pop, Media and Sexuality 1976–96*, London: Chatto and Windus.

Schwarzkopf, E. (1982), *On and Off the Record – a Memoir of Walter Legge*, London: Faber and Faber.

Slawson, W. (1985), *Sound Color*, Berkeley, CA: University of California Press.

Slobin, M. (1993), *Subcultural Sounds – Micromusics of the West*, Hanover, NH: Wesleyan University Press.

Spencer, N. (1996), Review of *Wildest Dreams*, *Observer*, 31 March.

Stanley, B. (1995), 'Viva la Europop', *Guardian*, 17 June.

Stockhausen, K. (1989) *Stockhausen on Music – Lectures and Interviews*, comp. R. Maconie, London: Marion Boyars.

Stravinsky, I. (1942), *Poetics of Music*, trans A. Knodel and I. Dahl, Cambridge, MA: Harvard University Press.

Strinati, D. (1995), *An Introduction to the Theories of Popular Culture*, London: Routledge.

Sutherland, S. (1985), 'Slave trade', *Melody Maker*, 2 November.

Tagg, P. (1991), *Fernando the Flute*, research report Liverpool: Institute of Popular Music.

Tamm, E. (1995), *Brian Eno – His Music and the Vertical Color of Sound*, New York: Da Capo Press.

Théberge, P. (1997), *Any Sound You Can Imagine – Making Music/Consuming Technology*, Hanover, NH: Wesleyan University Press.

Valéry, P. (1964), 'The Conquest of Ubiquity', trans. R. Manheim, in *Aesthetics*, New York: Pantheon Books.

Vulliamy, G. and Lee, E. (1976), *Pop Music in Schools*, London: Cambridge University Press.

Wallis, R. and Malm, K. (1990), 'Patterns of Change', in S. Frith and A. Goodwin (eds), *On Record: Rock, Pop and the Written Word*, London: Routledge.

Ward, P. (1995), 'Working in the Digital Domain', *Studio Sound*, November.

Warner, S. (1996), *Rockspeak! The Language of Rock and Pop*, London: Blandford.

White, A.L. (ed.) (1987), *Lost in Music: Culture, Style and the Musical Event*, London: Routledge and Kegan Paul, Sociological Review Monograph 34.

Whiteley, S. (1992), *The Space Between the Notes*, London: Routledge.

Winder, A. (1985), 'Propaganda', *Melody Maker*, 2 November.

Wishart, T. (1985), *On Sonic Art*, York: Imagineering Press.

Wishart, T. (1994), *Audible Design*, York: Opheus the Pantomime.

Wolff, J. (1987), '…', in R. Leppert and S. McClary, *Music and Society*, Cambridge: Cambridge University Press.

Zak III, A.J. (2001), *The Poetics of Rock – Cutting Records, Making Tracks*, London: University of California Press.

Zappa, F. with P. Occhiogrosso, (1989), *The Real Frank Zappa Book*, London: Pan Books.

Index

100 Greatest Number 1 Hits, The
    (television programme) 141
10cc 153
1984 (book) 109
90125 **62–74**, 76, 101, 141, 156
ABC 50
'Abzug' 115
Adam and the Ants 51, 61n
Adorno, Theodore xi–xii, 42
Adventures in Modern Recording 38n, 50,
    60n, 155
Age of Plastic, The 43, 48n, 50, 141
Air Studios 65, 101
Akai 24
Albee, Edward 93
Almond, Mark 122n, 142
AMS 101
'And You And I' 66
Anderson, Jon 62, 63, 64, 66, 67, 71, 156
Anderson, Laurie 100
Archies, The 79
Arp 29
Art of Noise, The xiv, 10, 60–61n, 70, 75,
    91–105, 110, 125, 129, 130, 139, 141
Art of Noises, The (Futurist Manifesto) 76,
    92–93
Atari 25
Atom Heart Mother 69
'Axel F' 107

'Baker Street' 7
Ballad of the Streets EP 122n
Ballard, J.G. 48n
Band Aid 106
Banks, Pete 62
Barraud, Francis 42
Barthes, Roland 42, 53, 110
Battery Studios 76
Bauhaus (pop group) 90n
Bay City Rollers, The 90n
BBC (radio and television) 12, 14, 15,
    82–3, 88, 90n

'Beat Box' 104n
Beatles, The 8
'Belfast Child' 122n
Below the Waste 93
Benjamin, Walter xii–xiii, 41, 48n
Berio, Luciano 63
Biddu 155
Big Generator 63
Birch, David 60n
Birchfield, Joel 56
Blackwell, Chris 125, 126
Blockheads, The 80
Boulez, Pierre 10, 17n, 97, 140
Bow Wow Wow 51, 54, 61n
Bowie, David 124
Brave New World (book) 109
Bremner, Rory 121n
British Board of Film Censors 82
Brown, Chuck 143
Brown, James 84, 105n, 129
Brüchen, Claudia 108, 110–11
Bruford, Bill 62, 63, 66
'Buffalo Gals' xiv, **50–61**, 98, 139, 141
Buggles, The xiv, 8, 38n, **41–9**, 50, 60n,
    62, 114, 141
Burgess, Richard 48n

Cabaret Voltaire 90n
Cage, John 154
Cardin, Pierre 123
Carlos, Wendy 107
Casio 24
'Changes' 66
Channel Four 76, 83, 141
Chaplin, Charlie 109
Charles, Tina 48n, 155
'Chase, The' 111, 115
Cinema (pop group) 64
C-Lab *see Notator*
Clinton, George 84
'Close (to the Edit)' 100, 101
Close to the Edge 62, 63, 66, 69, 74n, 101

'Close to the Edge' 66
Collins, Phil 24
Commentators, The 121n
Computer World 122n
Consolidated Talking Machine Company 42
Copeland, Stewart 114
'Crazy' 90n, 108
Creme, Lol 153
'Crossing (ooh the action), The' 133
'Cry' 106
Cubase 25, 37n
Curved Air 114

Dada 51–52
Darlow, S. 38n
'Days of Pearly Spencer, The' 122n
Dean, Roger 65
Debussy 149
'Demolition Man' 137n
Depeche Mode 91
Derrida, Jacques 53
Disney, Walt 93, 104
'Do They Know It's Christmas?' 106
Dolby, Tom 60n
Dollar 50
'Don't Cry – It's Only the Rhythm' 133–4
'Don't Touch Me There' 127
Dorper, Ralph 108, 122n
'Double Dutch' 50, 54
Downes, Geoff 41, 48n, 62, 114
Dr Dre 149
'Dr Mabuse' 108, 110, 111, 115, 122n
Drama 50, 60n, 62, 65, 73, 156
'Dream Within a Dream' 111, 114
'Duck for the Oyster' 52, 54, 55
Duck Rock xiv, **50–61**, 141
Dudgeon, Gus 153
Dudley, Anne 60n, 91
'Duel' 110, 111, **115–22**, 128, 139, 141
Dunbar, Sly 38n, 125
Dury, Ian 80
DX7 130

East Tennessee Hilltopers 56
Eddy, Duane 92
Edison, Thomas 48n, 72

Egan, Nick 60n
Eisler, Hans 42
'El San Juanera' 53, 54
Emmerson, Lake and Palmer 63
EMT 145
E-Mu 24
Epstein, Brian 50
Eurovision Song Contest 109
Experience Unlimited 143

Fairlight 69, 70, 89, 91, 98, 101, 104, 105n, 122n, 129–30, 139, 144
Fantasia 104
Ford, Henry 109
Fragile 62
Frank Pourcel Plays Abba 107
Frankie Goes To Hollywood xiv, 10, **75–90**, 108, 110, 114, 123, 127, 141, 147
Freytag, Susan 108
'Frog and the Princess, The' 124, 125, 131, 138n
'Frozen Faces' 111
'Funky Drummer' 129

Gaskin, Barbara 107
Gastwirt, Joe 106
Genesis 63
Gerrie, Malcolm 76
'Give Me Back My Heart' 60n
Glitter, Gary 79
Glitterbest 51
Glittering Prize 142n
'God Save the Queen' 51, 61n, 83
Godley and Crème 79, 106, 142
Gordon Giltrap Band, The 114
Gore, Lesley 107
Goude, Jean-Paul 124, 135
Gould, Glenn 36, 38n
Grammy Award 152
Great Rock 'n' Roll Swindle, The (film) 51, 52
Greatest Synthesizer Hits 107
Gregory, Glenn 114

Haig, Paul 115
'Hand Held in Black and White' 60n
Hardcastle, Paul 59, 100, 105n, 121n

Haring, Keith 53
Heartfield, John 122n
'Here I Go Again' 124
Herrmann, Bernard 115
His Master's Voice (painting) 42
History Mix Volume 1, The 142n
Hitchcock, Alfred 115
*Hollyridge Strings Play Instrumental
    Versions of Hits Made Famous by
    Elvis Presley, The* 107
Howe, Steve 62, 63, 114
Human League, The 91
Huxley, Aldous 109

'I am a Camera' 60n
'I Need a Man' 124
'I Wish It Could be Christmas Everyday'
    122n
'I'm not in Love' 153
In No Sense? Nonsense 93
In Visible Silence 93
Internationale Situationniste 60n
Into Battle with The Art of Noise 93, 99
'Into the Lens' 60n
Introspective 142n
'It Can Happen' 66
Italian House 109
'It's my Party' 107
ITV 13
'I've Seen That Face Before (Libertango)'
    137n

Jeczalik, Jonathan 70, 80, 91, 101
'Jewel' 111, **115–22**, 128, 139
'Jewelled' **116–22**
Jive Bunny 122n
'Jive My Baby Jive' 54
Johnson, Holly 78, 79, 80, 88, 90n
'Jones the Rhythm' 38n, 131, 135
Jones, Grace xiv, 75, 38n, **123–38**, 141,
    147
Jones, Tom 92

Kawai 24
Kaye, Tony 62, 64, 67
Kirkendale, Allen L. 114
Korg 24

Kraftwerk 91, 104n, 105n, 115, 122n, 150
Kraushaar, Bob/Bobbie 113–14

Lang, Fritz 109
Langan, Gary 60n, 64, 91, 152
Langer, Mutt 154
'Legba' 53, 54
'Let There Be Love' 122n
Lexicon of Love (The) 50, 74n, 161
Linn drum 83, 122n, 144
Lipson, Steve 80, 81, 112, 113, 114, 118,
    122n, 126, 127, 136, 143, 145, 152
Little Richard 124
Living My Life 125
'Living on the Road in Soweto' 55

Mackie 146
McLaren, Malcolm xiv, 10, **50–61**, 127,
    141, 156
McLaren, Norman 104
McLuhan, Marshall 53
McShane, Ian 124, 135, 138n
*Malcolm McLaren Presents the World
    Famous Supreme Team Show –
    Round the Outside! Round the
    Outside!* 61n
Man Machine, The 104n, 122n, 150
'Mandela Day' 122n
Marillion 114
Marinetti 76
Martin, George 36, 153
Massive Attack 150
Max Headroom 100, 105n
Mayhew, Henry 56
Meek, Joe 36
Meier, Dieter 13
'Merengue' 54
Merleau-Ponty, Maurice 42
Mertens, Michael 108
'Metal Postcard' 122n
Metropolis (film) 109
Michael, George 6
Mills, Gordon 50
Minogue, Kylie 35
'Mirror, Mirror (Mon Amour)' 60n
Mix, The 122n
Modern Times (film) 109

'Momento' 100, 122n
'Moments in Love' 100, 130
Monkeys, The 3, 90n
Moog 144
Moraz, Patrick 62
Morley, Paul 75, 91, 104n, 110, 135
Morris, William 12
Mosely, Ian 114
MP3 (online music distribution) 6
MTV 13, 48
Mud 8
'Murder of Love, The' 111, 114–15
Musicians' Union, The 47
Musique concrète 30, 69, 95, 99

National Association of Music Merchants
    (NAMM) 37n
New England Digital (NED) *see*
    Synclavier
Nightclubbing 38n, 125, 137n
'Nineteen' 59, 100, 105n, 121n
'N-N-Nineteen Not Out' 121n
Notator 25

'O Superman' 100
Oasis 8
'Obatala' 54
Offord, Eddy 101
Oldfield, Mike 107, 142
'Operattack' 125, 130, 131, 132
Orbit, William 108, 122n
Orwell, George 109
'Owner of a Lonely Heart' xiv, **62–74**, 98,
    139, 141

'P Machinery' 109, 111, 115
Padgham, Hugh 24
'Paranoimia' 105n
Parker, Colonel Tom 50
Parnes, Larry 51
Peel, John 78
Penman, I. 126, 135
Père Ubu 90n
Pet Shop Boys 105n, 142, 161
Pete, Piute 56
Phantom of the Opera, The (musical and
    film) 94

Pink Floyd 63, 64, 69
'Pocket Calculator' 115
Poe, Edgar Allen 110
Police, The 114
Pop Idol (television programme) 13
Pop Stars (television programme) 13
'Power of Love, The' 77
Propaganda 75, **106–22**, 123, 128, 139,
    141, 161
'Protection' 150, 155
Psycho (film) 115
Public Enemy 61n, 105n
'Pull up to the Bumper' 137n
'Punk it Up' 54

Q: Are we not men? A: We are Devo! 107

Rabin, Trevor 62, 64, 66, 67, 73
Radioactivity 122n
Rafferty, Jerry 7
Read, Mike 83, 90n
Reagan, Ronald 79
Reed, Lou 83
Reid, Jamie 51
'Relax' xiv, 10, **75–90**, 98, 114, 127, 139,
    141, 144
Residents, The 92
Richards, Andy/Andrew 80, 114
Robinson, Paul 74n
'Robots, The' 115
Roland 24, 122n, 144
Rolling Stones, The 107
Ross, Malcolm 115
Rotten, Johnny 51
Russell, Tony 56
Russolo, Luigi 76, 90n, 92–3, 104n
Rutherford, Paul 78

'Satisfaction' 107
Schaeffer, Pierre 95
Scream, The 122n
Scritti Politti 91
Seal 90n, 108, 142, 142n, 152, 153, 161
Secret Wish, A **110–22**, 128, 141
*See Jungle! See Jungle! Go Join Your
    Gang Yeah, City All Over! Go Ape
    Crazy* 54

'See the Lights' 122n
Sequential Circuits 24
Sex Pistols, The 51, 54, 61n, 79, 83, 127
Shakespeare, Robbie 38n, 125
Shakin' Stevens 8, 123
'Siberian Khatru' 66
Sidebottom, Frank 92
Simple Minds 112, 142, 161
Sinatra, Frank 90n
Siouxsie and the Banshees 122n
Slave to the Rhythm xiv, 38n, 112, 113,
    123–38, 139, 141, 143, 145, 147, 156
'Slave to the Rhythm' 126, 131, 137n,
    141, 147
Smith, Bessie 74n
Smith, Dave 24
'Song for Chango' 54
Sony 143, 144
Sorrell, Jonathan 114
'Sorry for Laughing' 111, 115
Soul Searchers, The 143
'Sound Sweep, The ' (short story) 48n
Sousa, John Philip 41
'Soweto' 54
Spector, Phil 34, 36, 153
Squire, Chris 62, 64, 66, 67
Steinberg *see Cubase*
Stewart, Dave 107
Stockhausen, Karlheinz 63
Switched-On Bach 107
Sylvian, David 114
Synclavier 81, 113, 129–31, 134, 137n,
    144

Tales from the Topographic Oceans 64
'Tell Laura I Love Her' 90n
Temperance Seven, The 8
Tenement Symphony 122n, 142n
Thatcher, Margaret 78
Thein, A. 114
Three Little Pigs 93
Time and a Word 64
'Time to Fear (Who's Afraid), A' 99, 100,
    102
Top of the Pops (television programme)
    12–13, 14, 15, 83, 155
TR808 144

Tube, The (television programme) 76, 77,
    83, 148
Tubes, The 127
Tubular Bells II 107, 142n
Turner, Tina 74n, 142, 161
Twiggy 124
'Two Tribes' 76–7, 79, 81, 90n

Union 63

Valance, Rickie 90n
Valéry, Paul xiii
Vaughan, Frankie 90n
'Video Killed the Radio Star' xiv, 8, **41–9**,
    71, 92, 139, 141
'Videotheque' 60n
View to A Kill, A (film) 123
'Violet' 147

Wakeman, Rick 62, 63
'Walk on the Wild Side' 83
'Walking in the Rain' 137n
Walkman (Sony) 31
Wall, The 64
Warhol, Andy 14, 17n, 51, 76
Warm Leatherette 125
'Weeping Willow Blues' 74n
Welcome to the Pleasuredome 77, 112,
    141, 145
Westwood, Vivienne 51
'What's Love Got to Do with It' 74n
'Whirlpool' 153
White, Alan 62, 64, 67
Who's Afraid of The Art of Noise? **91–105**,
    106, 111, 122n
'Who's Afraid of the Big Bad Wolf?' 93
Who's Afraid of Virginia Woolf? (theatre
    play and film) 93
Wildest Dreams 142n
Wishful Thinking 111, **116–22**
Wizzard 122n
Wood, Roy 122n
Woolley, Bruce 38n, 126
World Famous Supreme Team, The 55
'World's Famous' 54

Yamaha 24, 130

Yes xiv, 50, 60–61n, **62–74**, 91, 101, 106,
    141, 151, 156, 161
Yes Album, The 62
Yessongs 62
'You Were Always on My Mind' 105n

Zance – A Decade of Dance from ZTT
    108, 122n
ZTT (Zang Tuum Tumb) 75–9, 81, 83, 88,
    90n, 91, 93, 103, 106, 108, 109, 110,
    123, 125, 136, 148, 155